Contemporary
Young Children

MW01201003

Contemporary Challenges in Teaching Young Children provides both veteran and aspiring early childhood educators with the information and tools they need to build on their understanding of developmentally appropriate practice.

Teachers face many challenges, including family configuration, social and political stressors related to accountability requirements, funding shortages, and the resulting need to teach with fewer resources. This innovative book focuses exclusively on problem-solving at the classroom level and fosters creative methods of ensuring best practices are in place for *all* children, including those with limited experience in formal social settings and a lack of self-regulatory behaviors. Drawing on current research and their own wealth of experience, expert contributors cover topics from the critical importance of social-emotional learning to culturally responsive teaching to using technology to empower teachers and learners.

Written in accessible, non-technical language, this book addresses complex factors affecting child development, guiding readers through the best strategies for tackling real problems in their practice.

Gayle Mindes is Professor Emerita and recipient of the Via Sapientiae Award at DePaul University, Chicago, USA.

Contemporary Challenges in Teaching Young Children

Meeting the Needs of All Students

Edited by
Gayle Mindes

Routledge
Taylor & Francis Group
LONDON AND NEW YORK

First published 2020
by Routledge
52 Vanderbilt Avenue, New York, NY 10017

and by Routledge
2 Park Square, Milton Park, Abingdon, Oxon, OX14 4RN

Routledge is an imprint of the Taylor & Francis Group, an informa business

© 2020 Taylor & Francis

Library of Congress Cataloging-in-Publication Data
A catalog record for this title has been requested

ISBN: 978-1-138-31223-4 (hbk)
ISBN: 978-1-138-31226-5 (pbk)
ISBN: 978-0-429-45835-4 (ebk)

Typeset in Bembo
by Deanta Global Publishing Services, Chennai, India

Contents

Preface

Teachers today face a very complex society, whether in rural, suburban or urban environments. The context is shaped by the social and economic trends of our global world, along with the demands of governments, the public, and families. While teachers always responded to demands, today's teacher is often asked to do more with less. That is, accountability and service demands are increasing, while support services and expectations for teacher performance increase. At the same time, young children living in our complicated world present more intricate profiles requiring individualized assessment, intervention, and teaching. As early childhood educators, we rise to this challenge. We come to the field with a love of children, an upbeat spirit, and a creative energy. We strive for the development of all of the learners in our sphere—classroom, childcare center, or school.

This book is guided by a vision to discuss issues facing early childhood educators and to provide food for thought and implementation. So, what are the factors influencing our particular work? What are the social, economic, political, and personal factors that facilitate or impede our work? In each of the following chapters, readers will be able to learn about strategies to implement and be guided to additional research. Questions guiding the chapters are: How do we understand children? How do we support their individual needs? How do we understand the social lives of children? What are the important theoretical foundations? These overall questions are explored in each of the following chapters:

The "Introduction" situates the issues for contemporary society.

Chapter 1, "Practical Strategies for Navigating Complex Systems," features the teacher as the center of the bioecological model, providing clues for successfully navigating the teacher's world.

Chapter 2, "Social-Emotional Learning is Foundational," presents social-emotional learning as the anchor for academic and social success in childcare and school settings.

Chapter 3, "Culturally Responsive Teaching in Early Childhood," shows how to maximize teacher interactions so curricula works for *all* children, especially those from diverse cultures and ethnic backgrounds.

Chapter 4, "Scaffolding Multilingual Learners in Early Childhood Classrooms," provides strategies and examples for mentoring young multilingual children to success in the English-driven curriculum.

Chapter 5, "Migrant and Refugee Children," offers ways to understand the migration process and different cultures, giving examples to facilitate bicultural and transnational identities in the classroom while establishing relationships with families.

Chapter 6, "Challenging Behaviors in the Classroom," gives practical strategies for helping children who have suffered traumatic experiences, who often present challenging behavior.

Chapter 7, "Supporting Exceptional Children and Their Families," explains the benefits of inclusive classrooms for all young children and presents differentiated ideas.

Chapter 8, "Changing Curricular Trends in Early Childhood Education: Addressing the Needs of All Children," shows how to engage in developmentally responsive teaching and offers a particular focus on exploratory learning opportunities and arts integration.

Chapter 9, "Playful Learning," calls for teachers to create opportunities for play, with examples of ways to connect to standards and required assessment systems.

Chapter 10, "Using Technology to Empower Teachers and Learners," emphasizes ways to use technology in the best interests of young children and for the individualization of instruction.

Chapter 11, "Mirrors, Windows, and Springboards: Choosing and Using Quality Literature with the Young Children We Know," delivers practical advice for choosing and using books to connect to all young children.

Chapter 12, "Mathematics to Promote Critical Thinking," outlines ways to understand early math and to use it to facilitate child learning, with practical ideas throughout.

Chapter 13, "'But Why?' Considerations for Encouraging Scientific Thinking in the Preschool Classroom," explains how to promote inquiry learning with examples for the science center, incidental science, and informal science.

Chapter 14, "Studying Social Studies and Visual Literacy to Foster Identity and Community," shows where the social studies fit in early childhood programs with examples for using visual literacy and studying community.

Chapter 15, "The Strength in Strategy: Planning for High-Quality Professional Learning Communities," gives concrete ideas for keeping our practice alive with support from mentors and colleagues.

"Conclusion: Succeeding in the Face of Challenges" sums up the contemporary challenges with optimism for the future.

About This Book

This book is written for the teacher who wants to understand the broad range of issues associated with providing educational experiences, including all young children in inclusive environments, while collaborating with families. Accordingly, the book reflects the knowledge base of early childhood education. It provides illustrations of responsive developmentally appropriate practice for prospective teachers, as well as perspectives for experienced teachers to reflect upon best practices in our contemporary society. The book approaches present-day challenges from research and practitioner experts, representing the voices across our field. It is written in nontechnical language based on current research.

Organization of the Book

The book is organized beginning with a look at contemporary issues facing teachers, followed by the teacher in the bioecological system. The next chapters focus on the foundation of social-emotional learning, culturally responsive teaching, multilingual children, migrant and refugee children, those who have experienced trauma, and young children who are exceptional. We turn then to the curriculum with a discussion of meeting the needs of all children, followed by play to capture children's curiosity, and the utilization of technology. The next chapters give strategies for best practice with children's literature, early math, preschool science, social studies, and visual literacy, concluding with a focus on keeping our work alive with professional learning communities.

Meet the Authors

Bridget Amory, EdD, is an experienced educator and administrator who is passionate about collaborating with colleagues and families to improve the educational outcomes for children of all ages. She is currently the Director of PK-12 Student Learning in the Milford (DE) School District, grateful that she gets to work alongside a dynamic team of dedicated professionals to serve a diverse population of learners. She is also an adjunct instructor at Wilmington College (DE), helping to develop curricula and prepare pre-service educators.

David Banzer is the Education Coordinator at Erie Neighborhood House, where he works with preschool teachers in their implementation of curricula and supports their professional learning. He previously taught preschool for eight years. He earned an M.Ed. in Early Childhood Education from the University of Illinois at Chicago, is currently a doctoral student at UIC majoring in Educational Psychology, and is a member of the Math at Home/Early Math Matters research team. His work focuses on early math and its connection to other STEM content areas through project-based approaches, presenting this work at state and national early childhood conferences.

Sarah Bright is a doctoral student at DePaul University, where she is pursuing a Doctor of Education (EdD) in the Curriculum Studies and Instruction program. She has worked in a variety of roles within educational publishing and curriculum development, with a focus on using technology in curriculum development for early elementary gifted students, and is a research associate at Erikson Institute and Northwestern University. Bright has a BA from the University of Toronto and an MA from New York University.

Marie Ann Donovan is Associate Professor of Teacher Education at DePaul University. She anchors courses in early reading and children's literature. Her research focuses on professional identity development in vocational education settings, as well as early childhood professional education pathways across two- and four-year degree programs. She serves as an associate editor for the *Illinois Reading Council Journal*, coauthoring its column on the intersection of classroom and school libraries in fostering children's literacy. She also serves as the program director for Early Childhood Education at DePaul and chairs the Faculty Advisory Council to the Illinois Board of Higher Education.

Dominic F. Gullo is a professor of early childhood development and education. He has worked in the profession for over 35 years as a Head Start and public school classroom teacher as well as a university professor and researcher. Dom's areas of specialization and research include early childhood curriculum and assessment, school readiness, risk and resiliency in early childhood, and early childhood school reform. Dom has held many leadership positions in the field with professional associations and has consulted widely with schools throughout the United States and abroad. He has published widely and presented his work both nationally and internationally.

Ravi Hansra is the founder of Hansra Consulting and Advisory Services (HCAS), with over 17 years of education experience. HCAS provides support to educational organizations regarding strategic planning, professional learning, curriculum design, and evaluation. Prior to HCAS, she served as CPIO at the YMCA of Metro Chicago, overseeing early learning, Youth Safety and Violence Prevention, Community Schools, and Signature Programming. Prior to the Y, Dr. Hansra was a Leadership Development Consultant at Rush University, a professor at DePaul University, and a high-school English teacher. She has experience leading organizational change, strategic planning, leadership development, curriculum design, and evaluation.

Nancy Hashimoto is a doctoral student in Early Childhood Education at DePaul University in Chicago, IL, where she also earned her bachelor's in Early Childhood Education and her master's in history. She is the parent of a first grader with Autism Spectrum Disorder and a preschooler. Her doctoral studies focus on autism in early childhood and its intersection with the family. Particular interests include resiliency, sibling interactions, social/ emotional development, neurological development, and parenting children with autism.

Marisha L. Humphries, Ph.D. is Associate Professor in the Department of Educational Psychology at the University of Illinois at Chicago and a licensed clinical psychologist. Dr. Humphries' research seeks to develop an integrated approach to studying African American children's normative and prosocial development, and to utilize this basic research to create culturally and developmentally appropriate school-based behavior-promotion programs. Her work examines African American children's emotional and social competence, and the ways in which schools can support children's development in this area. Dr. Humphries' work considers the contextual and cultural factors associated with children, families, and schools.

Gayle Mindes is Professor Emerita of Education at DePaul University in Chicago. She taught in the pre-service early childhood programs there, as well as in the doctoral program for Early Childhood Education and Educational Leadership. Mindes, a life-long urban educator, writes and speaks on the topics of assessment, challenging behavior, social studies, and kindergarten. Recent books include *Assessing Young Children, 5th ed.* (with L.A. Jung, 2015) and *Teaching Young Children with Challenging Behavior* (Ed., 2018). She is a consulting editor for the National Association for the Education of Young Children (*naeyc*) and has publications on kindergarten for *naeyc*.

Karen Monkman, Professor, Educational Policy and Comparative International Education at DePaul University, works on equity and social justice issues, including those related to migration and education. Her work spans all age and educational levels and learning, both in and out of school. Selected publications include *Globalization and Education* (with Nelly Stromquist, 2014 and 2000), "Social and Cultural Capital in an Urban Latino School Community" (in *Urban Education*, with Margaret Ronald and Florence Délimon, 2005), and "Literacy on Three Planes" (in *Bilingual Research Journal*, with Laurie MacGillivray and Cynthia Carla Leyva, 2003).

Larissa Mulholland is a critical early childhood professional committed to social justice. She has worked closely with diverse children and families, which has informed her approach to workforce development, both as director of a Reggio-inspired teacher education program and currently as the Master Teacher at the Ounce of Prevention's Educare center in Chicago. Her work is based in sociocultural theories of education and development and the implications of early childhood education policy and curriculum for social equity and agency. Mulholland is currently a doctoral student in the DePaul School of Education.

Julie Parson Nesbitt is a doctoral student in early childhood education at DePaul University in Chicago. Her research focuses on trauma-informed education. Publications include "A Cool Baby and a Good One, Too: Reflections of a White Mom" (in *What Does It Mean to Be White in America?*, 2016), and a review of *Closing the School Discipline Gap* (in *Education Review*, 2015). Parson Nesbitt gave a panel presentation on trauma-informed education at the 2016 Network for Public Education national conference. She works with the community organization Parents 4 Teachers and received Gwendolyn Brooks' "Significant Illinois Poet" award.

Mark Newman is Professor of Social Studies Education at the National College of Education, National Louis University. He has written and edited articles and books on maps, photographs, primary sources, and various historical and geographical topics. He is co-author of a book on visual literacy. Newman has been awarded several National Endowment for the

Humanities grants and was Director of a Library of Congress Teaching with Primary Sources project. In 2016, he won the National College of Education Distinguished Teaching Award.

Anne Pradzinski is an Assistant Professor at National Louis University where she works with pre-service teachers in Early Childhood and Elementary Education. As an educator with a focus on STEM learning, she has taught at multiple levels from toddlers to teenagers. Prior to teaching at the college level, Anne taught middle school science and US history in a large, suburban public school district. Currently pursuing her PhD at the University of Illinois at Chicago, her research focuses on how early childhood educators approach science teaching and learning in preK classrooms. Additionally, she had presented locally and nationally on the topics of early math teaching/learning and early childhood professional development.

Megan Schumaker-Murphy, Ed.D. has 15 years of experience in early childhood education as a special education teacher, early interventionist, and teacher educator. She completed her doctorate at DePaul University in Chicago in June 2019 with a dissertation entitled "Fathers' Experiences in Early Intervention: Marooned in the Kitchen or Member of the Team." A practitioner at heart, Schumaker-Murphy's research focuses on working collaboratively with families with children with developmental differences. At the YMCA in Chicago, Schumaker-Murphy mentored early childhood practitioners with a focus on anti-bias education and culturally relevant teaching. She begins an appointment as Assistant Professor at Salem State University, Salem MA in September 2019.

Kathleen M. Sheridan, PhD, is an associate professor in the College of Education at the University of Illinois in Chicago. Dr Sheridan has presented and published her research in numerous venues. Her current research focuses on effective professional development in early math for early childhood professionals. Her grant funded early math professional development project can be seen at www.mathathome.org. She is currently working on a similar STEM professional development project that focuses on early science.

Janet E. Thompson, M.A., is Director of the NAEYC-accredited Early Childhood Lab School at the UC Davis Center for Child and Family Studies, a program that emphasizes responsive adult-child interactions, reflective practice, and the design and use of outdoor environments to enhance learning. As an early childhood educator, her interests focus especially on the growth of social and emotional competency and its contributions to early learning. She was a lead author of California's Preschool Learning Foundations and Curriculum Frameworks for Social-Emotional Development and Social Sciences, as well as writing on *The Role of the Administrator* for its companion Preschool Program Guidelines.

Ross A. Thompson is Distinguished Professor of Psychology at the University of California, Davis, where he directs the Social and Emotional Development Lab. Thompson studies the development of positive social motivation in young children, including prosocial behavior, conscience (moral) development, and emotion understanding. He also writes on the applications of developmental science to practice and policy, including children in poverty, early childhood mental health, and early education. Ross and Janet E. Thompson were lead contributors to the California Preschool Learning Foundations in Social-Emotional Development and History-Social Science, and also contributed to the California Preschool Curriculum Frameworks in each area.

Liliana Barro Zecker is a language and literacy researcher. Her work describes the language development of monolingual and multilingual children in home and school settings. Recently, she has collaborated with classroom teachers documenting teacher inquiries as they relate to the teaching/learning processes observable in multilingual classrooms. Zecker has experience working as a K-8 elementary, ESL, and special education teacher. She completed her MA degree in Learning Disabilities at Northwestern University and obtained her doctorate from The University of Michigan in the Combined Program in Education and Psychology, with an emphasis in Language and Literacy. She is an Associate Professor in the College of Education Teacher Education Department at DePaul University.

Editor's Acknowledgment

Thanks to the children, families, teacher candidates, doctoral students, and colleagues who have influenced my thinking over the years. I appreciate the dialog that has served to expand and challenge my thinking. Special thanks to the contributors who make this a practical book with teachers at the center: Bridget Amory, David Banzer, Sarah Bright, Marie Ann Donovan, Dominic F. Gullo, Ravi Hansra, Nancy Hashimoto, Marisha L. Humphries, Karen Monkman, Larissa Mulholland, Julie Parson Nesbitt, Mark Newman, Anne Pradzinski, Megan Schumaker-Murphy, Janet E. Thompson, Ross A. Thompson, and Liliana Barro Zecker—friends, colleagues, and experts who delivered research-based, thoughtful and practical advice. They bring wisdom, a can-do spirit, and a variety of voices to this project. Their voices, challenges, and critiques encouraged my thinking and provided a solid footing for the editing. And thanks always to my mentor for sharper writing—my son, Jonathan.

Gayle Mindes, 2019

Editor's Introduction

Facing the Challenges in Your Classroom

Gayle Mindes

Figure 0.1 Early childhood teachers at work.

A teacher these days gets it from every direction. Wanda comes to first grade for the first time in her life in January; Billy wants to draw a rainbow and there are only black markers. You asked the principal for help with Jimmy, a second-grader, who shows signs of learning disabilities; the consultant can fit you in on an afternoon next semester—end! The childcare director emails you to say quarterly individualized assessment reports were due three days ago. As the school day ends, the principal calls you to meet a parent whose six-year-old is chronically late. Other books describe what's going on in the world making teaching difficult, but try citing poverty statistics to Irene, who's in first grade and is struggling with staying in her seat, or telling Arthur, who can't hold a pencil, why his favorite music teacher won't be coming to the school anymore due to funding cuts. Or explaining to families you can't wait with their child after 6:00 pm because you are going to your second job (Figure 0.1).

Today's early childhood teacher is increasingly alone out there. The cavalry is not coming. Teachers need answers to the problems they face on a daily basis. This book provides these answers by focusing on the teacher as the center of the classroom. We address the specific issues teachers face and offer problem-solving skills, strategies, and answers. Our focus is teacher-centered, because we believe early childhood teachers are resilient and resourceful in their efforts to serve children and their families. We gathered experts to help teachers with the myriad issues facing early childhood educators serving young children in multiple educational environments—childcare centers, home childcare, public and private PK–3rd-grade settings. While there are many monographs and books on the topics in this volume, none focus exclusively on problem-solving at the classroom level. The various emphases of these other writings are on the curriculum, the child, the child's behavior, and sometimes on the family.

In this book, we focus on the teacher as the indispensable leader for the classroom. Contemporary societal and local community issues may be making you feel isolated and assailed, but the experts recruited for this handbook provide concrete ideas to help you in your practice. The information and tools provided assist you in building on your understanding of responsive developmentally appropriate practice, showing you how the ideas can work in your classroom. We focus a lens on practice to promote innovative problem-solving to ensure best practices for all young children. In this way, the book seeks to reduce your personal stress. For you are among the teachers who aspire to be effective, helpful educators for all the children in your community.

The themes represented in this book were derived from the challenges faced in all settings. Experienced experts in their respective fields were chosen who can consider and conduct research as well as link research to practice. The voices in this volume are distinct, focusing on various settings and ages in our complex landscape of early childhood education. If you see yourself in the above exemplars of challenges or other challenging situations in our contemporary society, this book will ensure you remain committed to teaching the young children you love.

"Practical Strategies for Navigating Complex Systems" starts you off with Megan Schumaker-Murphy's strategies for managing individual stress, system demands, and ways to influence systems, while understanding yourself and others in the system. Included is a workflow tool.

Thinking About the Children

In "Social-Emotional Learning is Foundational," Ross Thompson and Janet E. Thompson illustrate ways to promote the development of children's self-regulatory behaviors and the conflict-management and coping skills necessary to succeed in the social environment of the classroom. Thompson and Thompson show the connections of social-emotional learning to school readiness and academic success. You can learn strategies to support self-regulation, emotion-understanding and social skills for classroom success for your students.

"Culturally Responsive Teaching in Early Childhood" by Marisha L. Humphries tackles head-on the notion of colorblind ideology about young children and shows how the teacher's role is central to making learning effective for children from underrepresented racial and ethnic groups. You will see ways to understand and implement culturally responsive teaching. The culturally relevant teaching strategies highlighted show their importance for the achievement and development of culturally and linguistically diverse children.

"Scaffolding Multilingual Learners in Early Childhood Classrooms" by Liliana Barro Zecker links pedagogical principles to effectively support multilingual children toward multiliterate development. Besides specific strategies for effective instruction, Zecker includes children's work samples illustrating best practice. Zecker writes with the knowledge of our educational system built on English-focused learning and achievement, often with short-term interventions for multilingual learners.

In "Migrant and Refugee Children" by Karen Monkman and Larissa Mulholland, you learn the paths of migration and about who comes to the U.S. Monkman and Mulholland illustrate ways to support im/migrant children and ideas for building relationships with parents. Ways to support transnational identities are also described.

"Challenging Behaviors in the Classroom" by Julie Parson Nesbitt provides classroom strategies for children affected by trauma, who often bring challenging behavior to the classroom. Parson Nesbitt describes alternative healing practices and ways to build a trauma-informed school, and cautions about practices that do not work.

"Supporting Exceptional Children and Their Families" by Nancy Hashimoto shows inclusive classroom strategies to foster social, emotional and cognitive development so young children can feel welcomed, a sense of belonging, and valued. Hashimoto includes differentiated instruction, intentional social engagement, and the appreciation of difference as ways to encourage young children with special needs to thrive. Practices to understand and support parents are also included.

Curriculum and Strategies

In the leadoff to this discussion, "Changing Curricular Trends in Early Childhood Education: Addressing the Needs of All Children," Dominic F. Gullo delineates why a "one size fits all" approach to curricula does not fit our world today. Gullo shows how to use early learning standards for developmentally responsive teaching. Central to Gullo's illustrations are exploratory learning activities and the integration of the arts in the curriculum.

To anchor curricular practices in play, Bridget Amory in "Playful Learning" demonstrates how to engage children in play and connect play with standards.

Amory delineates how to fit play into required assessment systems, justify the curricular practice, and ways to celebrate play.

"Using Technology to Empower Teachers and Learners" by Sarah Bright brings critical arguments for including technology as a learning tool and why using it is important for the future of young children. Included are illustrations of digital tools for teachers to use to adapt curricula. You will learn the value of digital devices and content as a tool for creation, communication, and building community.

"Mirrors, Windows, and Springboards: Choosing and Using Quality Literature with the Young Children We Know" by Marie Ann Donovan illuminates the way to use books as mirrors and windows for the children we serve. Donovan provides tools for analyzing your current literacy materials and resources for finding new materials. Finally, Donovan shows learning strategies using books, with a focus on the role books play in diversifying the curriculum to ensure culturally relevant practice.

Kathleen M. Sheridan and David Banzer take us to "Mathematics to Promote Critical Thinking." Sheridan and Banzer illustrate the underlying concepts in early math, and ways to implement teacher-directed and learning-center activities in the classroom. Links to National Council of Teachers of Mathematics (NCTM) standards and resources for additional activities are provided.

Anne Pradzinski confirms curiosity as the driver in child learning in "'But Why?'" Pradzinski illustrates science in the early childhood classroom, and ways to build inquiry into incidental science and informal science. Pradzinski brings up the use of non-fiction science books and illustrates ways to support inquiry learning—asking questions, experimenting, evaluating evidence, and asking more questions. Links to both Next Generation Science Standards and recommendations from the National Science Teachers Association (NSTA) are included.

In "Studying Social Studies and Visual Literacy to Foster Identity and Community," Mark Newman uses visual learning to demonstrate the power of this tool. Newman explains the role of social studies in promoting identity and community. He begins with the story behind a drawing of a family, a common early education activity involving children in applying accumulated knowledge, experiences and skills, which facilitates children reaching the highest level of Bloom's Taxonomy—the production of new or original work. Newman illustrates classroom activities and strategies to foster identity and community.

Megan Schumaker-Murphy and Ravi Hansra remind us in "The Strength in Strategy: Planning for High-Quality Professional Learning Communities" of the excitement and power of keeping our practice alive by studying with colleagues facing the same challenges that we do. Illustrated for you is planning with Understanding by Design (UbD), incorporating reflective practice, and demonstrate personalized practice.

Tools and Ideas from Experts

This book assembles top experts in early childhood who offer their recommendations gleaned from over 500 years of combined experience in research and practice across the landscape of early childhood environments. With an emphasis on the teacher, the heart of any educational program, you are positioned to use the strategies in this book to enhance your work with children and families. Each contributor is united in themes undergirding high-quality programs for young children and their families. The themes start with a commitment to responsive developmentally appropriate practice. Essential aspects of this practice include respect for cultural and learning diversity, and the inclusion of children with diverse abilities and those representing various social-economic, ethnic, racial, and gender identities. Our role as teachers is to collaborate with families and to implement programs meeting early learning standards in environments supporting inquiry learning while employing technology and other interventions to support differentiated instruction. As teachers we work in systems requiring accountability, measured sometimes in ways we view as problematic. We draw support from colleagues who share and nurture our efforts to be life-long learners, those who champion our successes and weep with us over challenges unmet. So, dive into this book of concrete ideas for meeting the challenges you find in your practice.

1 Practical Strategies for Navigating Complex Systems

Megan Schumaker-Murphy

As teachers, we know children don't develop in isolation. Rather, all domains of their development are impacted by their environments and the systems making up those environments. The most well-known framework of this concept is Bronfenbrenner's (1979; Bronfenbrenner & Morris, 1998) bioecological systems model. Generally, teachers are presented with examples of systems models placing students at the center of the conceptual model to call our attention to the myriad factors impacting learning development. In this chapter, the focus is on teachers and the multiple systems impacting our professional and personal development. When we take the time to understand and reflect on these factors, we can better manage the expectations and impact created by each system level. This allows us to plan strategies and to meet systems expectations in ways that aren't as disruptive to best teaching practices. Teachers can develop coping mechanisms and structures within themselves and their microsystems to buffer against potential negative impacts from the stress created by systems outside our own control.

Understanding the Bioecological Systems Model

The bioecological systems model is usually drawn as a series of concentric circles with an individual in the center circle. Each larger circle represents a system impacting the development and well-being of the individual at the center. The farther the circle from the individual, the less control and reciprocity exist in the relationship between systems at that level and the person in the center. Closest to the individual is the microsystem, then the mesosystem, the exosystem, and finally the macrosystem. The chronosystem, which represents time, is the final level in the bioecological systems model. The chronosystem is not represented as one of the concentric circles, but rather as an overlay impacting systems at all levels.

In the center of our model is you, the teacher. This chapter presents a generalized model with systems many teachers encounter. As you read, it's important for you to reflect on what your personalized bioecological model looks like. Each teacher's experience varies and even the systems we have in common may impact individual teachers differently. For example, almost all teachers interact with special educators. Depending on the microsystem-level relationship you have with the special educator, the meso-level relationships of the people in the microsystem and how they interact with the special educator, and the exo- and macrosystem factors impacting special education provision at your school, this relationship may be quite positive and supportive for you. Perhaps, if you are working in a well-funded district with an adequate number of special education teachers to meet student need, and you are paired with a special educator who shares your values and ideas about best practice in education and who has strong, positive relationships with students and their families, you will feel supported and your personal and professional development will be positively impacted. Conversely, if your school district has more students with special educational needs than it has special educators to provide assigned IEP minutes, and you are paired with a special educator who is burned out and negatively views students and families, the two of you may fundamentally disagree about how to meet the needs of the children in your classroom. When this happens, your personal and professional development can be negatively impacted.

At the center of our bioecological systems model is the individual. Everyone is made of a personal biological, cognitive, emotional, and behavioral characteristic set. These characteristics both influence and are products of development (Bronfenbrenner & Morris, 1998). For example, Ms. Awashthi, with an easy-going temperament, will likely experience more pleasant interactions with the occupational therapist assigned to provide special education minutes for several children with autism and attention deficit hyperactivity disorder (ADHD) in her classroom. As a result, Ms. Awashthi will be more likely to learn about and try new approaches to learning and classroom management. Through repeated, positive interactions with the occupational therapist working with students in her classroom, Ms. Awashthi will master the use of more effective teaching strategies with her students. The more effective teaching and management strategies build a foundation for increased feelings of self-efficacy and more positive interactions with students in the teacher's microsystem. Conversely, Mr. Milligan is slow to warm and struggles with depression. He may have difficulty building a working partnership with the same occupational therapist. The symptoms of Mr. Milligan's depression could impact his ability to find the energy and motivation to try new strategies offered by the occupational therapist. As a result, Mr. Milligan's interactions in his microsystem, both with the occupational therapist and his students, are more likely to be negative because he did not develop the knowledge and skills to meet their behavioral and educational needs. Consequently, Mr. Milligan's negative interactions with the occupational therapist and the classroom management challenges occurring in his microsystem can cause more stress and negative emotional reactions. These factors will exacerbate Mr. Milligan's existing mental health challenges, continuing to impact negatively his relationships with others in his microsystem.

Directly outside of the individual is the microsystem. The microsystem is made up of teachers' interactions with others and personal relationships. This system includes personal relationships with romantic partners, the teacher's own children and their caregivers, siblings and parents, and anyone else the teacher interacts with regularly in their personal life. Professional relationships are also situated in the microsystem. These relationships with our principals, school support staff, coworkers, teacher coaches, special education staff and our students and their caregivers are part of our microsystems. Most teachers have quite large microsystems. Microsystems also change frequently. After all, every autumn, teachers' microsystems grow by at least 20 children and their caregivers. This leaves teachers with many interpersonal relationships impacting their personal and professional development. According to Bronfenbrenner (1979), when one member of your microsystem undergoes a developmental change, you'll experience a change as well. For example, if your teaching assistant goes to a conference and learns new methods of supporting positive classroom behaviors without yelling, his development as a more competent classroom manager will help you as the classroom teacher to grow as well. Perhaps the assistant teacher will share those strategies with you and you'll improve your management skills as a team. Or maybe your assistant's increased competency in managing classroom behavior frees you to spend less time managing behavior and more time planning for project-based learning.

Many of the people in your microsystem have relationships with each other. These relationships make up the next system in the bioecological systems model, the mesosystem. The mesosystem is "a system of microsystems" (Bronfenbrenner, 1979, p. 25). This system represents how your microsystems interact with each other. The outputs of each of these relationships in the mesosystem impact the individual at the center of the model by mitigating or exacerbating existing stressors or by creating them. For teachers, this can mean how students interact with each other, how the teaching assistant in your classroom and your student teacher interact, and the nature of the relationships your school administrator has with your students' parents. In your personal life, the relationship your children have with your romantic partner exists in your mesosystem. A major part of your mesosystem is the interrelationship between your work setting and home. A common mesosystem-level challenge I and many other educators face is the difference between my school calendar and my daughter's school calendar. When the vacation days on our calendars don't align, the discrepancy creates stress for me as I have to find quality childcare and miss the extra time with my daughter. When teachers' calendars do align with their own children's schools, stress may arise because a teacher isn't able to drop her children off for the first day of school because it is also her own first day of school.

Beyond the mesosystem sits the exosystem. Entities in the exosystem impact the person at the center without any direct interactions with that person. The teachers' union at your school is situated in the exosystem, as are the superintendent of your district and the school board. These groups negotiate your salary and benefits and have the power to dictate the curriculum, both of which impact your day-to-day life, but as a teacher at the center of the model, you don't interact directly with them. Other examples of exosystem-level units impacting teachers are state-level education policies and funding streams, state boards of education and teacher licensing requirements and exams, university teacher preparation curricula, packaged curricula, including The Creative Curriculum® (Teaching Strategies, 2016), and textbook and educational testing companies such as Pearson and Routledge. Each of these systems impacts teachers although teachers rarely interact directly with the systems other than to submit paperwork, take exams, or implement their curriculum. The media is also in the exosystem. Movies like *Dangerous Minds*, memes of exhausted teachers throwing papers, and news coverage of the local teachers' strike contribute to a larger, societal value of teachers and our identities as educators.

The cultural views we hold about teachers are in the macrosystem, represented by the last and largest of the concentric circles. This system encompasses all the other systems and includes the cultural ideologies upon which the other systems are built. Within the macrosystem lie societal beliefs about the goals of education, what kinds of skills our students should learn in schools, and what level of prestige is given to teachers. American attitudes about inclusion and special education and culturally and linguistically diverse learners are positioned in the macrolevel system level. The Common Core State Standards emerged as a result of macro-level systems. Together with the Council of Chief State School Officers, the National Governors' Association pushed for unified standards for college and career readiness (Common Core State Standards Initiative, 2018). If you are a teacher in one of the 41 states that adopted Common Core, this macro-level initiative impacts the curriculum chosen in your exosystem, which then in turn impacts the instructional interactions you have in your microsystem.

The final component of the bioecological systems model is the chronosystem. It accounts for the ways that cultural ideologies and bodies of knowledge shift over time. Bronfenbrenner added the chronosystem to acknowledge the impact that these shifts have on systems at every level and thus on individual development. A chronosystem-level factor significantly impacting early childhood teachers is the scientific research completed in the last 30 years, establishing a foundation for understanding how young children best learn and develop, and of course how all the systems around the children impact their development (Allen & Kelly, 2015). One significant example emerging in recent years is the understanding of the prevalence and impact of trauma on overall health in the United States. Beginning in 1998 (Felitti et al.), researchers began to connect childhood trauma to changes in the brain and body impacting development and health over lifetimes. Initial data from this CDC-Kaiser Permanente study found about two-thirds of people, regardless of education or socioeconomic status, experienced at least one adverse childhood experience. Understanding of the prevalence and impact of Adverse Childhood Experiences (ACES) continues to expand our perception of what constitutes ACES (Institute for Safe Families, 2013) and how ACES impact individual health and development throughout a person's life (Anda et al., 2006).

Another component of the chronosystem is the stage in the individual's career. This accounts for the variance in the impact of each system depending on the person's age and life-cycle events. For example, if you are a new grad entering your first year of teaching, your chronosystem demonstrates that the impact each system has on your professional development is different from what would be the case for a veteran teacher two years from retirement.

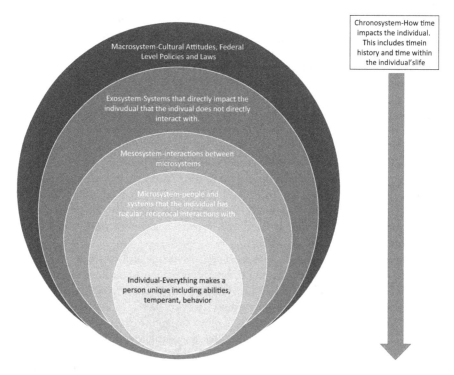

Figure 1.1 Adapted from Bronfenbrenner, U. (1979) The ecology of human development. Cambridge, MA: Harvard University Press and Bronfenbrenner, U. & Morris, P.A. (1998) The ecology of development process. In W. Damon (Series Ed.) & R.M. Lerner (Vol. Ed.), *Handbook of Child Psychology: Vol. 1. Theoretical Models of Human Development* (5th ed. 939–991). New York: John Wiley.

This chapter provides an example bioecological systems model for a Chicago Public Schools Head Start teacher. It will be helpful for you to review this example and create a draft of your own bioecological systems model before continuing to the next section of this chapter (Figure 1.1).

Individual and Microsystem-Level Strategies for Managing System Demands

The number of systems successful teachers must work in can be overwhelming. In fact, in a study exploring stress and teacher burnout in a midwestern urban city, 93% of teachers reported that they are highly stressed (Herman, Hickmon-Rosa & Reinke, 2018). Of these teachers, 60% reported healthy coping mechanisms and low teacher burnout while the teachers without adequate coping skills reported high levels of burnout. The symptoms of burnout extend beyond emotional exhaustion and result from stressful interactions between the individual and the systems wherein she develops. These systems manifest at the individual level and can include insomnia, fatigue, anxiety, depression, and apathy, along with intense feelings of anger and frustration (Leiter, 2005). Additional physical symptoms associated with professional burnout are body pain and high blood pressure (Mariammal, Amith, & Sornaraj, 2012). Prolonged occupational stress and feelings of burnout are linked to diabetes, heart disease, and strokes (Mariammal, Amith, & Sornaraj, 2012)

It's important not to place the blame for burnout on teachers themselves. Our systems models show that in many instances, causes of high teacher stress come from meso-, exo-, and macro-level structures. As discussed above, factors within the individual are both a product of developing within a systems context and influence the way the individual teacher develops within the systems, creating a cycle of developmental influence. While teachers may not be in a position to change these structures, we are able to develop coping mechanisms and structures at the individual and microsystem levels to foster resilience in ourselves and the teachers around us. Teachers can address their individual-level stress responses proactively and reactively using a variety of coping mechanisms.

Proactive Strategies for Managing Individual Stress

Proactively, teachers can integrate self-care practices into their daily routines including eating well, exercising, and practicing mindfulness and meditation. Planning for these activities helps to ensure that busy teachers make time for them (Center for Early Childhood Mental Health Consultation (CECMHC), n.d.). Teachers can also use planning to maximize their productivity, so they are able to meet assessment and other deadlines established by structures within their exosystems.

We've all heard the saying that we should put our own oxygen masks on before we help anyone else with their mask. While it may have become commonplace, the sentiment is definitely true. In my interactions with teachers, I often see them skipping lunches, sacrificing sleep, not taking sick days when they're ill, and giving up time at the gym or time with family and friends in favor of spending time working. Most teachers, including me, are guilty of making these sacrifices more often than is good for us. In the moment, when the deadline for entering data into the online portfolio assessment system is fast approaching, these sacrifices often feel like the best option. Not taking care of ourselves in the short term can contribute to burnout in the long term (CECMHC, n.d.).

Two of the most effective coping mechanisms for proactively managing stress caused by any level of your systems model are exercise (Shepard, 1996; Gerber, Lindwall, Lindegård, Börjesson, & Jonsdottir, 2013), and mindfulness (Brown & Ryan, 2003).

Some teachers enjoy exercise, but time is a barrier to getting in a workout. If this is the case for you, adding exercise to your weekly schedule or incorporating exercise into time with family and friends will help ensure that exercise doesn't fall by the wayside as you manage interactions with various systems. It's also a fun way to combine another effective coping mechanism, spending time with people who understand you (CECMHC, n.d.), into your routine. While writing my dissertation, the only exercise I found myself getting was when my girlfriends suggested we turn our weekly coffee dates into walk and talks. I found myself feeling renewed after each walk even though I always dreaded putting on my walking shoes because I felt so tired. Teachers can tap into the positive relationships in their microsystems for encouragement to make sure they are making time for these kinds of proactive coping mechanisms.

If you and the people closest to you are not naturally inclined to exercise, one strategy for making sure that you exercise regularly is to incorporate it into your daily classroom routine. In early childhood education, the curriculum usually addresses physical activity and development. In birth-to-five classrooms, gross motor time is planned as a part of the everyday learning experience. When you plan activities like obstacle courses, dance parties, or races for your students, you can participate instead of watching from the sidelines. Even ten minutes of cardiovascular exercise at a time is beneficial to your health (Centers for Disease Control, 2018). As a bonus, these positive interactions help to build and maintain strong relationships with the students in your microsystem. As a teacher coach, I also find that literally jumping into a classroom dance activity helps to facilitate positive relationships between me and the teachers I work with. There's nothing like a little silliness during music and movement time to show your coworkers you're in the thick of early childhood teaching with them.

Mindfulness practices seem to be getting a lot of buzz lately in the exosystem, with media coverage, books, podcasts, and Internet resources. The essence of mindfulness is to be present in the moment so that you are able to recognize your current emotional state, what caused that emotional state, and how your body feels while you are in that state, often using calming or relaxation techniques to calm your mind and body when you are experiencing stress (Singh, 2010). An excellent lay definition of mindfulness is "Mindfulness is a skill... where you learn to see what's happening in your head right now, clearly, so that you don't get yanked around by it" (Harris, 2016). Taking time for mindfulness doesn't mean that a teacher will sit quietly with an empty mind for 20 minutes. Rather, it means being fully present in the moment, taking note of your emotional state and employing healthy coping mechanisms to acknowledge it and move on. A review of available literature focused on teachers and mindfulness found that teachers who use the practice have positive mental health outcomes (Emerson et al., 2017). One such study found that teachers who practiced mindfulness consistently reported decreased stress and symptoms of burnout (Roeser, 2013).

As a bonus for busy or overwhelmed teachers, mindfulness only takes a few minutes. It can be practiced alone or with people from your microsystem. One mindfulness curriculum adopted by Chicago Public Schools, the Calm Classroom® (Luster & Luster, 2008), offers a series of three-minute mindfulness activities that can be done with young children through primary grades. Each of these activities helps the teacher and children focus on their bodies and breathing. If your school doesn't have an adopted mindfulness curriculum a variety of resources to guide you through mindfulness activities exists, including the book *Happy Teachers Change the World: A Guide for Cultivating Mindfulness in Education* (Hanh & Weare, 2017), which gives short lesson plans for classroom mindfulness activities. Classrooms utilizing mindfulness practices showed a 23% decrease in challenging behaviors after the first year (Luster & Luster, 2017).

If you want to practice mindfulness but aren't sure where to start or don't have the resources to purchase a curriculum, the Center for Early Childhood Mental Health Consultation publishes an open source short packet called *Taking Care of You: Providers* (Nyklicek & Kuijpers, 2006). This packet provides a quick and easy guide to determining what causes your stress, what your personal indicators and symptoms of stress are, and how you can act to reduce your stress. This tool can be completed proactively, before teachers feel stress, and referred back to as teachers react to stress caused by their interactions with other systems.

Whatever your preferred method to ensure self-care, research demonstrates it's key in preventing burnout and managing stress within individuals.

Managing Your Microsystems

Even the most physically fit and mindful teachers will sometimes find themselves struggling to manage relationships in their microsystems, especially because teachers maintain such large professional microsystems. One way to lay a foundation for positive microsystem-level interactions is to adopt a strengths-based mentality. The strengths-based teacher develops positive relationships with students, families, and coworkers by focusing on their positive characteristics and skills, taking a culturally competent approach to understanding others and their behavior (Green, McAllister, & Tarte, 2004). Strengths-based teachers strive to empower and build the capacity of others by leveraging these strengths. When you enter into relationships with people in your microsystem with a strengths-based focus, you see each member of your microsystems positively, thus making it easier to have pleasant and productive interactions with them. As you interact within each microsystem, you're impacting the development of the other person within that microsystem. A strengths-based mindset helps to ensure your impact on the development of others is positive.

You'll likely encounter many people in your microsystem, making it challenging to maintain a strengths-based relationship with them. This is when your individual practices of self-care and mindfulness come in handy. None of us can control the behavior of others, but we can seek to understand in culturally competent ways. For example, in some Latinx, Asian, and African cultures, coming to school to talk with a teacher is seen as deeply disrespectful. In many homes coming from these cultures, families consider teachers experts; therefore, family members will not engage with teachers in the same way that families who identify with the dominant American culture might. In families with strong ties to one of these cultures, the family caregivers may view their duties as an engaged family to get the child to school on time every day with the appropriate school supplies (Halgunseth & Peterson, 2009). Other families may struggle with any number of other issues including work schedules, immigration status, or transportation. When viewed through a deficit-based lens, you may feel deeply frustrated with their lack of involvement in their children's education. When you learn more about each family's capacities and belief systems, your view and moreover your interactions with each of these families becomes much more strengths-based. These interactions become a strengths-based relationship that allows for reciprocal capacity building.

Adopting a strengths-based mindset doesn't mean that you won't ever struggle with your microsystem relationships and it certainly isn't always easy to do. However, it will help you engage more successfully with students, families, and coworkers, and hopefully your development as an educator will thrive as a result.

Working with Your Mesosystems

There are times when, no matter your own mindset or work toward cultivating positive relationships in your microsystem, the relationships between microsystems will cause strife in your professional life or in your ability to maintain a work/life balance. Sometimes, there isn't much that you can do to mitigate these conflicts. When this occurs, mindfulness and self-care become very important, so you don't become burned out as a result of stressful mesosystem-level conflicts. In some cases, through your modeling of strengths-based interactions and mindfulness practices, you can help build the capacities people in your microsystems bring with them into their own relationships with others. For example, when you model mindfulness with your students, they'll exhibit fewer challenging behaviors. Improved classroom behaviors can positively impact the class's relationship with the art teacher, for example so that after art class each week you will not have to debrief about your students' poor behavior in the art room.

For students who exhibit challenging behaviors or have special learning needs, your modeling of strengths-based language and interactions with families and other school staff will help to support positive relationships between children and families and children and school staff.

Navigating Exosystems and Their Expectations

Unlike factors in the micro- and meso-level, it is unlikely that you will have strong reciprocal relationships with structures in the exosystem. These are systems impacting you but you can't usually control or impact yourself. For example, many school districts have a pay matrix determining your level of annual compensation. In Chicago, the Chicago Teachers' Union and the Chicago Board of Education negotiate to determine salary amounts and fringe benefits as well as the number of hours a day children attend school and the maximum number of children allowed in each classroom. The school board sets the academic calendar as well. These decisions have a direct impact on teachers, but rarely do individual teachers have a direct voice in determining the outcomes (although some teachers do have the opportunity to participate more actively in their teachers' unions).

One major challenge presented by the exosystem for many teachers can be interacting meaningfully with prepackaged curricula. For the teacher at the center of our example model, the Head Start block grantee in Chicago, DFSS requires the use of the Creative Curriculum® (Teaching Strategies 2016), a project-based approach to learning with young children. The Creative Curriculum® is paired with an online assessment system called Teaching Strategies Gold® (Teaching Strategies, 2016). Both are aligned with Illinois State Early Learning Standards and National Head Start Standards (National standards are technically in the macrosystem but in this case influence curriculum choices in the exosystem). As a result, the teacher at the center of this model must utilize a project-based approach to learning that is monitored with a fidelity checklist (Figure 1.2).

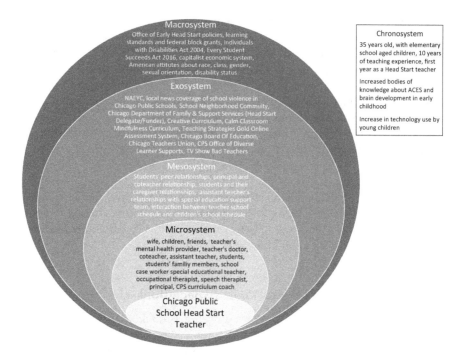

Figure 1.2 Sample bioecological system model of a Chicago Public School Head Start Teacher.

Additionally, the teacher must provide documentation for each student for 38 objectives (spread across 78 indicators) four times per year. If this teacher has a half-day Head Start program like the one at Swift Elementary School, it means the teacher must complete documentation for each of the 38 objectives for 40 students. That's over 6,000 pieces of documentation to enter per school year! While it is certainly best practice to use portfolio-based assessments for preschool children and most teachers know their students well enough to determine their levels of development in each area, it can be overwhelming to collect that many pieces of documentation and upload them into an online system. To successfully navigate this exosystem-level requirement, one strategy I learned from a group of curriculum coaches I worked with is to create a workflow plan for yourself (Ramos-Castillo, Danner, & Watson, personal communication, 2018). A workflow plan is just an outline of what kinds of documentation you will collect during the week, how you will collect it, and what classroom staff will be responsible for collecting it and uploading it into the online system. A workflow plan also outlines what you will do during your allotted planning time each week. Workflow plans can be as detailed or as sparse as you like and can be stored in your lesson plans, a bullet journal, phone calendar or even on a sticky note on your desk. The important thing about workflow plans is while you allow for changes as needed, you stick to the plan as much as possible. That way, you aren't frantically collecting and inputting documentation notes and neglecting lesson planning at the end of each quarter. Workflow also ensures you're following best practices for early childhood assessment by providing ongoing, authentic assessments of children's learning that you can access to inform lesson planning. The workflow plan also helps with the mesosystem-level challenge of work/life balance, which remains a struggle for me and every other teacher I've ever met (Figure 1.3).

A strengths-based mindset is helpful when engaging with exosystem-level influences as well as in the micro- and mesosystems. Learning standards, packaged curricula, and required assessment practices are meant to be tools to help

Daily
- Take anecdotal notes and collect work samples for documentation of student learning
- Interpret formative assessment data and respond to students' immediate learning needs
- Urgent family communication
- Mindfulness and self-care

Weekly
- Teaching team meetings (all adults in the classroom)
- Lesson plan and materials prep
- Student documentation Plan (developmental doman of focus for the week, which children to document on particular days)
- Plan the planning time (what will you do during nap time, enrichment classes, etc)
- General family communication

Monthy
- If using online assessment system, run documentation status report and plan to take anecdotal notes and work samples to fill in gaps. If using paper portfolios, eyeball documentation to establish gaps and make plan to collect anecdotal notes and work samples to fill in gaps.
- Review and plan changes to learning environment
- Meet with curriculum coaches and special education team
- Class level reflection: What do your students do well? What skills do they need more support with?

Figure 1.3 Sample work flow plan.

Preschool Teacher Workflow Example

Week Of:	Observation Focus	Monday	Tuesday	Wednesday	Thursday	Friday
9/24-9/28	Social Emotional Development/ Fine Motor/literacy	Children to Observe: JM, AR, JE, AN Planning time Use: Email AN's occupational therapist and note home about something good that happened today, File last week's observations into student portfolios	Children to observe: BB, ZD, AH, KP Planning time use: Print children's sign in sheet and put in entrance, prep circle time materials for children's info web about worms, reserve books about insects from library, call pet store to see if we can get worms donated.	Children to Observe: AS, DS, ES, JS ALL-Collect children's sign in sheet and use their name writing for portfolios Planning time: Meet with AN and JM speech therapist	Children to Observe: TT, BU, DU, HV Planning time: Review children's info web about worms, lesson plan for week of 10/1-10/5 with worm study, Add pictures related to worm study to AN communication binder	Children to observe: AW, CW, FY, PY Planning time: Gather materials to add/omit from learning centers for next week, email AN family about communication binder success this week. Send Week in Review email to families
10/1-10/5	Language and Literacy	Children to observe: Children to Observe: JM, AR, JE, AN, ZD Planning time: email check in with JM family, file last week's observations in portfolios	OUT: Loose parts PD	Children to observe: BB, AS, DS, ES, JS Planning time: Print photos from Aquarium Monday for worm study documentation wall display	Children to observe: AH, TT, BU, DU, HV Planning time: lesson plan for week of 10/8-10/12, find nonfiction for nonfiction read aloud about worms	Children to observe: KP, AW, FY, PY Planning time: Email check in with AN family, Send Week In Review email to families

Preschool Teacher Workflow Example.

teachers use best practices in education. While I don't advocate and wouldn't like using a scripted curriculum, I do appreciate that packaged curricula like the Creative Curriculum are meant to be used as resources for teachers to ensure high-quality learning interactions with students. Most packaged curricula allow for flexibility to differentiate learning or to integrate your own ideas. Starting with a lesson plan from a packaged curriculum can help build your capacity as a teacher by supporting the teaching of a subject that is new to you. Teaching Strategies Gold® helps teachers to identify children's learning needs and provides sample activities to target specific skill development. In addition to building capacity through the provision of evidence-based lesson plans, using these plans as a springboard can free time to interact with students during learning center or music and movement play, use district-provided planning time for entering student documentation and assessment data, or to leave work in time to have dinner with your family.

Understanding and Advocating in Your Macrosystem

The system individuals have the least direct impact upon is the macrosystem. As a teacher, one the most important things we can do for ourselves is to take time to reflect and understand how the beliefs of the dominant culture shape our own identity and the ways our culture impacts our teaching and interactions with those in our microsystems. This reflection builds our capacity for mindfulness practices and our ability to interact with others in strengths-based ways. When we question our own assumptions about what is "normal" we become more inclusive in our microsystem practices.

In addition to cultural practices, national laws and policies are in the macrosystem. As teachers, we have a responsibility to advocate for laws and policies that support best practices in education. We can use the resources provided to us by exosystem-level systems like the National Association for the Education of Young Children to support our advocacy. This advocacy can happen in ways that feel small but have an impact on election outcomes, including voting in the interest of sound educational policies in national elections or in more immediately visible ways such as participating in a school walk-out to bring attention to the issue of gun violence in schools.

Using the Chronosystem to Gain Understanding of Yourself and Others

The final component of Bronfenbrenner's bioecological systems model that teachers interact with is the chronosystem. This system helps to contextualize how every other system in our model impacts us and often has the potential for a more neutral impact than some of the other system levels. For example, your age, life, and work experience all sit in the chronosystem. On their own, each of these factors is neutral, but they still have the potential to impact your personal and professional development as they change the way you interact with the other systems in your model. Potentially negative events in the chronosystem are events like war and natural disasters. When these potentially negative events occur, it's important to invest time in self-care and to employ mindful strategies to cope with these events.

The last interaction with the chronosystem is our interaction with our current bodies of knowledge, which is generally positive as more information is always helpful. An increase in the body of knowledge around how young children learn best and an increased awareness of the long-term impacts of ACEs lead to positive changes in policy at the macro- and exosystem levels.

Putting It All Together

Arguably, teachers have large and potentially overwhelming bioecological systems models. Therefore, it is important to take time to understand how organizations and structures at each level of the model empower teachers to successfully manage the interactions and expectations that take place in the day-to-day practice of teaching young children.

References

Allen, L., & Kelly, B.B. (Eds.). (2015). *Transforming the Workforce for Children Birth Through Age 8: A Unifying Foundation*. Washington, DC: The National Academies Press.

Anda, R.F., Felitti, V.J., Walker, J., Whitfield, C.L., Bremner, J.D., Perry, B.D., Dube, S.R., & Giles, W.H. (2006). The enduring effects of abuse and related adverse experiences in childhood. A convergence of evidence from neurobiology and epidemiology. *European Archives of Psychiatry and Clinical Neuroscience, 56*(3), 174–186.

Bronfenbrenner, U. (1979). *The Ecology of Human Development*. Cambridge, MA: Harvard University Press.

Bronfenbrenner, U., & Morris, P.A. (1998). The ecology of development process. In W. Damon (Series Ed.) & R.M. Lerner (Vol. Ed.), *Handbook of Child Psychology: Vol. 1. Theoretical Models of Human Development* (5th ed., pp. 939–991). New York: John Wiley.

Brown, K.W., & Ryan, R.M. (2003). The benefits of being present: Mindfulness and its role in psychological well-being. *Journal of Personality and Social Psychology, 84*(4), 822–848

Centers for Disease Control and Prevention. (2011). Strategies to Prevent Obesity and Other Chronic Diseases: The CDC Guide to Strategies to Increase Physical Activity in the Community Atlanta, GA: U.S. Department of Health and Human Services

Centers for Disease Control and Prevention. (2018). How much physical activity do you need? Retrieved from: https://www.cdc.gov/physicalactivity/basics/adults/index.htm

Center for Early Childhood Mental Health Consultation. (n.d.). Taking care of ourselves: Providers. Retrieved from: https://www.ecmhc.org/documents/TakingCare_ProviderBk_final.pdf

Common Core State Standards Initiative. (2018). Development process. Retrieved from: http://www.corestandards.org/about-the-standards/development-process/

Emerson, L.M., Leyland, A., Hudson, K., Rowse, G., Hanley, P., & High-Jones, S. (2017). Teaching mindfulness to teachers: A systematic review and narrative synthesis. *Mindfulness, 8*(5), 1136–1149.

Felitti, V.J., Anda, R.F., Nordenberg, D., Wililamson, D.F., Spitz, A.M., Edwards, V., Koss, M.P., & Marks, J.S. (1998). Relationship of childhood abuse and household dysfunction to many of the leading causes of death in adults: The Adverse Childhood Experiences (ACE) study. *American Journal of Preventative Medicine, 4*(4), 245–258.

Gerber, M., Lindwall, M., Lindegård, A., Börjesson, M., & Jonsdottir, I. (2013). Cardiorespiratory fitness protects against stress-related symptoms of burnout and depression. *Patient Education and Counseling, 93*(1), 146–152.

Green, B.L., McAllister, C.L., & Tarte, J.M. (2004). The strengths-based practices inventory: A tool for measuring strengths based service delivery in early childhood and family support programs. *Families in Society: The Journal of Contemporary Social Services, 85*(3), 326–334.

Halgunseth, L.C., & Peterson, A. (2009). *Family Engagement, Diverse Families, and Early Childhood Education Programs: An Integrated Review of Literature.* Washington, DC: NAEYC.

Hanh, T. N., & Weare, K. (2017). Happy Teachers Change the World: A Guide for Cultivated Mindfulness in Education. Berkeley, CA: Parralax Press .

Harris, D. (host). (2016, December 20). *10% Happier* [Audio podcast]. Retrieved from: https://www.stitcher.com/podcast/abc-news/10-happier/e/48594709

Herman, K.C., Hickmon-Rosa, J., & Reinke, W.M. (2018). Empirically derived profiles of teacher stress, burnout, self-efficacy, and coping and associated student outcomes. *Journal of Behavioral Interventions, 20*(2), 90–100.

Institute for Safe Families. (2013). Findings from the Philadelphia urban ACE study. Retrieved from: http://www.instituteforsafefamilies.org/sites/default/files/isfFiles/Philadelphia%20Urban%20ACE%20Report%202013.pdf

Leiter, M.P. (2005). Perception of risk: An organizational model of occupational risk, burnout, and physical symptoms. *Anxiety, Stress & Coping, 18*(2), 131–144.

Luster, J. & Luster, J. (2008). *Calm Classroom.* Carol Stream, IL: Still Moment Publishing. Edit

Luster, J., & Luster, J. (2017). Using Calm Classroom to improve behavior in Chicago public schools: Year 1 Behavioral Data Scores Interim Report K-8th grade. Retrieved from: https://cdn.shopify.com/s/files/1/2220/4227/files/i3_Study_1st_Year_Preliminary_Behavior_Data_Results.pdf?9714121052525255435

Mariammal, T., Amitha, A., & Sornaraj, R. (2012). Work-influenced occupational stress and cardiovascular risk among teachers and office workers. *Journal of Chemical and Pharmaceutical Research, 4*(3), 807–811.

Nyklicek, I., & Kuijpers, K. (2006). Psychological mindedness predicts outcome of a mindfulness-based stress-reduction intervention (abstract). *International Journal of Behavioral Medicine, 13*(2), 179–179.

Roeser, R.W., Schonert-Reichl, K.A., Jha, A., Cullen, M., Wallace, L., Wilensky, R., Oberle, E., & Thomson, K. (2013). Mindfulness training and reductions in teacher stress and burnout: Results from two randomized, waitlist-control field trials. *Journal of Educational Psychology, 105*, 787–804.

Shephard, R.J. (1996). Worksite fitness and exercise programs: A review of methodology and health impact. *American Journal of Health Promotion, 10,* 436–452.

Singh, N.N. (2010). Mindfulness: A finger pointing to the moon. *Mindfulness, 1*(1), 1–3.

Teaching Strategies. (2016). The Creative Curriculum for Preschoolers (6th ed.). Bethesda, MD: Teaching Strategies.

2 Social-Emotional Learning is Foundational

Ross A. Thompson and Janet E. Thompson

Figure 2.1 Children learning social rules of group behavior.

Learning how to teach does not end with an academic degree or a teaching credential. In some respects, it just begins. A novice teacher may be well prepared by courses in teaching strategies and supervised practica, but much of learning how to teach derives from daily encounters with developing young learners in the complicated social environment of a classroom. Lesson plans to encourage developing language or number skills sometimes have to compete with the other needs of the student. One child does not seem capable of sitting still and consequently has difficulty focusing on the activity. Another carries into the classroom the emotional turmoil of parents with financial problems. A third is excluded by other children because of his aggression, which identifies him as a problem in the eyes of teachers as well. These social, emotional, and self-regulatory challenges are not ancillary to the task of learning: they are central to it. Yet most teachers feel more capable of promoting emergent literacy and numeracy than conflict management, self-regulation, or coping skills in young children. And having come to the classroom well prepared with lesson plans for developing cognitive skills, novice teachers find that they must devote more attention than they had expected to developing social and emotional skills (Figure 2.1).

Once the importance of social-emotional learning to achievement is recognized, the question is how to support this kind of learning. Does a teacher create classroom lessons on emotion understanding as s/he does for how plants grow? Does the teacher look for "teachable moments" when children are in the midst of self-regulatory problems to coach better skills, even though children may be upset or distracted? Does the teacher look for later occasions for reflection on an earlier emotional meltdown? Should all of these strategies be used by a thoughtful teacher of social-emotional learning?

These are the questions that are the focus of this chapter. We begin by considering how, and why, educators, researchers, and the public have gradually begun recognizing the importance of social-emotional learning to young children's school readiness and academic success. We then turn to specific domains of social-emotional learning—self-regulation, emotion understanding, and social skills—to understand why they are important to classroom success, and what approaches teachers can take to strengthen these capabilities in young children. The chapter closes with some concluding comments.

The Importance of Social–Emotional Learning

Educational researchers have gradually recognized the importance of social-emotional learning to school achievement. As early as 2005, Gilliam (2005) reported that nearly seven out of every 1000 enrolled preschoolers were expelled due to behavioral problems in the classroom, a rate that was higher than the national rate of expulsion for K-12 students. These were often the students who would benefit most from remaining in the classroom. Kindergarten teachers also reported that they were concerned about children in their classes who lacked the self-regulatory and social-emotional capacities for getting along with others and following instructions (Rimm-Kaufman, Pianta, & Cox, 2000). These are often the children most deemed unready for school because of these self-regulatory and social-emotional difficulties.

But at the same time, Duncan and his colleagues reported that only measures of preschool cognitive competence were important to individual differences in early elementary school academic performance. By contrast, preschool measures of social-emotional development and behavior problems were not important to early academic success (Duncan, Dowsett, Claessens et al., 2007). This widely publicized report concluded that efforts to improve school readiness should be devoted primarily to enhancing young children's thinking, reasoning, and number skills. Subsequent analyses showed, however, that when academic achievement was considered beyond school entry, persistent behavior problems were as important as reading and math scores for predicting high-school dropout (Magnuson, Duncan, Lee, & Metzger, 2016). One reason, therefore, for early attention to emerging emotional and behavior problems is that if they are unaddressed in early childhood they are likely to increase and have compounding effects on children's classroom conduct. In the words of one of the authors' blog post, "[a]ddressing behavior problems of 5- to 12-year-olds is as important for their future schooling as teaching them math and language" (Duncan, 2016).

This conclusion is shared by an increasing number of educational researchers (Rock & Crow, 2017). A study by the Baltimore Education Research Consortium of more than 9,000 students reported that by third grade, children who had been assessed as not socially and behaviorally ready in kindergarten were significantly more likely to have been retained in grade, received special educational services, or been suspended or expelled (Bettencourt, Gross, & Ho, 2016). Indicators of social and behavioral readiness included teacher reports of young children following classroom rules, maintaining positive relationships with peers and adults, cooperating in group activities, showing empathy and concern for peers and adults, and using appropriate coping skills. Jones, Greenberg and Crowley (2015) obtained kindergarten teacher reports of the social-emotional skills of more than 750 children and found that early socioemotional competence predicted important outcomes later in life, including high-school graduation and early adult employment, and helped to reduce the probability of receiving public assistance in early adulthood, involvement with the criminal justice system, and substance abuse. An important feature of this study is that the researchers controlled for other influences that could be related to these outcomes, including family socioeconomic status, life stresses, neighborhood quality, academic achievement, and behavior problems, and found that beyond these influences, kindergarten social-emotional skills uniquely forecasted later adult outcomes.

Summarizing these and other findings, a recent consensus report from a consortium of leading researchers in this field concluded that "[s]ocial, emotional, and cognitive capabilities are fundamentally intertwined—they are interdependent in their development, experience, and use" and this is why early social-emotional competencies are foundational to academic success (Jones & Kahn, 2017, p. 7). The consortium also noted that social and emotional skills are malleable: they can be taught and developed throughout life. Similarly, a distinguished consensus committee commissioned by the National Research Council to study early learning concluded: "[s]ocioemotional competence increasingly is viewed as important for a child's early school adjustment and for academic success at both the preschool and K-12 levels" (Committee on the Science of Children Birth to Age 8, 2015, p. 139).

There are other reasons for growing public and professional attention to the role of social-emotional learning in academic success. With increasing numbers of young children showing signs of chronic stress, educators are realizing how significantly the emotional, behavioral, and self-regulatory problems created by persistent stress can impede learning—not just for the child but also for the entire group (Thompson, 2014). The growing call for educational accountability, coupled with the focus of early educators on the whole child, means that behavioral and emotional problems such as these must be addressed if children are to become proficient learners. The whole-child focus also means that the daily classroom schedule for young children cannot be as narrowly focused on cognitive, mathematical, language, and scientific skills as might be true with older children. Along with calls for recognizing the importance of play is an awareness that developing self-regulation, emotion understanding, social skills, and competencies in group participation are also part of the formal and informal curriculum for young children.

Taken together, we have come a long way from the days when educators of young children had to defend their commitment to social-emotional learning in the context of calls for increased attention to language and mathematical learning. Now that the importance of social-emotional learning is recognized, what do we do about it?

Nurturing Social-Emotional Learning

When we think of "social-emotional learning" we are considering a wide variety of interrelated capabilities, including cooperation, following directions, emotion regulation, conflict resolution skills, communicating feelings and needs, recognizing and responding constructively to others' emotions, impulse control, creating and maintaining positive relationships with peers and teachers, understanding social cues, flexibility in social interactions, conscience and moral understanding, emotion knowledge, group participation, friendship with peers, taking responsibility for one's actions, self-awareness and self-confidence—and the reader could probably add to this list. Each of these capabilities is relevant to how children learn and behave in the classroom, but it can be daunting to any teacher to consider how to encourage healthy development in all of these skills.

It can be helpful, therefore, to think of social-emotional learning in terms of a smaller set of general competencies (Jones, Zaslow, Darling-Churchill, & Halle, 2016). In the sections that follow, we focus on three: self-regulation, emotion understanding, and social skills.

Self-Regulation

Individual differences in self-regulation have significant consequences for school success because these differences affect many aspects of how young children behave in the classroom. *Behavioral* self-regulation (sometimes called impulse control) affects how well children can sit still for circle time or manage the transition from individual work to group activity. *Emotional* self-regulation is important to how children respond to everyday peer provocation or manage frustration. *Attentional* self-regulation affects young children's capacities to remain focused on what the teacher is saying or on an independent learning task. *Cognitive* self-regulation influences how well children can mobilize their thinking skills in a problem-solving challenge and persist if their initial solutions are unsuccessful. Self-regulation is thus relevant to a variety of social-emotional learning capacities.

Although we can distinguish between behavioral, cognitive, attentional, and emotional self-regulation, these capacities are interconnected for several reasons. One reason is that they are based on the maturation of common brain areas, particularly in the prefrontal cortex (Blair, 2002; Diamond, 2002). Another reason is these different forms of self-regulation are jointly affected by children's experiences, such as the stresses children encounter from living in poverty (Hackman & Farah, 2009). Children who experience chronic stress exhibit multiple kinds of self-regulatory problems because of how persistent stresses affect brain and behavioral development (Thompson, 2014). A third reason is that when children have difficulty with one form of self-regulation, it can affect other kinds of self-regulation, such as when children who have difficulty quieting themselves for a learning activity also have difficulty focusing their attention and concentrating their thinking. A teacher's observation that some young children seem to have multiple self-regulatory challenges is consistent with how individual differences in self-regulation develop.

We can define self-regulation as the ability to internally manage one's attention, thinking, emotions and behavior without external control. The emphasis on internal rather than external control makes us think of self-regulation as self-control. Another way of thinking of self-regulation that is especially pertinent to young children is this: it consists of doing what *doesn't* come naturally (Thompson, 2009).

For educators of young children, the development of self-regulation presents a good news/bad news story. On one hand, the preschool and early elementary school years are a period of rapid growth in self-regulation and thus a time when educators can contribute to strengthening these skills (Best & Miller, 2010; Zelazo & Carlson, 2012). On the other hand, the development of self-regulation is an extended process, lasting into early adulthood owing to the slow maturation of the prefrontal brain regions on which self-regulatory capacities are based (Best & Miller, 2010). Both conclusions are important for educators of young children to keep in mind. While there is much that can be done to foster the growth of self-control in young children, the brain regions related to self-regulation are still at a primitive stage of maturation in early childhood, and it is important to have appropriate developmental expectations for children's management of their behavior, emotions, thinking, and attention.

Self-Regulation and Executive Functions

It can be helpful to unpack self-regulation into its components to better understand how these capacities contribute to young children's management of themselves. Researchers think that self-regulation consists of at least three components that they call *executive functions*. What are executive functions? A formal definition is that executive functions are cognitive skills that enable self-controlled, goal-directed thought and behavior (Best & Miller, 2010). Less formally, one might think of executive functions as like the mind's air traffic control system (Center on the Developing Child, 2011). Just as an airport's air traffic control system manages the departure and arrival of multiple flights to avoid crowded runways or delays, the mind's air traffic control system coordinates the multiple mental activities we must use simultaneously in everyday social or learning situations to avoid making mistakes. For adults, it is easy to think of the value of executive functions as we use them in multitasking, ignoring distractions in order to concentrate, monitoring others' reactions while socially interacting with them, or engaging in emotional self-control during an argument. Once we realize how important executive functions are to adult capacities for self-regulation, it is easy to see how their development is essential to children's abilities to act and think in ways that are socially appropriate and help them achieve their goals.

The primary cognitive skills that constitute executive functions include:

- *Inhibition*: the ability to resist a strong inclination to do one thing and instead do what is most appropriate or needed. Difficulty inhibiting initial impulses are at the root of many self-regulatory problems for young children, whether this involves using actions rather than words when frustrated, blurting out an answer rather than raising one's hand, or getting distracted rather than staying on task.
- *Mental flexibility:* the ability to switch perspective, attention, or mental focus. Self-regulation often involves being able to switch gears easily, such as understanding how a disagreement looks from the other person's perspective, transitioning from a favorite activity to a different activity, or looking at a problem from a different perspective to create a new solution.
- *Working memory:* the ability to hold information in mind while mentally working on it. Young children are still learning how to deliberately use their memory abilities, and self-regulatory problems can derive from limitations in working memory, such as forgetting instructions after beginning to carry them out, not remembering whose turn it is, or failing to connect a peer's emotional outburst with something that happened earlier in the day.

These (and other) executive functions work together. For adults, everyday social interaction engages mental flexibility (considering how the other person is thinking about the conversation), inhibition (determining the right, albeit insincere, response), and working memory (weighing a person's comment in light of a recent experience). The same is true of young children. When instructed by a teacher to clean up and get ready to go outside, the teacher may discover after five minutes that although some children are ready to go, several are still working on the prior activity (mental flexibility), others cleaned up but were distracted by a new activity (inhibition), and a few cleaned up but have forgotten to get ready to go outside (working memory). The obstacles that young children face in self-regulation are many!

Because of the importance of executive functions to self-regulation, studies show that they are also important to school achievement. In one study, preschool children who showed stronger executive function skills were also higher on standardized tests of literacy, vocabulary, and math. Moreover, growth in executive functions from the fall to the spring was associated with growth in emergent literacy, vocabulary, and math skills over the prekindergarten year (McClelland, Cameron, Connor, Farris, Jewkes, & Morrison, 2007). Similar findings were reported in a study of children in Head Start, which also showed that an intervention program strengthened executive function skills which, in turn, contributed to improvements over time in children's prereading competencies (Bierman, Nix, Greenberg, Blair, & Dometrovich, 2008). It is not surprising, as noted earlier, that problems associated with self-regulation are among the most prevalent reasons that kindergarten teachers regard certain children as not ready for school (Rimm-Kaufman et al., 2000).

Early childhood stress, often associated with family adversity such as economic difficulty, is associated with poorer executive functions (Noble, McCandliss, & Farah, 2007). and there is some evidence that these self-regulatory difficulties contribute to lower achievement in reading and math in the early elementary grades (Sektnan, McClelland, Acock, & Morrison, 2010). For this reason, promising intervention programs have been developed to strengthen self-regulatory skills in these children through curricular modules focused on improving self-control, problem-solving skills, and emotion understanding (Bierman et al., 2008) or through teacher training in behavioral management techniques, coupled with expert consultation (Raver, Jones, Li-Grining, Metzger, Champion, & Sardin, 2008). Early evidence indicates that when these programs are used appropriately, preschool children show gains in self-regulation and also improvements in their academic performance.

Supporting the Development of Self-Regulation in Young Children

Teachers in a preschool or early elementary classroom therefore have many reasons for strengthening self-regulatory skills in the children they teach. Here are some of the strategies they can use:

- *Developmentally appropriate expectations* are the first step. Parents of young children expect far greater self-control from them than is warranted on the basis of developmental science and research into brain development (Newton & Thompson, 2010). This is likely to be true also of those who work with young children in classrooms and other out-of-home settings. One reason for inappropriate expectations for young children's self-regulation is that things would be so much *easier* if children followed directions faithfully, kept their emotions in check, and reliably took turns – and since there are often one or two children in the group who do so, we expect that the rest of the children should be capable of doing so also. (It turns out that these self-regulated children may have a temperamental quality called *effortful control* that boosts their self-regulatory capability (Kochanska & Knaack, 2004).) It is important to keep in mind that the brain areas that support self-regulation in young children are still very immature, because without this awareness, it can become easy to perceive typical young children as being defiant or stubborn when they have difficulty controlling their emotions when distressed, become distracted during a long period of trying to sit still, lose their way when trying to follow complex multistep instructions, or have difficulty sharing materials that they have waited a long time to use.

- *Use "do" rather than "don't" statements when guiding children.* It is natural for adults to use prohibitions to deter inappropriate or impermissible behavior, such as "stop shouting" or "don't run indoors." But these instructions require inhibition, one of the executive functions that is only slowly maturing at this age. If teachers instead instruct children about what they should do instead—"use your indoor voice" or "walk so you don't run into others"—children can more easily enact these alternatives, which happen also to be incompatible with the inappropriate behavior.

- *Help children use words to regulate their behavior and thought.* We are familiar with the injunction "use your words when you're mad" as a guard against children expressing their frustration aggressively. Words are also a means of self-control in other situations. Young children can use self-talk to keep them focused on a science project ("First I dig a hole in the soil ... then I put in the seed and cover it up to see if it will grow. But now I need to water the seed ...") or a prereading activity ("What rhymes with cow?"). At this age, words have a self-regulatory effect because of the mental activity required for using language for self-instruction, and when language is used in this manner in a group activity, it also serves as a self-monitor.

- *Engage children in activities that provide practice in self-regulation* including games such as "Simon Says" and "Red Light Green Light." There are other activities that also enhance young children's self-regulation, such as sociodramatic play in which children must monitor their roles and the progress of the narrative (sociodramatic play is also an excellent stimulus to social skills), pauses in the schedule for children to plan their next activities (especially if planning needs to be done in a group in which different goals and desires have to be coordinated), and the availability of a quiet space (with storybooks) where children can retreat when they feel the need for an opportunity to regroup.

To a surprising extent, the capacity of young children to exercise self-regulation depends significantly on how the classroom space is organized, how the daily schedule is structured, and how teachers help in managing the number of self-regulatory demands a group setting presents for children. Each of these elements of a child's school experience can provide external support for the internal challenges of self-regulation. Thus when teachers create a daily schedule that is predictable (while being flexible), signal the approach of a transition between activities (so children can prepare for it), alternate quiet activities with more active periods, create a physical environment that is calming and orderly, and themselves model emotional self-control, cognitive flexibility, and attentional focus, young children are more capable of regulating their feelings, behavior, thinking and attention. While the brain's capacities for self-control are slowly maturing, in other words, children benefit from external support in developing their own self-regulation.

Emotion Understanding

One of the most important achievements of early childhood is developing understanding of people's feelings. Emotion understanding is more than just identifying the emotions in facial expressions or knowing the situations that evoke different feelings. It also involves understanding the causes of different emotions, the consequences of feeling angry or happy, and the significance of another's emotions for oneself. The latter is important because it is the basis for developing empathy and compassion for the experience of others and the growth of a genuinely human connection to another's experience that curbs aggressive and violent conduct (Thompson, 2011). Emotion understanding is thus a key ingredient for many social-emotional competencies, including developing positive relationships with peers and teachers, friendship, conflict resolution, emotion regulation, a sense of responsibility, and even moral conduct.

The early childhood years are a period of astonishing growth in emotion understanding (Pons, Harris, & de Rosnay, 2004; Thompson & Lagattuta, 2006). This may seem surprising to those of us who were taught that young children are egocentric and have difficulty distinguishing their own feelings and perspectives from those of others. But researchers today have a very different view: from early in life, young children have a very nonegocentric awareness that others' feelings, desires, and perspectives are different from the child's own (Wellman, 2014). It is true that young children often *act* in an egocentric manner, but when they resist sharing or are inconsolable until satisfied, this may reflect limited emotion self-regulation rather than egocentrism. Even a one-year-old is aware that another person may not be paying attention to what interests the child (this is why infants point at things). She or he also looks to the emotional expressions of a trusted adult to determine whether an unfamiliar person is safe or dangerous when the child is uncertain. These early achievements are the beginning of a fascinating journey of discovering how people's mental states—their focus of attention, desires, emotions, goals, intentions, thoughts and beliefs—affect their behavior. These discoveries unfold in the early childhood years, and researchers call this developing "theory of mind" (Wellman, 2014).

Emotions are an important element of the mental states that affect people's behavior. Infants and toddlers become proficient at identifying basic emotions in facial expressions and vocal intonations and responding appropriately to them. They enlist those emotions in their appraisal of everyday events, in part because they have learned that emotions are "about" objects and events (in other words, people don't just feel happy or angry; rather, they feel happy *about* something that has happened, or angry *at* someone). Somewhat later, young preschoolers learn that emotions are connected to other mental states like desires and goals (people feel happy when they get what they want, and sad when they don't), and by the age of five, they also learn that emotions are based on beliefs that may be mistaken (such as feeling sad by misunderstanding when the parent was due to arrive). In fact, children of this age also realize that emotions can be evoked by mental events alone (for example, recalling a sad event can make someone feel sad).

During the preschool years, young children are also learning about emotion regulation, which they believe can be accomplished by restricting exposure to emotionally arousing situations (e.g., covering the eyes and ears or getting away) or seeking support from an adult. By the early elementary years, however, they also learn emotion regulatory strategies that involve mental distraction (thinking happy thoughts) or changing goals (playing a new game after losing). As they are entering elementary school, children also begin to understand that emotions are not always shown but may be hidden or faked, such as when a child looks happy rather than annoyed when receiving an undesired gift. Older children also realize that people can feel more than one emotion in a situation (such as simultaneously feeling excited and anxious while boarding a roller coaster), and how personality characteristics can affect emotional reactivity (Maya is usually cheerful, but Josh gets angry quickly).

These advances in emotion understanding are important contributions to social understanding. They help young children gradually appreciate the diverse causes of others' feelings: not only immediate events but also previous events, thoughts about past events, and even personality characteristics contribute to the emotion we observe in another. These causes have implications for how emotions can be managed. Developing emotion understanding also helps young children gain insight into the complexity of people's behavior: emotions can be hidden, for example, and thus internal experience can remain private (and others can be fooled about how someone feels or thinks). Moreover, the insights that young children glean into others' emotional experiences provide them with perspective on their own emotions. Although it can be difficult to apply your rapidly developing emotion knowledge to your own feelings, with adult assistance young children can reflect on why they're feeling sad or angry (was it the peer's behavior, or something that preceded it?) and how best to manage strong feelings.

As these examples illustrate, insight into emotion can be assisted by activities with adults who can help to identify the feelings of other people (and the child), their causes, and emotion regulatory strategies. Here are some approaches adults can use:

- *Provide words for the emotion and talk about its causes*, because of the value of language in developing young children's concepts about emotion. Sometimes it is best to have these conversations at the moment that emotions are witnessed or experienced because the event is more immediate to the child. But sometimes it is best to wait for a later occasion, when feelings have calmed, to review with the child what happened and why, because then the child may be more capable of taking perspective on the experience and enlisting his or her knowledge to apply to that incident. In these situations, talking with sympathetic understanding of how another person felt and why, even if the feelings were disruptive, can help children adopt a more compassionate attitude toward another's feelings. With children of all ages, it can be helpful first to solicit the child's understanding of what was witnessed or felt before providing the adult's perspective. It can also be helpful to generalize from specific experiences to broader realities ("David got mad when you knocked over his block buildings. People don't like it when other people ruin their work.").

- *Seek opportunities to role-play emotional experiences and their consequences.* In fact, this is what young children themselves do spontaneously, such as in sociodramatic play. "Trying on" strong feelings and their results while playing a role can provide a forum for exploring what it is like to feel that way, what actions result, and strategies for emotion regulation, as well as considering the effects of emotion on how people get along. Storybook reading and puppet play can be enlisted for similar purposes, especially when children are encouraged to imagine how the story characters felt in different circumstances, and why.

- *Model and talk about your own emotions and your experience of them.* Young children are like sponges for new understanding of how people feel and think, and when we talk openly about these mental states and their effects on our actions, it advances their theory of mind. Talking about a recent disappointing experience or using words to say how you felt when children were especially helpful, or conversing about how you manage the frustration of dropping a tray of beads as you are cleaning them up together can give young children significant insights into emotion and its consequences.

- *Help children appreciate the individuality of their own emotional experiences, and those of others.* Young children are aware of the differences in personality among their peers, but putting these into words and encouraging children's thinking about how their own personality affects their emotions and behavior can help children understand emotions better, and also understand themselves ("You like to jump into games fast, but Nina likes to watch for a while first.").

Social Skills

Central to social-emotional learning are social skills: the capacities for cooperation, conflict negotiation, friendship, sensitivity to others' feelings, responsible conduct, and other skills that enable children to get along with others and be a contributing member of the group. We consider social skills last because they are based on the capacities for self-regulation and emotion understanding earlier discussed. With emotion understanding comes the child's comprehension of why we treat others with consideration and respect; with self-regulatory ability comes the capacity to enact positive, constructive social behaviors even in situations where they conflict with self-interest. Developmental changes in social skills derive from many things, including growth in social understanding, knowledge and memory for social expectations, a sense of oneself as a group participant, the incentives provided by close relationships, and other ingredients—but central are the child's developing capacities for self-regulation and growing understanding of emotions.

A teacher's efforts to strengthen social skills in young children is a significant contributor to academic success because at school, children's learning occurs in a group setting in which social interactions and relationships color the experience of learning. This is vividly illustrated by studies showing that children who develop warm, positive relationships with their kindergarten teachers and with other children are more excited about learning, more positive about coming to school, more self-confident, and achieve more in the classroom than do children who experience more troubled or conflicted relationships with their teachers or other children (Ladd, Birch, & Buhs, 1999; see review by Thompson & Raikes, 2007). The connection between classroom relationships and academic achievement is especially strong for children who are otherwise at risk for academic difficulty because of the support and motivation these relationships can provide.

To encourage the development of social skills in young children, here are some of the strategies that teachers can use:

- *Coach children in successful peer interactions* by engaging children in problem-solving solutions. Rather than immediately suggesting a strategy for cooperation, such as turn-taking or compromise, a teacher can begin by putting into words the feelings, desires, goals, expectations or other mental states that underlie the conflict, drawing on the child's developing theory of mind to understand why he or she is having trouble getting along with another child. The teacher can also ask the child to suggest possible solutions to the difficulty and help them choose one to try—and then check back to see how well it is being implemented. On other occasions, teachers can look for instances of cooperative, constructive peer interaction and underscore the reason why such conduct is desirable ("I notice that Maria helped Jeon find the book he needed, and that means that you *both* can do your work now."). Above all, the teacher can verbalize his or her observations of children's behavior with other children to put into words what children are doing and the reasons why.
- *Build a classroom community with shared responsibility for "our" room.* Young children are gradually building a sense of themselves not only as individuals but also as members of a group, and classroom experiences can help them understand the roles and responsibilities involved in group membership. This can involve, for example, gently reminding children that everyone

should be involved in cleaning up, even when they were not personally responsible for the mess. It can involve enlisting children's participation in group decision-making, such as choosing a name for a classroom pet and engaging in a democratic process like voting to make the final choice. It also involves helping children understand classroom rules and the reasons for them ("we raise hands during circle time because that gives everyone a chance to be heard and everyone a chance to listen").

- *Engage children in classroom projects that require cooperation with one or more other children.* Social skills are developed in social interaction when young children have direct experience with negotiation, compromise, turn-taking, persuasion, and devising other solutions to the disagreements that inevitably arise. When they are doing so in the context of an overall goal, such as completing a shared project, it can motivate greater efforts to understand and the work through differences. Depending on the age of the child, teachers can encourage children to devise their own solutions to difficulties rather than appealing for an adult's assistance.
- *Engage children's families.* Social skills are developing at home as well as in the classroom. Regular communication with families about the social-emotional aspects of children's experiences in preschool or elementary school can help families support the growth of cooperation, empathy, responsibility, and other capabilities.

Concluding Comments

The widening recognition that social-emotional learning is foundational draws renewed attention to the preschool or early elementary classroom as an environment for learning. Amid calls for greater academic attention to emergent literacy, number skills, and scientific reasoning, it can be easy to think of young children as individual learners disconnected from the social environment in which they are learning, and as cognitive beings who do not need also to develop emotional and self-regulatory capacities. If we instead regard the classroom through the eyes of young children, in which the challenges of managing to interact successfully in a complex environment of other children and adults are comparable to (and sometimes more daunting than) mastering letters and numbers, the importance of the classroom as a forum for social-emotional learning becomes clearer.

It is not just the *content* but also the *manner* of learning that distinguishes social-emotional learning. Teachers can create lessons on cooperation and people's feelings as they do lessons on minerals and rocks. But because social-emotional learning is based on young children's lived experience, many additional opportunities to foster learning emerge spontaneously from the interactions of children with peers and adults in the classroom, and wise teachers take advantage of these opportunities. This is, in a sense, the implementation of emergent curriculum for learning about emotions, people, and the self. Moreover, it is sometimes best when teachers make learning opportunities out of shared discussion of events in the recent past that posed emotional challenges or involved social conflict, when young children's passions have cooled and their ability to reflect is greater. All of these forms of guidance are important to social-emotional learning (McClelland, Tominey, Schmitt, & Duncan, 2017; Moreno, Nagasawa, & Schwartz, 2018).

With the science of social-emotional learning sufficiently clear to demonstrate its importance both to classroom learning and to young children's well-being (see also Thompson & Raikes, 2007), the challenge—but also responsibility and opportunity—for teachers is understanding how to deeply incorporate social-emotional learning into young children's classroom experiences. Since those learning opportunities exist in every child's school day, this is a wonderful challenge to confront.

References

Best, J.R., & Miller, P.H. (2010). A developmental perspective on executive function. *Child Development, 81*, 1641–1660.

Bettencourt, A., Gross, D., & Ho, G. (2016). *The Costly Consequences of Not Being Socially and Behaviorally Ready by Kindergarten: Associations with Grade Retention, Receipt of Academic Support Services, and Suspensions/Expulsions*. Baltimore, MD: Baltimore Education Research Consortium.

Bierman, K.L., Nix, R.L., Greenberg, M.T., Blair, C., & Dometrovich, C.E. (2008). Executive functions and school readiness intervention: Impact, moderation, and mediation in the Head Start REDI program. *Development and Psychopathology, 20*, 821–843.

Blair, C. (2002). School readiness: Integrating cognition and emotion in a neurobiological conceptualization of children's functioning at school entry. *American Psychologist, 57*, 111–127.

Center on the Developing Child. (2011). *Building the Brain's "Air Traffic Control" System: How Early Experiences Shape the Development of Executive Function*. Working Paper number 11. Retrieved from: https://developingchild.harvard.edu/resources/building-the-brains-air-traffic-control-system-how-early-experiences-shape-the-development-of-executive-function/

Committee on the Science of Children Birth to Age 8: Deepening and Broadening the Foundation for Success. (2015). *Transforming the Workforce for Children Birth Through Age 8: A Unifying Foundation*. Washington, DC: National Academies Press.

Diamond, A. (2002). Normal development of prefrontal cortex from birth to young adulthood: Cognitive functions, anatomy, and biochemistry. In D.T. Stuss & R.T. Knight (Eds.), *Principles of Frontal Lobe Function* (pp. 466–503). New York: Oxford University Press.

Duncan, G.J. (2016, October 20). Addressing behavior problems of 5- to 12-year-olds is as important for their future schooling as teaching them math and language (blog post). Retrieved from: https://www.childandfamilyblog.com/child-development/behavior-problems-future-schooling/

Duncan, G.J., Dowsett, C.J., Claessens, A., Magnuson, K., Huston, A.C., Klebanov, P., Pagani, L.S., Feinstein, L., Engel, M., Brooks-Gunn, J., Sexton, H., Duckworth, K., & Japel, C. (2007). School readiness and later achievement. *Developmental Psychology, 43*, 1428–1446.

Gilliam, W.S. (2005). *Prekindergarteners Left Behind: Expulsion Rates in State Prekindergarten Systems.* Foundation for Child Development Policy Brief Series, number 3. New York: Foundation for Child Development.

Hackman, D.A., & Farah, M.J. (2009). Socioeconomic status and the developing brain. *Trends in Cognitive Sciences, 13,* 65–73.

Jones, D.E., Greenberg, M., & Crowley, M. (2015). Early social-emotional functioning and public health: Relationship between kindergarten social competence and future wellness. *American Journal of Public Health, 105,* 2283–2290.

Jones, S.M., & Kahn, J. (2017). *The Evidence Base for How We Learn: Supporting Students' Social, Emotional, and Academic Development.* Consensus statements of evidence from the Council of Distinguished Scientists, National Commission on Social, Emotional, and Academic Development. Washington, DC: The Aspen Institute.

Jones, S.M., Zaslow, M., Darling-Churchill, K.E., & Halle, T.G. (2016). Assessing early childhood social and emotional development: Key conceptual and measurement issues. *Journal of Applied Developmental Psychology, 45,* 42–48.

Kochanska, G., & Knaack, A. (2004). Effortful control as a personality characteristic of young children: Antecedents, correlates, and consequences. *Journal of Personality, 71,* 1087–1112.

Ladd, G.W., Birch, S.H., & Buhs, E.S. (1999). Children's social and scholastic lives in kindergarten: Related spheres of influence? *Child Development, 70,* 1373–1400.

Magnuson, K., Duncan, G.J., Lee, K.T.H., & Metzger, M.W. (2016). Early school adjustment and educational attainment. *American Educational Research Journal, 53,* 1198–1228.

McClelland, M.M., Cameron, C.E., Connor, C.M., Farris, C.L., Jewkes, A.M., & Morrison, F.J. (2007). Links between behavioral regulation and preschoolers' literacy, vocabulary, and math skills. *Developmental Psychology, 43,* 947–959.

McClelland, M.M., Tominey, S.L., Schmitt, S.A., & Duncan, R. (2017). SEL intervention in early childhood. *The Future of Children, 27,* 33–47.

Moreno, A.J., Nagasawa, M.K., & Schwartz, T. (2018). Social and emotional learning and early childhood education: Redundant terms? *Contemporary Issues in Early Childhood,* in press.

Newton, E.K., & Thompson, R.A. (2010). Parents' views of early social and emotional development: More and less than meets the eye. *Zero to Three Journal, 31,* 10–15.

Noble, K.G., McCandliss, B.D., & Farah, M.J. (2007). Socioeconomic gradients predict individual differences in neurocognitive abilities. *Developmental Science, 10,* 464–480.

Pons, F., Harris, P.L., & de Rosnay, M. (2004). Emotion comprehension between 3 and 11 years: Developmental periods and hierarchical organization. *European Journal of Developmental Psychology, 1,* 127–152.

Raver, C.C., Jones, S.M., Li-Grining, C., Metzger, M., Champion, K.M., & Sardin, L. (2008). Improving preschool classroom processes: Preliminary findings from a randomized trial implemented in Head Start settings. *Early Childhood Research Quarterly, 23,* 10–26.

Rimm-Kaufman, S.E., Pianta, R.C., & Cox, M.J. (2000). Teachers' judgments of problems in the transition to kindergarten. *Early Childhood Research Quarterly, 15,* 147–166.

Rock, L., & Crow, S. (2017). Not just "soft skills": How young children's learning and health benefit from strong social-emotional development. Washington, DC: Too Small to Fail.

Sektnan, M., McClelland, M.M., Acock, A., & Morrison, F.J. (2010). Relations between early family risk, children's behavioral regulation, and academic achievement. *Early Childhood Research Quarterly, 25,* 464–479.

Thompson, R.A. (2009). Doing what *doesn't* come naturally: The development of self-regulation. *Zero to Three Journal, 30*, 33–39.

Thompson, R.A. (2011). The emotionate child. In D. Cicchetti & G.I. Roissman (Eds.), *The Origins and Organization of Adaptation and Maladaptation. Minnesota Symposium on Child Psychology* (vol. 36, pp. 13–54). New York: Wiley.

Thompson, R.A. (2014). Stress and child development. *The Future of Children, 24*, 41–59.

Thompson, R.A., & Lagatutta, K. (2006). Feeling and understanding: Early emotional development. In K. McCartney & D. Phillips (Ed.), *The Blackwell Handbook of Early Childhood Development* (pp. 317–337). Oxford: Blackwell.

Thompson, R.A., & Raikes, H.A. (2007). The social and emotional foundations of school readiness. In D.F. Perry, R.F. Kaufmann & J. Knitzer (Eds.), *Social and Emotional Health in Early Childhood: Building Bridges Between Services and Systems* (pp. 13–35). Baltimore, MD: Paul H. Brookes Publishing Co.

Wellman, H.M. (2014). *Making Minds: How Theory of Mind Develops*. New York: Oxford.

Zelazo, P.D., & Carlson, S.M. (2012). Hot and cool executive function in childhood and adolescence: Development and plasticity. *Child Development Perspectives, 6*, 354–360.

3 Culturally Responsive Teaching in Early Childhood

Marisha L. Humphries

Figure 3.1 Children learning together.

Almost half of the children in the U.S. are under eight years old, with 30.7% of these children being five years of age or younger (National Kids Count, 2018b). In 2017, approximately 51% of children under the age of five were from underrepresented racial and ethnic groups (including bi- and multi-racial children) with Latino/Hispanic (26%) and Black/African American (14%) representing the majority of the children in this group (National Kids Count, 2018a). Despite the increase in the number of children from diverse racial and linguistic backgrounds, teachers are struggling to provide a responsive, high-quality educational experience for culturally and linguistically diverse (CALD) children (Durden, Escalante, & Blitch, 2015). Generic, high-quality teaching alone is not sufficient to educate a diverse population of young children entering educational and childcare settings. To provide a positive learning environment, teaching practices must incorporate the cultural knowledge, experiences, learning, and communication styles of CALD children. This chapter will examine the need for culturally responsive teaching in early childhood educational settings to promote equity and opportunity for young children (Figure 3.1).

High-Quality Early Childhood Education and Care

High-quality early childhood teaching and care go beyond meeting the basic needs of young children: these high-quality strategies also provide young children with opportunities for meaningful learning activities and language development, and work to foster close, caring relationships between children and their teachers. The essential characteristics of high-quality early childhood education and care include teachers providing sensitive and stimulating interactions and developmentally appropriate activities for young children (Burchinal, 2011; Rhodes & Huston, 2012).

The focus on high-quality educational standards is steeped in educational practices that have traditionally not included issues of culture and diversity. High-quality early childhood practices have yielded positive outcomes for all groups of children. However, current conceptions of high-quality education in early childhood settings are still not providing significant outcomes for CALD children. Perhaps there is a need to examine different types of quality in early childhood to identify the high-quality practices needed to yield significant educational outcomes for CALD children. For instance, two types of quality emerged in the evaluation of early childhood education: *structural* and *process* quality (Reid & Kagan, 2015). Research on high-quality early childhood education largely focuses on *structural* quality as it relates to class size, teacher-child ratio, and teacher credentials. *Process* quality research focuses on teacher-child interactions and emotional support. This includes teachers acknowledging and supporting students, and providing them with positive verbal (i.e., praise and encouragement) and non-verbal (i.e., smiles and nods) feedback. Issues of culture, diversity, and equity are also factors in *process* quality; however, these factors are rarely addressed when examining issues of high-quality in research or educational practices for young children.

High-Quality for Who?

Many educational and child development organizations (e.g., National Association for the Education of Young Children, National Head Start Association, Zero to Three) indicate in their position or mission statements that teachers and care-providers of young children must have the professional capacity to meet the diverse needs of their students (Reid & Kagan, 2015). High-quality early childhood education entails practices that are targeted to children's needs (Yoshikawa, Wuermli, Raikes, Kim, & Kabay, 2018). It includes nurturing and sensitive care and high expectations of all children. Unfortunately, CALD children are less likely to attend high-quality early childhood facilities or receive high-quality care (Burchinal & Cryer, 2003; Magnuson & Waldfogel, 2005). Furthermore, when the focus is on children's cultural, racial/ethnic and linguistic needs, there is often opposition to such efforts. Many will argue that engaging in such cultural practices will reduce the quality of the educational experiences children are receiving. Or cultural instructional practices are seen as "add-ons' to traditional high-quality educational practices. Despite what many educators believe, utilizing a cultural lens in education is not antithetical to high-quality instruction. High-quality early childhood education must support young children's socio-cultural development and awareness to create positive learning experiences and success (Durden et al., 2015).

Colorblind Ideology for Young Children

Schools and educators are sources of racial information for the students they serve (Lewis, 2001). However, there is often resistance to addressing issues of race, ethnicity, and culture in education, and this is especially true in early childhood. Educators often have the erroneous assumption that acknowledging and embracing race equates to treating certain groups poorly or engaging in discriminatory and racist behavior. In addition, there is a lack of acceptance of how race is woven into the fabric of U.S. society, which impacts children and the systems serving children. Not only are issues of race ignored or not addressed, but there is no attempt to challenge or dismantle racist practices and oppression in education and care spaces. This lack of acknowledgment allows teachers to not only avoid racial realities, but also allows the teacher to avoid personal understanding and perceptions of race.

This is called a colorblind ideology, whereby there is a denial of racial differences by emphasizing sameness and a denial of racism by pushing the belief that everyone has equal opportunities (Neville, Awad, Brooks Flores, & Bluemel, 2013). Individuals who embrace a colorblind ideology attempt to operate from a space where race does not matter and believe race is unimportant in everyday interactions.

Many teachers who embrace a colorblind ideology will contend, "I don't see color," "I teach all my students the same," "A good teacher can teach all students," "Race is not a factor in teaching," and "Young children don't see race." All of these statements indicate that race is neutral and does not matter in the lives of young children. Colorblindness ignores the fact that all individuals, including children and teachers, are cultural beings. And we are all impacted by our cultural context. Yes, even young children see race; they are not blind to race. Children as young as three to five years old can categorize individuals by race and have developed racial biases (Aboud, 2008). These racial biases are not the direct result of young children learning them from their parents (Winkler, 2009); instead, children adopt the racial biases they are exposed to in society by way of school, literature, media, and social interactions. When teachers and schools ignore the culture of their students, they are invalidating children's humanity. A colorblind ideology is a fantasy at best, where one pretends to live in a world where racism and oppression do not exist, and dangerous at its worst. Avoiding conversations about race helps to strengthen young children's bias and stereotypes about race and ethnicity, which is the opposite of what many colorblind educators believe they are doing with their "color-free" approach.

Many will argue issues of cultural diversity, especially as it relates to race and ethnicity in early childhood education, is unnecessary. Young children are perceived as "pure" and "innocent," and adults should not bias or pollute them with issues of race and culture. Teachers who have this perspective believe race is absent or not relevant in children's early life and educational experiences. This chapter rejects this ideology. Instead, this chapter starts from the space that racial, ethnic and language diversity are important in the lives of young children. As such, the focus is on why integrating cultural diversity into early education is critical for the success of CALD children.

Many underestimate young children's awareness and understanding of racial messages and dynamics. Children learn from their experiences in society that whiteness is normalized and privileged in the U.S. (Winkler, 2009). Researchers note young children are quite aware and have developed sophisticated, age-related understandings of racial and ethnic issues (Boutte, 2018; Delpit, 2017). Therefore, it is our responsibility as early childhood teachers to address cultural, linguistic, and racial issues in our practices in order to truly provide a high-quality educational experience for all children.

Culturally Responsive Teaching

Neither society nor classrooms are neutral spaces, therefore education is not a neutral process (Boutte, 2018). Education, like all facets of society, is impacted by ideologies including those related to race, linguistics, and oppression. Reid and Kagan (2015) argue that quality and equity are intertwined and must be considered together. In order to provide high-quality early childhood education and care, teachers must include equity in their instruction. Race and culture are recognized as significant factors in the learning process—factors that facilitate achievement. Irvine (2009) contends the reason many culturally diverse students fail is due to the lack of connection teachers make between children's knowledge and cultural perspective and curricular content. Culturally responsive teaching (CRT) utilizes the "cultural knowledge, prior experiences, frames of reference, and performance styles of ethnically diverse students to make learning environments more relevant to and effective for them" (Gay, 2010, p. 31). This cultural knowledge includes the sociocultural background of not only the children but also their settings, neighborhoods, and families (Gay, 2013). As such, instructional practices need to be informed by this localized cultural and contextual specificity. Teachers who engage in CRT acknowledge the unequal distribution of power and privilege in our society. Public systems including educational systems that are supposed to help children and families have in many instances denied CALD children opportunities for success (The Annie E. Casey Foundation, 2014). The promotion of justice in educational practices challenges the –isms in our society (Irvine, 2009). The intentional engagement in CRT is crucial for young children's educational achievement and socio-cultural development (Durden et al., 2015).

As noted previously, issues regarding culture and race are often absent from early childhood settings as many teachers believe young children should be "protected" from race. Teachers' engagement in a traditional colorblind orientation in early childhood classrooms is in direct opposition to CRT. CRT takes a positive approach to teaching CALD children by focusing on equity and opportunity as opposed to what has become the "standard" in education, a deficit approach that engages in "gap gazing." Gap gazing focuses problem-solving efforts and resources on closing the achievement gap of CALD children as opposed to disrupting and dismantling the disparities in opportunities leading to the achievement gap for CALD children (Iruka, Curenton, & Durden, 2018). A culturally relevant pedagogy places culture at the center of both instruction and learning, and utilizes CRT to engage and facilitate achievement among CALD children. Culture and language are critical elements of education; their inclusion starts from planning, continuing to instruction and then assessment (Ladson-Billings, 1999).

CRT is effective, high-quality instruction from a cultural perspective that connects children's lived cultural experiences to content standards. Students' cultural knowledge and ways of learning are incorporated into the classroom and instruction. This includes behavioral expressions of knowledge, beliefs, and values that recognize the significance of race and culture in learning.

CRT is a developmental process where educators are learning over time (Gay, 2013). There is a struggle as one learns and begins to make sense of issues of power and privilege in their own personal identities and in how it impacts their teaching. Due to the on-going learning nature of CRT, many early childhood teachers may feel unequipped to engage in this type of work. This includes not just a lack of skill to engage in CRT teaching strategies, but also the inability to identify and access culturally relevant instructional materials (Gay, 2013). A list of strategies (by no means exhaustive) facilitating the implementation of CRT in early childhood settings is provided (see Table 3.1). Early childhood teachers must have the capacity to effectively teach in diverse early childhood classrooms (Reid & Kagan, 2015).

Table 3.1 Strategies and resources to engage in Culturally Relevant Teaching (CRT)

Classroom books and materials relevant to diverse racial and ethnic groups
Classroom books and materials in languages of the young children in your classroom
Encourage home language use in the classroom
Teachers should learn phrases in children's home language and use in the classroom and
    to engage with parents/caregivers
Teachers must be willing to engage in discussions about race, ethnicity, linguistics, social
    class, etc.
Teachers must educate themselves on issues of race and culture
Teachers need to raise strengths-based questions –
    What are the strengths of this family?
    What are the strengths of this family's cultural background?
    How do I capitalize on the child's and their family's strengths to educate the child?
        (Iruka, Curenton & Eke 2014).
Professional development and coaching for early childhood teachers to implement CRT
Directors must ask their teachers explicit questions about culture and language as it relates
    the young children in their early childhood settings
Website provides a listing of multicultural and urban children's literature by
    developmental age- http://www.kidslikeus.org/
Website provides resources for educators to teach issues of diversity that focuses on social
    justice and anti-bias. Teaching Tolerance - https://www.tolerance.org/

Approaches to Culturally Responsive Teaching and Practice

One approach placing culture at the center of work with young children and families is the culturally responsive, anti-bias family engagement (CRAF-E4). To help early childhood educators work successfully with diverse families, CRAF-E4 utilizes the cultural knowledge, experiences, and communication styles of CALD children and their families while also acknowledging the social injustice, inequality, and prejudice children and families experience (Iruka, Curenton, & Eke, 2014). The four Es in the CRAF-E4 approach are Expectation, Education, Exploration, and Empowerment. Teachers must have high expectations for CALD children. This requires teachers to both identify and raise their implicit and explicit educational and behavior expectations of CALD children. The second E, Education, focuses on having educators help families support their children's optimal development. Educators also need to explore how to partner and value families. And finally, educators utilizing this framework empower families on ways to advocate for their children to address issues of social justice and injustice.

As evidenced by the CRAF-E4 model, engaging in culturally relevant practice is not just focused on topics of cross-group similarities, ethnic foods, holidays and customs, or using colloquial language and pop culture in the classroom (Irvine, 2009), but also must address issues of inequality and oppression (Gay, 2013). CRT is not tokenism whereby heroes of a particular racial or ethnic group are plastered on classroom or school walls and highlighted during that group's "month" (e.g., books and posters about Martin Luther King Jr or Barack Obama in February, Maya Lin and Michelle Kwan in May, Cesar Chavez or Sonia Sotomayor in October, and Sacagawea and Crazy Horse in November). The inclusion of cultural and linguistic components at the surface level without real understanding and integration into teachers' instructional practices often has the opposite effect to what was intended. Teachers must engage young children in age-appropriate conversations about these issues. For example, real discussions about the impact of societal and governmental actions on immigration on children and families. CRT needs to be incorporated not only into teachers' instructional practices and the curriculum, but also child and classroom assessments and evaluation, along with early childhood teachers' professional development (Iruka et al., 2014).

The Role of the Teacher in CRT

A review of the literature revealed teachers know little about racism, oppression, and structural inequality (Sleeter, 2001). This helps to explain why the process of teaching from a CRT perspective is initially uncomfortable as teachers have to acknowledge and address issues of oppression and privilege and learn to teach toward equity and social justice. Such teaching begins with teachers identifying and reflecting on their personal identities and the multiple identities of the young children in their classrooms. CRT is both critically reflective and intentional (Durden et al., 2015). Highlighting the need for teachers to have ongoing professional development as it relates to teaching for equity. Teachers and schools committed to providing a culturally relevant educational experience for their young children must develop a strengths-based perspective of CALD children their families, communities, and culture.

The National Association for the Education of Young Children's (NAEYC) first ethical principle of doing no harm provides support for CRT. The principle states that those in early childhood teaching shall not engage in practices that harm children emotionally or physically, or that are disrespectful of, exploit or intimidate children (NAEYC, 2011). Boutte (2018) utilizes this principle as justification for why early childhood teachers need to examine their instructional practices to determine if they are appropriate for Black and other CALD children. Boutte contends that traditional educational practices rooted in a White-privileged, Eurocentric framework can cause social and emotional harm to African American children, and children from other racial and ethnic minority groups. Low expectations, including a lack of texts about and perspectives of diverse cultural groups, unawareness of cultural expressions of behavior, and harsh discipline (including suspension and expulsion from early childhood settings; Gilliam, Maupin, Reyes, Accavitti, & Shic, 2016) contribute to the "harm" CALD children are exposed to in early childhood settings. For example, Black children's behavior is often viewed more negatively and harshly by their teachers (Gilliam et al., 2016). Children speaking a primary language other than English are often punished or assumed to be less capable of academic achievement (Pettit, 2011) in educational settings which value and privilege English. The core values of NAEYC's (2011) standards of ethical behaviors indicate children are best supported in the context of their culture where there is respect for diversity among children, families, and professionals.

Many teachers may agree cultural diversity is important but do not understand how to incorporate cultural diversity into early childhood classrooms. Furthermore, few teachers actually implement or engage in teaching that supports diverse cultural perspectives in early childhood classrooms, aside from the occasional ethnic potluck or cultural holiday celebration. As a result, teachers may resist CRT due to a lack of knowledge and access to resources supporting the diverse cultures of children in their classrooms. Effective instruction is responsive to the diverse cultural backgrounds of all students in the classroom (Gay, 2002; Kidd, Sánchez, & Thorp, 2008). CRT uses a cultural frame of reference or lens for instruction and curriculum content (Gay, 2013) while providing children with access to resources and opportunities. This can include utilizing young children's home language in the classroom and instructional practices that match the learning styles of CALD children (e.g., oral storytelling, communal goals). An example of an instructional strategy that honors a communal orientation is cooperative learning activities. In a cooperative learning activity, teachers can create groups of students with different abilities who are tasked with sorting manipulatives into categories created and defined by the student groups.

Given many teachers do not share the cultural or linguistic background of their students, these teachers will need explicit cultural examples. Teachers will need to learn the diverse strengths of CALD children and their communities, and how to use this information to improve children's educational achievement. For some teachers this is counter to how they have been trained to think about the education of CALD children. Early childhood teachers' attitudes, beliefs, and experiences impact the quality of care and educational experiences they provide to the young children in their classrooms (Rhodes & Huston, 2012). Therefore, teachers who have limited or negative beliefs about CALD children are unable to provide the high-quality education and care environment that CALD children not only need but deserve.

Teachers' own cultural and educational background can bias them against children and families who come from different backgrounds than their own (Iruka et al., 2014). For instance, when teachers identify "the right way" for children to learn and behave they are relying on a culturally determined standard that may not align with the cultural background of the children in their classrooms. This may prevent them from engaging in a strengths-based perspective allowing for culturally relevant teaching. CRT requires teachers to be intentional and reflective (Durden et al., 2015).

This self-reflection practice allows teachers the opportunity to understand their own cultural identities, the cultural background of CALD children, and the interaction between teachers and children's cultural background. Questions that may arise during this reflective process include, "What do I believe are the causes of achievement difficulties of various culturally and linguistically diverse children?" "How do my own family and educational background influence my expectation of CALD children and families?" "How do my own family and educational background influence my teaching practice?" "Can I identify how specific beliefs about CALD children are embedded in my instructional practice and behavior expectations?" As teachers engage in this reflective practice, it will allow them to begin to replace deficient perceptions and beliefs of CALD children with more positive perceptions and beliefs of CALD children and their families (Gay, 2013). For example, as a result of participating in a study about culturally relevant teaching in early childhood classrooms, early childhood teachers became more aware of their students' cultural and linguistic backgrounds (Durden et al., 2015). Some of these teachers were also observed to engage in more culturally relevant practices in the classroom. Engaging in CRT requires teachers to be aware of and reflective on their multiple identities (i.e., racial, ethnic, cultural, linguistic, gender, etc.) and the intersectionality of their identities with the identities of their students and families (Cochran-Smith, 2004; Durden et al., 2015).

Conclusion

Teaching is a sociopolitical practice where the classroom can be a place of equity, justice, and opportunity (Banks, 1993; Durden et al., 2015). Implementing equity-based instruction creates a positive learning environment for CALD children. Early childhood teachers can improve the achievement potential of CALD children by teaching through the children's cultural lens (Gay, 2013). When CALD children are provided with the opportunity to develop an identity of excellence, they are more able to be successful in early childhood settings (Humphries & Iruka, 2018).

References

Aboud, F.E. (2008). A social-cognitive developmental theory of prejudice. In S.M. Quintana & C. McKown (Eds.), *Handbook of Race, Racism, and the Developing Child* (pp. 55–71). Hoboken, NJ: John Wiley & Sons.

Banks, J.A. (1993). Multicultural education: Historical development, dimensions, and practice. *Review of Research in Education, 19*, 3–49.

Boutte, G. (2018). Teaching about racial equity issues in teacher education programs. In I.U. Iruka, S. Curenton & T. Durden (Eds.), *African American Children in Early Childhood Education: Making the Case for Policy Investments in Families, Schools, and Communities* (pp. 247–266). Emerald Group Publishing Limited.

Burchinal, M. (2011). Differentiating among measures of quality: Key characteristics and their coverage in existing measures. *Research to Policy, Research to Practice Brief OPRE.*

Burchinal, M.R., & Cryer, D. (2003). Diversity, child care quality, and developmental outcomes. *Early Childhood Research Quarterly, 18*, 401–426.

Cochran-Smith, M. (2004). *Walking the Road: Race, Diversity, and Social Justice in Teacher Education.* New York: Teachers College Press.

Delpit, L. (2017). Seeing color. In W. Au, B. Bigelow & S. Karp (Eds.), *Rethinking Our Classrooms: Teachers for Equity and Justice* (vol. 1, 2nd ed., pp.158–160). Milwaukee, WI: Rethinking Schools.

Durden, T.R., Escalante, E., & Blitch, K. (2015). Start with us! Culturally relevant pedagogy in the preschool classroom. *Early Childhood Education Journal, 43*(3), 223–232.

Gay, G. (2010). *Culturally Responsive Teaching: Theory, Research, and Practice* (2nd ed.). New York: Teachers College, Columbia University.

Gay, G. (2013). Teaching to and through cultural diversity. *Curriculum Inquiry, 43*, 48–70.

Gilliam, W.S., Maupin, A.N., Reyes, C.R., Accavitti, M., & Shic, F. (2016). Do early educators' implicit biases regarding sex and race relate to behavior expectations and recommendations of preschool expulsions and suspensions. *Research Study Brief*, Yale University, Yale Child Study Center, New Haven, CT.

Iruka, I.U., Curenton, S.M., & Durden, T.R. (2018). Introduction. In I.U. Iruka, S. Curenton & T. Durden (Eds.), *African American Children in Early Childhood Education: Making the Case for Policy Investments in Families, Schools, and Communities* (pp. 3–13). Emerald Group Publishing Limited.

Iruka, I., Curenton, S., & Eke, W. (2014). *The CRAF-E4 Family Engagement Model: Building Practitioners' Competence to Work with Diverse Families*. Academic Press.

Irvine, J.J. (2009). Relevant: Beyond the basics. *Teaching Tolerance, 36*, 41–44.

Kidd, J.K., Sánchez, S.Y., & Thorp, E.K. (2008). Defining moments: Developing culturally responsive dispositions and teaching practices in early childhood preservice teachers. *Teaching and Teacher Education, 24*(2), 316–329.

Ladson-Billings, G. (1999). Preparing teachers for diversity. In L. Darling-Hammond & G. Sykes (Eds.), *Teaching as the Learning Profession* (pp. 86–123). San Francisco, CA: Jossey-Bass.

Lewis, A.E. (2001). There is no "race" in the schoolyard: Color-blind ideology in an (almost) all-white school. *American Educational Research Journal, 38*(4), 781–811.

Magnuson, K.A., & Waldfogel, J. (2005). Early childhood care and education: Effects on ethnic and racial gaps in school readiness. *The Future of Children, 15*, 169–196.

National Association for the Education of Young Children (NAEYC). (2011). *NAEYC Code of Ethical Conduct and Statement of Commitment: Position Statement*. Washington, DC: National Association for the Education of Young Children.

National Kids Count. (2018a). Child population by race and age group. Annie E. Casey Foundation. Retrieved from: https://datacenter.kidscount.org/data/tables/8446-child-population-by-race-and-age-group?loc=1&loct=1#detailed/1/any/false/871,870,573,869,36,868,867,133/68,69,67,12,70,66,71,13|/17077,17078

National Kids Count. (2018b). Child population by single age. Annie E. Casey Foundation. Retrieved from: https://datacenter.kidscount.org/data/tables/100-child-population-by-single-age?loc=1&loct=1#detailed/1/any/false/871,870,573,869,36,868,867,133,38,35/42,43,44,45,46,47,48,49,50,51,52,53,54,55,56,57,58,59,60,61/418

Neville, H.A., Awad, G.H., Brooks, J.E., Flores, M.P., & Bluemel, J. (2013). Color-blind racial ideology: Theory, training, and measurement implications in psychology. *American Psychologist, 68*(6), 455–466.

Pettit, S.K. (2011). Teachers' beliefs about English language learners in the mainstream classroom: A review of the literature. *International Multilingual Research Journal, 5*(2), 123–147.

Reid, J.L., & Kagan, S.L. (2015). *A Better Start: Why Classroom Diversity Matters in Early Education*. Washington, DC: Poverty & Race Research Action Council.

Rhodes, H., & Huston, Al. (2012). Building the workforce out youngest children deserve. *Social Policy Report, 26*, 1–26.

Sleeter, C.E. (2001). Preparing teachers for culturally diverse schools: Research and the overwhelming presence of whiteness. *Journal of Teacher Education, 52*, 94–106.

The Annie E. Casey Foundation. (2014). *Race for Results: Building a Path to Opportunity for All Children.* Kids Count Policy Report, Baltimore, MD. Retrieved from: https://www.aecf.org/m/resourcedoc/AECF-RaceforResults-2014.pdf#page=3

Winkler, E.N. (2009). Children are not colorblind: How young children learn race. *PACE: Practical Approaches for Continuing Education, 3*, 1–8.

Yoshikawa, H., Wuermli, A.J., Raikes, A., Kim, S., & Kabay, S. (2018). Toward high-quality early childhood development programs and policies at national scale: Directions for research in global contexts. *Social Policy Report, 31*, 1–36.

4 Scaffolding Multilingual Learners in Early Childhood Classrooms

Liliana Barro Zecker

Increasingly, teachers of young children find their students are growing in multilingual environments. Thus, as they plan instruction, they need to meet the diverse needs of students who, despite English not being their native or home language, are expected to succeed academically in English. Ideally, research proposes, students would be able to learn in dual-language environments, where the two languages, home and English (e.g., Spanish/English, Chinese/English), are given equal emphasis. The goal of these programs is bilingualism and biliteracy for all. In the last decade, the number of dual-language programs in the US has grown exponentially but nevertheless, to date, the majority of English Language Learners (ELs) attending US schools do not have access to solid dual-language programs throughout their K-12 experience. Generally speaking, most bilingual education programs, while increasingly respecting students' home languages and diverse cultures, aim at supporting students' development in English so that, in turn, students can make gains in academic achievement and be successful at schools where the main language of instruction is English.

English Learners and Academic Success

Tapping into Students' Linguistic Repertoires—Translanguaging

Researchers have been looking at what works best to enhance the schooling success of multilingual students for decades. The foundational concepts molding the way we think about English learners' acquisition of English and their ability to succeed in school stem from James Cummins's research (2005, 2008). Early on, Cummins drew the distinctions between two kinds of *language competencies—**social** language and **academic** language abilities—that ELs need to tackle to be able to do well in English-predominant school environments.

Cummins argued that ELs are to develop Basic Interpersonal Communication Skills (BICS). BICS refer to social, mostly oral conversational language, the type of communication that often includes many cues to the listener (i.e., gestures, facial expressions) and is context-embedded language (i.e., shared references, often concrete). It takes ELs approximately two years to conquer BICS.

But social language competency is not enough for academic success. ELs need to gain Cognitive Academic Language Proficiency (CALP): the academic language that characterizes school talk and texts. When teachers lecture, during classroom discussions, and when students read and write academic texts, there is less face-to-face interaction than during informal conversations; non-verbal clues (i.e., gestures, facial expressions) tend to be absent or at least less prominent than during casual social talk. Academic language is often more reliant on abstract concepts than social talk; reading and writing demands are high as textbooks are above the language proficiency of the students. Often too, cultural and linguistic knowledge is needed to comprehend fully the content of school discourse. Cummins' (2005) investigations indicate that it takes five to seven years for ELs to become competent in academic language use.

After years of researching bilingual education programs and observing ELs' academic achievement, Cummins (2008) began to emphasize the importance and power of cross-language transfer. More recently, the field has used the term *translanguaging* to describe what bilinguals do when they access different linguistic features or modes of the autonomous languages they know in order to maximize successful communication (García, 2009). In other words, multilingual individuals draw from their multiple linguistic repertoires (or databases) to communicate effectively.

Despite the widely recognized effectiveness and the recent widespread growth in the number of dual-language or two-way immersion bilingual programs offered across the US (Steele et al., 2017), in reality, the vast majority of US bilingual education programs still operate under the (often tacit) premise that language mixing is to be avoided or that languages are to be kept separate in a somewhat rigid, pre-established way (i.e., by assignment, by content area, by time of the day). Teachers are strongly encouraged to teach monolingually—not to mix—and students, generally speaking, are asked to show knowledge monolingually. On any given curricular task (e.g., writing) or at given curricular times (e.g., morning is in English, afternoon is in Chinese), it is suggested to both teachers and students that they choose and stay within the confines on one linguistic code. Mixing languages is discouraged. This separate-language policy runs against the grain of what teachers and students tend to do and what happens naturally in most classrooms to secure accurate communication (Cummins, 2008; Hornberger & Link, 2012; Reyes, 2012).

As a result, teachers often feel conflicted, given the restrictive policies and the entrenched fear of translation-as-a-crutch, about implementing or encouraging teaching and learning that allows for translanguaging. But researchers explain that:

"Translanguaging is about *communication*, not about *language* itself. There are times when we need to be language teachers, focusing on accuracy in English so that our learners can pass exams and be taken as proficient speakers in wider society. Much of the time, though, we are working with students to explore concepts, add to their knowledge, make connections between ideas and to help them make their voices heard by others. This is often about *communicating*, and this is where using *all* our language resources can be very valuable."

(NALDIC EAL Journal.org https://ealjournal.org/
2016/07/26/what-is-translanguaging/)

Numerous studies show that translanguaging is a naturally occurring communication phenomenon in bilingual classrooms—it just happens—and that it is an effective tool for teaching and learning (Blackledge & Creese, 2010; García, 2009, 2014; García, Flores, & Woodley, 2012; García & Kleifgen, 2010; García & Sylvan, 2011; García & Kano, 2014; García & Leiva, 2014; Hornberger & Link, 2012). In contrast to restrictive and often unspoken one-language-at-a-time principles, researchers argue for a more adaptable approach. They propose that second language teaching and learning (oral language as well as reading and writing) require flexibility (Creese & Blackledge, 2010; Cummins, 2008; Guo & Mackenzie, 2015). Hornberger & Link (2012) explain "welcoming of translanguaging in classrooms is not only necessary, but desirable educational practice [...] to build on the communicative repertoires and translanguaging practices of students, their families, and communities" (p. 1). When translanguaging is accepted as a valid form of communication of knowledge, when teachers and students allow languages to "lean on each other" to optimize communication, ELs gain communicative competency (i.e., they understand and communicate better). Lozano Lenis (2015) summarizes what the literature on translanguaging and education indicates: "Based on this research we can say that translanguaging builds deeper thinking, provides students with more rigorous content, affirms multiple identities, and at the same time develops the language needed to perform specific academic tasks" (p. 58).

As a result, gone are the days when teachers aimed at suppressing students' home language/s and avoided translation (Dworin, 2006). Having access to more than one language system (i.e., vocabulary, grammar, etc.) is considered an asset rather than a hindrance (Reyes, 1992; 2012). Teachers have access to a plethora of ideas about techniques, routines, and strategies that they are advised to apply to support the academic growth of multilingual students by tapping into their rich and multiple linguistic repertoires (Souto-Manning & Martell, 2016).

ECE Pedagogy for English Learners—*What To Do? How To Do It?*

Responsive Pedagogy in ECE Classrooms

Research shows that the majority of Early Childhood Education (ECE) teachers are generally knowledgeable about Second Language (SL) learning and relevant bilingualism pedagogies (Baecher & Jewke, 2014; Cabezas & Rourke, 2014). However, surveys indicate that some ECE teachers are unclear about some assumptions regarding early bilingualism that have now been debunked (Genesee 2009; Gonzalez, 2016). When polled, many ECE teachers recognized that working effectively with ELs is "a lot like working with early childhood students" (Baecher & Jewke, 2014, p. 49). That is, many of the strategies applied in early childhood education (e.g., emphasis on hands-on activities supported by highly contextualized language, strong focus on vocabulary development, multisensory engagement, simplified language of commands) resemble those recommended to work with ELs to support their second language acquisition. Yet a significant number of ECE teachers expressed ongoing concern about how to:

(1) use specific teaching approaches/strategies
(2) assess ELs' cognitive, social and emotional needs and
(3) effectively communicate fluently with ELs and parents when teachers do not know the home language (Cabezas & Rourke, 2014).

It is important for pre- and in-service ECE teachers to continue to grow their repertoire of skills and abilities that are specific to SL pedagogy, to learn more about young ELs' typical patterns of language learning and acquisition so that they can better support ELs' growth as effective language users and, as a result, their academic achievement (Baecher & Jewke, 2014; Cabezas & Rourke, 2014; Zepeda, Castro, & Cronin, 2011). This is particularly important in light of Snow's (2014) recent comments on how the adoption of Common Core State Standards is likely to impact the education of multilingual students, especially the youngest ELs:

> A looming worry about the implementation of CCSS in the US is that … opportunities in the classroom to build student knowledge are being ignored. *This danger starts in early childhood programs where pressures to teach English to speakers of other languages and to teach the basic, small domain literacy skills may well leave no time for knowledge-building activities such as reading aloud and discussing topics introduced through books read, or taking field trips, or engaging in science observations and conversations.* We will have done our students no great service if we teach them to read words accurately and fluently but deprive them of the information they will need to truly comprehend complex texts.
>
> (Snow, 2014, p.15. Emphasis added)

The most emphasized principle in effective second-language learning pedagogy (Cabezas & Rourke, 2014; Zepeda, Castro, & Cronin, 2011) is the importance of supporting **vocabulary development**. Research on multilingual learners shows that vocabulary knowledge is the single best predictor of academic achievement (Feldman & Kinsella, 2005). Teachers of ELs are advised to keep vocabulary development at the center of instruction, making each possible opportunity a vocabulary-building one, picking up and extending word meanings in every possible way, using a variety of supporting techniques. Alongside the stress on vocabulary building, other well-known strategies to effectively scaffold language learning amongst ELs include:

1 Using **visual and other non-verbal cues** in concrete, experiential, multisensory, hands-on learning experiences embedded in a **thematic context.**
2 Tapping into **the child's first language as a tool to support learning**, encouraging parents to use the home language for communication.
3 Providing **ample social learning** opportunities both among children working with each other as well as teacher-student strong modeling of language use.

The section below provides concrete examples or models of curricular routines carefully planned and deployed so as to meet the needs of and support the language development of young ELs. These routines were observed in early childhood classrooms populated by ELs who, as is often the case, displayed different levels and types of language competencies in English.[1] Some of the ECE classrooms were in dual-language program settings but the majority were not. Some of the teachers were able to speak the students' home language, but many were not able to communicate fluidly with students and/or parents. Most of the examples contain English/Spanish cognates but all the activities are applicable to SL regardless of the students' home language background. The majority of the examples revolve around an Interactive Read Aloud (IRA), and show how teachers integrate the SL responsive pedagogy principles listed above.

Interactive Read Alouds: Curricular routines that are perfect springboards into responsive SL pedagogy

Interactive Read Alouds (IRA) of picture books are among the most common curricular events in ECE classrooms. IRAs are recognized fertile routines to support the language development of young children. They are particularly beneficial for young English learners given that IRAs, as curricular routines, have the potential to meet all the requisites of SL recommended instructional best practices explained earlier. That is, centered around texts (picture books) that are usually selected in connection to a curricular **theme** (e.g., Tall Tales, Fairy Tales, Butterflies, Sea Animal Life, Halloween), IRAs are highly **social interactive** meaning-making events. IRA discussions are strongly **focused on vocabulary** learning and rely heavily on **visual/non-verbal clues** as well as students' own prior knowledge and experiences (including their multilingual repertoires or knowledge of other language/s).

  IRAs are rich early first- and second-language acquisition opportunities given the inherent high contextualization provided by the illustrations (i.e., the pictures help students understand/deduce the meaning of words, plot, character traits, sequence of events, etc.) and other non-verbal cues, such as changes in intonation, emphasis, and characters' voices, introduced by the reader (the teacher or other more-able reader). IRAs expose young students to language that is more complex than oral exchanges; they are likely to include the academic language and scientific concepts (see Cummins CALP above) that are needed to attain and make progress in academic achievement (Leung, 2008; Massaro, 2017).

Vocabulary and Interactive Read Alouds

Day in and day out, as teachers plan vocabulary work around a given text, inevitably they ask themselves how many and which words they should/can cover. Because it is impossible to cover all words needing coverage, research suggests teachers use a three-tier approach allowing them to sort the words into three categories (Beck, McKeown, & Kucan, 2008; Kindall, 2009):

Tier I.   Words: Likely known, might need slight clarification.
Tier II. Words: Need to discuss directly so students engage in meaning making.
Tier III. Words: Might need to clarify but not work specifically as they are not essential to the topic/theme/text understanding.
Teachers then concentrate their efforts on Tier II Words.

It is important to note, at this point, what is known about the *strategies that are not effective when working on vocabulary building*. Research indicates that copying and reciting dictionary or teacher-provided definitions, the "use-the-word-in- a-sentence" activity, and repeated practice spelling of the target vocabulary words, are the least effective instructional strategies for promoting vocabulary growth. Definitions are not how we think of word meanings when we face or we are asked to explain what we know about an uncertain word. Rather, learners try to connect the unknown word to a known context or other words that do not mean the same but are in some way related to it.

Thus, vocabulary lessons should be focused on learning meaning (not spelling or definitions) and creating semantic networks: relations between words that go together or belong to the same semantic field because of conceptual relations (i.e., they belong to the same group, they share some traits, they can be linked conceptually). Building on students' existing knowledge, helping them connect the new to the known, helps students solidify those connections. Students need multiple exposures to vocabulary words for learning to happen. Providing students with examples and non-examples of a given term and discussing connections between words are far more effective for retention and transfer of new word knowledge than rote memorization of definitions or using target words in sentences (Figure 4.1).

Classroom Examples

The examples below show how teachers can use the vocabulary found in different texts and, while conducting IRAs, tap into the words that appear in the

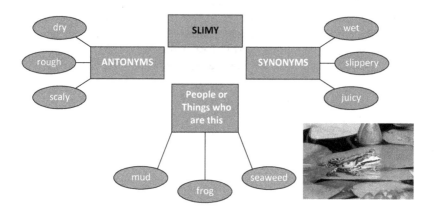

Figure 4.1 Word map.

text and use them as springboards into related vocabulary, building semantic networks of connected words, even when those related terms do not appear in the text. In effective programs, IRAs are not stand-alone curricular events, at least not most of the time. Effective teachers plan for IRAs that are connected to the central topic or theme that unifies the curriculum into units (e.g., Winter Animals and their Habitats, Human Body). This cohesive alignment of read-aloud texts and the rest of the ideas/concepts children encounter during the course of the day as they work in other areas of the curriculum (e.g., science) help reinforce vocabulary learning and the understanding of academic concepts through repeated exposure.

Based on an Interactive Read Aloud of *Come on, Rain!* (Hesse, 1999), teachers can start with the most common words associated with rain and a storm, most of which appear in the book or are likely to be associated by students with their experiences of rain. Notice that the words range in difficulty, allowing teachers to adapt to students' diverse language competencies. Some novice ELs might just need *umbrella, clouds* and *wet*, while others might be ready to consider the differences between *thunder* and *lightning*.

Using images, teachers can connect to other, more advanced vocabulary, which can be linked to the pertinent images and be made a naming or matching game (picture to label, if students can process print) at a center or to take home to play with the family (Figures 4.2 to 4.4).

The example below describes how a teacher can work contrasting *The Three Little Pigs* (Seibert, 2002) tale to *The True Story of The Three Little Pigs* (Sciezka & Smith, 1996) and connect to a unit that deals with Habitats and Climate. Initially, using some of the words in the text, the teacher expands students' vocabulary by introducing more specific terms that refer to dwellings (e.g., mansion, house, apartment) (Figure 4.5).

The discussion can be extended to materials often used in the construction of varied types of housing (e.g., mud, bricks, cement, adobe). Often, throughout

WORD ASSOCIATIONS

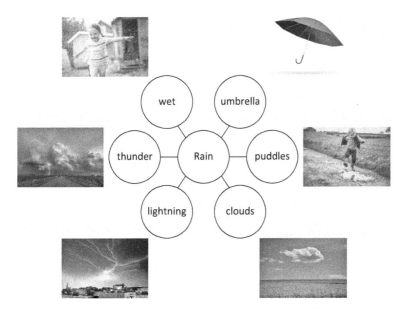

Figure 4.2 Words associated to rain.

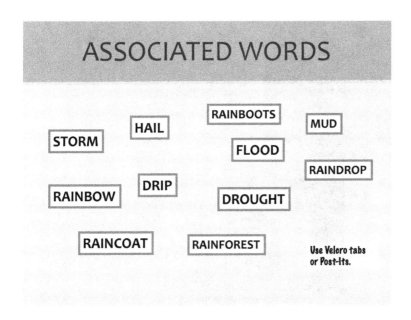

Figure 4.3 Associated words.

Figure 4.4 Illustrations for associated words.

Learning better words

Hut

PALACE-palacio

MANSION-mansión

HOUSE

APARTMENT-apartamentos

Figure 4.5 Learning better words.

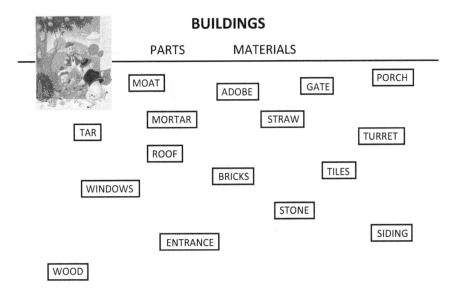

BUILDINGS

PARTS   MATERIALS

MOAT

ADOBE   GATE   PORCH

MORTAR   STRAW

TAR   TURRET

ROOF

BRICKS   TILES

WINDOWS

STONE

SIDING

ENTRANCE

WOOD

Figure 4.6 Buildings, materials, and parts.

these discussions, teachers can take advantage of cognates (e.g., cement = *cemento* in Spanish). The discussion can also be extended to parts of the buildings that require precise labels (e.g., entrance, gate, porch, moat) (Figure 4.6).

In this particular unit, the teacher chose to discuss the desert—one of the landscapes the story described. A connection was made to the temperature typical of deserts and the discussion shifted to words that denote different degrees of heat. Students can compare/contrast temperature words, learning about more nuanced vocabulary (e.g., hot, warm, tepid), organizing the words on a semantic gradient that can be adjusted to reflect different levels of vocabulary knowledge (Figure 4.7).

During the discussion, students provided examples of context in which those terms would be used, often in a way of recognition task (comprehension preceded expressive use of known vocabulary). So, the teacher would read a statement, when possible in conjunction with an image, and asked students to deem the statement TRUE or FALSE by showing thumbs up or down.

The teacher says:

- *We need boiling water to make tea.*
- *Always use tepid water for a baby bath.*
- *Nothing grows in the scorching desert weather* (Figure 4.8).

Similar strategies were observed when the teacher used *Cinderella* as the basis for an IRA. Often, although teachers worry about IRAs that revolve around commercialized, well-known tales, they are still students' favorites and thus

Figure 4.7 Semantic gradient.

Figure 4.8 Extending semantic networks.

highly engaging. How can teachers go beyond the known plot to push for greater understanding and more thoughtful discussion of these well-known texts? In this case, the teacher decided to expand students' vocabulary knowledge, focusing on the words *glass slipper*. The teacher expanded in a way that allowed for a wide range of students' language knowledge, discussing different types of shoes (e.g., clogs, boots), materials shoes are made of (e.g., leather, rubber), and specific labels for parts of shoes (e.g., eyelet, heel) (Figure 4.9 to 4.11).

Often, labeled diagrams are helpful in these kinds of vocabulary expansion activities (Figure 4.12).

Similar work was done during the IRA with *Brave Irene* (Steig, 2011) in a 2nd–3rd-grade class. The teacher gauged that students would know that "the wind *blows*…" So, she discussed at greater length the actions and roles attributed to the wind in the text, all words that add nuance.

Stretching Cinderella

- Kinds of shoes
- What shoes are made of
- Parts of a shoe

Figure 4.9 Stretching Cinderella vocabulary discussion.

Figure 4.10 Stretching Cinderella vocabulary discussion.

Because the teacher felt her students were ready, she highlighted and explicitly discussed all the -ed endings that indicate past tense in English, a morphological concept that needs to be emphasized for many ELs whose home languages do not mark past tense in the way English does (Figure 4.13).

Another term that the teacher expanded on when discussing *Brave Irene* (Steig, 2011) was *clutching* (as a springboard to discuss how "we *carry* things in

WORD SORTS

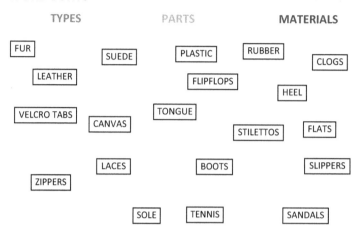

Figure 4.11 Stretching Cinderella vocabulary discussion.

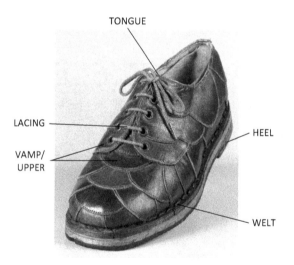

Figure 4.12 Labelled diagram.

different ways"). For extended discussion and repeated exposures to the word the teacher used the following activities, one heavily verbal, the other more dependent on visual cues (Figure 4.14).

"*Look at these pictures and say clutching if that is happening*" (Figure 4.15).

Similar work was done during an Authors' Study Unit organized around the *Mirette on the High Wire* series (McCully, 1997). The first story takes place at a *boarding house*, hence the vocabulary work included a comparison of different kinds of lodging facilities such as *hotels, motels, hostels, dorms, lodges, bed*

Learning better words

whirl(ed)

squall(ed)

yodel(ed)

wallop(ed)

shook

fac(ed)

wrench(ed)

ripp(ed)

wrestl(ed)

howling

twist(ed)

swallow(ed)

snatch(ed)

Figure 4.13 Extending vocabulary and structural analysis.

• If any of the things I say are examples of **clutching,** say clutching. If
  they are not examples of clutching, stay quiet.

  • Holding on tightly to a purse.
  • Holding a fistful of money.
  • Softly petting a cat's fur.
  • Holding on to branches while climbing a tree.

Figure 4.14 Examples and non-examples.

Clutching?

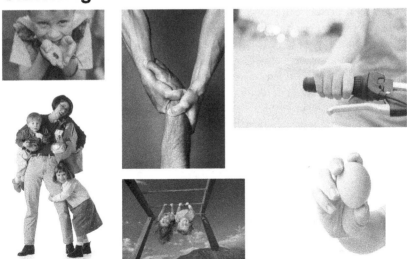

Figure 4.15 Clutching/not clutching.

JUGGLERS   MIME

TRAPEZE ARTIST

Figure 4.16 Stretching semantic networks.

and breakfasts, etc. Similarly, students were presented with images and videos of *jugglers*, *mimes*, *actors*, and *acrobats*, and discussed the differences and overlap between their performances and places of work (Figure 4.16).

Most of the strategies described above allow for individualized instruction, tailored to the different students' needs and competencies. Instruction should be differentiated, adjusting the vocabulary introduced and discussed according to the students' age and their various levels of language proficiency. Not all students need to *know*, remember, and/or use in expressive forms all the words. While vocabulary work is initially teacher-led in connection to an IRA, it can eventually become portable games (e.g., picture sorts, charades, picture/word match, Pictionary) or activities. In that way, students can continue to engage with the words as they work with an older buddy, a volunteer, a classroom partner, or at home. In other words, the examples above are all social engagements and allow for more advanced language users to model language for novices.

Research indicates that young language learners initially key into basic terms that are prototypical (Anglin, 1985). For instance, young children first master *big* and *small* to refer to size dimensions. *Big* refers to a lot of size; *small* refers to not too much size or lack of it. Later on, they learn how to understand and express the meaning of more specific vocabulary that relates to size (e.g., tiny, enormous). The same is true of second language learners. English learners, of all ages, tend to use and focus on basic, prototypical terms initially, and do not have more nuanced meanings in their comprehension and expression (Tocowicz, 2014). Exposing ELs to related, nuanced, more specific vocabulary should be a main goal of vocabulary instruction given its impact on oral language, reading comprehension, and written expression.

Thematic Units and Workshop

Often, ECE teachers embed IRAs into thematic curricular units (Schutz & Zecker, 2017; Zecker, Schutz, & Barbour, 2006) and use Reading and Writing Workshop structures (Calkins, 2018) to facilitate student engagement. These units allow students to build social as well as academic linguistic competence in English. The examples below come from a kindergarten Sea Animal Life unit in a dual language classroom.

The teacher included daily IRAs in English and Spanish, highlighting cognates whenever possible. Most of the IRAs were done with expository (informational) texts. During these IRAs, students were presented with the idea that when reading information books, the reader often does not read cover to cover. Often, the teacher modeled getting to the table of contents and figuring out where to find the information for a particular topic (e.g., what dolphins eat; whales and families). Students were able to explore all the IRA texts during their independent reading time. At times, students went through reference-type books about marine life and oceans, and would put down post-its with comments on them, a first step towards research gathering.

As the unit progressed, teacher and students composed lists about animals that were created as part of shared writing. They added to these as they learned more, and then at the very end of the unit, they typed them up and turned them into a book for each student—along with a picture of each animal' (Figure 4.17).

There were hands-on experiments (e.g., a blubber glove), songs on charts that supported vocabulary building as well as fluency, and some games that used the vocabulary and the concepts learned. Dramatizing was used to build conceptual knowledge (e.g., echolocation). After the group talked about the kinds of things marine biologists might record in their lab or observation notes, the teacher created little observation notebooks for students to use during a field trip to the aquarium.

Interactive writing sessions modeled the All About books genre. Each morning during morning meeting, a new page was created as a group, including a labeled diagram (Figure 4.18).

As a final project, students produced an All About or expert book on a sea animal of their own choice. The expert book was also heavily scaffolded during a daily writing workshop, when the teacher discussed and modeled the genre and students got to try different strategies and skills. At any given time,

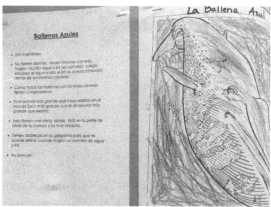

Figure 4.17 Lucas' take-home book.

Figure 4.18 Opportunities for children to label a drawing collaboratively.

throughout these activities, students were encouraged to use the language of their choice to participate in the activities, and often their texts showed translanguaging.

Nursery Rhymes and Word Play

Throughout any ECE curriculum, teachers are likely to include numerous opportunities for children to come in contact, follow along, and join in with nursery rhymes and word-play activities. When heavily supported by visuals (pictures) and gestures, these activities are considered best practices to promote and build phonological and phonemic awareness (specific awareness of the speech sounds of the language). Both types of awareness are at the root of literacy development. Teachers should be cautious about an overemphasis on repetitive language activities that focus on the form of language (how sounds and letters correspond).

Numerous articles have commented on the increasing focus on academics in ECE curricula (Bassok, Latham, & Rorem, 2016). This stress on academics and conventional forms is particularly evident in the transformation of early literacy curricula that inappropriately emphasize, both in instruction and assessment, conventional literacy behaviors. Many years ago, the work on emergent literacy (Teale & Sulzby, 1986) sketched the developmental progression that is typical of literacy learning amongst young children. Paris (2005) further clarified for teachers the difference between constrained and unconstrained reading skills. Constrained literacy skills, such as learning the letters of the alphabet or their sounds, are limited sets of knowledge—learning the letter sounds—that are mastered in brief periods of development. Unconstrained skills, such as vocabulary and making inferences, never stop growing. Despite all that we know about early developmental patterns in language and literacy acquisition, currently, four- and five-year-olds are expected to read and write conventionally a specific number of words by the end of the school year. The new emphasis of ECE curricula demands that young children conquer constrained literacy skills; it defies the well-documented developmental patterns. As they plan their work with young ELs who are learning the oral language on which literacy development stands, ECE teachers are most effective when they focus on the function of language and literacy, building the foundation of unconstrained skills (making sense, thinking critically, understanding the message of the text), those that require deep thinking and will continue to evolve over time.

Conclusion

In summary, young English learners make giant leaps in language learning when they are immersed in an environment that respects their diverse linguistic repertoires and scaffolds their growth in the different kinds of register that students need to conquer in order to be successful communicators in the different contexts (i.e., social, academic) in which they participate. Daily engagement in developmentally appropriate, meaningful curricular routines that foster vocabulary growth and critical thinking around academic concepts while considering multilingual students' linguistic diversity and resources is at the root of academic success.

Note

1   The author would like to thank Dr K. Schutz and Ms. K. Barbour, selfless collaborators as the data shared here was collected in their classrooms.

References

Anglin, J.M. (1985). The child's expressible knowledge of word concepts: What preschoolers can say about the meaning of some nouns and verbs. In K.E. Nelson (Ed.), *Children's Language: Volume 5. Hillsdale.* New Jersey: Erlbaum.

Baecher, L., & Jewkes, A. (2014). TESOL and early childhood collaborative inquiry: Joining forces and crossing boundaries. *Journal of Early Childhood Teacher Education, 35*(1), 39–53 (1090–1027 print/1745–5642 online doi.

Bassok, D., Latham, S., & Rorem, A. (2016). *Is Kindergarten the New First Grade?* AERA Open

Beck, I.L., McKeown, M.G., & Kucan, L. (2008). *Bringing Words to Life.* New York: The Guilford Press.

Cabezas, C., & Rourke, E. (2014). How do early childhood teachers understand and support the needs of young English language learners? *Asia-Pacific Journal of Research in Early Childhood Education, 8*(1), 57–78.

Calkins, L., & TCRWP. (2018). *Units, Tools and Methods for Teaching Reading and Writing.* New Hampshire: Heinemann.

Creese, A., & Blackledge, A. (2010). Translanguaging in the bilingual classroom: A pedagogy for learning and teaching? *Modern Language Journal, 94*(1), 103–115.

Cummins, J. (2005). Teaching for Cross-Language Transfer in Dual Language Education: Possibilities and Pitfalls. Presented at TESOL Symposium on Dual Language Education: Bogazici University, Istanbul, Turkey. September 23, 2005.

Cummins, J. (2008). Teaching for transfer: Challenging the two solitudes assumption in bilingual education. In J. Cummins & N.H. Hornberger (Eds.), *Encyclopedia of Language and Education Vol. 5: Bilingual Education* (2nd ed.). Boston: Springer Science + Business Media.

Dworin, J. (2006). The family stories project: Using funds of knowledge for writing. International Reading Association, 510–520

Feldman, K., & Kinsella, K. (2005). *Narrowing the Language Gap: The Case for Explicit Vocabulary Instruction.* New York: Scholastic.

García, O., (2009). Education, multilingualism and translanguaging in the 21st century. In A. Mohanty, R. Panda & T. Skutnabb-Kangas, (Eds.), *Multilingual Education for Social Justice: Globalising the Local* (pp. 128–145). New Delhi: Orient Blackswan.

García, O., Flores, N., & Woodley, H.H. (2012). Transgressing monolingualism and bilingual dualities: Translanguaging pedagogies. In A. Yiakoumetti (Ed.), *Harnessing Linguistic Variation for Better Education* (pp. 45–76). Bern: Peter Lang.

García, O., & Kano, N. (2014). Translanguaging as process and pedagogy: Developing the English writing of Japanese students in the US. In J. Conteh & G. Meier (Eds.), *The Multilingual Turn in Languages Education: Benefits for Individuals and Societies* (pp. 258–277). Bristol: Multilingual Matters.

García, O., & Kleifgen, J.A. (2010). *Education Emergent Bilinguals: Policies, Programs, and Practices for English Language Learners.* New York: Teacher's College Press.

García, O., & Leiva, C. (2014). Theorizing and enacting translanguaging for social justice. In A. Blackledge & A. Creese (Eds.), *Heteroglossia as Practice and Pedagogy.* Dordrecht: Springer.

García, O., & Sylvan, C. (2011). Pedagogies and practices in multilingual classrooms: Singularities in pluralities. *Modern Language Journal, 95*(iii), 385–400.

Genesse, F. (2009). Early childhood bilingualism: Perils and possibilities. *Journal of Applied Research on Learning, 2*(Article 2), 1–21.

Guo, K., & Mackenzie, N. (2015). Signs and codes in early childhood: An investigation of young children's creative approaches to communication. *Australasian Journal of Early Childhood, 40*(2), 78–87.

Hesse, H. (1999). *Come on, Rain!* New York: Scholastic Press.

Hornberger, N., & Link, H. (2012). Translanguaging in today's classrooms: A biliteracy lens. *Theory into Practice, 51*(4), 239–247 (In L. Zecker (Ed.), *Rethinking Language Teaching and Learning in Multilingual Classrooms*).

Kindle, K. (2009). Vocabulary development during read alouds: Primary practices. *The Reading Teacher, 63*(3), 202–211.

Leung, C. (2008, March 1). Preschoolers' acquisition of scientific vocabulary through repeated read-aloud events, retellings, and hands-on science activities. *Reading Psychology, 29*(2), 165–193.

Lozano Lenis, M.E. (2015), *Translanguaging and Identity in a Kindergarten Classroom: Validating Student's Home Culture and Language in an English-Only Era.* Doctoral Dissertations. 511. Retrieved from: https://scholarworks.umass.edu/dissertations_2/511

Massaro, D. (2017). Reading aloud to children: Benefits and implications for acquiring literacy before schooling begins. *The American Journal of Psychology, 130*(1), 63–72. (University of Illinois Press. Retrieved from: https://www.jstor.org/stable/10.5406/amerjpsyc.130.1.0063 Accessed: 03-10-2018 23:08 UTC).

Mc Cully, E.A. (1997). *Mirette on the High Wire.* London: Puffin Books.

Mc Cully, E.A. (2000a) *Mirette and Bellini cross Niagara Falls.* London: Puffin Books.

Mc Cully, E.A. (2000b) *Starring Mirette and Bellini.* London: Puffin Books.

Paris, S.G. (2005). Reinterpreting the development of reading skills. *Reading Research Quarterly, 40*, 184–202.

Reyes, M. (1992). Challenging venerable assumptions: Literacy instruction for linguistically different students. *Harvard Educational Review, 62*(4), 427–447.

Reyes, M. (2012). Spontaneous biliteracy: Examining Latino students' untapped potential. *Theory into Practice,* 51(4) (In L. Zecker (Ed.), *Rethinking Language Teaching and Learning in Multilingual Classrooms*)

Schutz, K., & Zecker, L.B. (June, 2017). *Writing Workshop in a Two-Way Immersion Kindergarten Classroom.* Poster presentation at the 11th International Symposium on Bilingualism, University of Limerick, Limerick, Ireland.

Sciezka, J., & Smith, L. (1996). *The True Story of the Three Little Pigs.* Puffin Books.

Seibert, P. (2002). *The Three Little Pigs.* Carson-Dellosa Publishing Group.

Snow, C. (2014). Language, literacy and the needs of the multilingual child. *Perspectives in Education, 32*(1). htpp://www.perspectives-in-education.com

Souto-Manning, M., & Martell, J. (2016). *Reading, Writing, and Talk: Inclusive Teaching Strategies for Diverse Learners, K-2*. New York: Teachers College Press.

Steele, J., Slater, R., Zamarro, G., Miller, T., Li, J., Burkhauser, S., & Bacon, M. (2017). *Dual-Language Immersion Programs Raise Student Achievement in English*. Santa Monica, CA: RAND Corporation. Retrieved from: https://www.rand.org/pubs/research_briefs/RB9903.html.

Steig, W. (2011). Brave Irene. New York: McMillan

Teale, W., & Sulzby, E. (1986). *Emergent Literacy: Writing and Reading*. New Jersey: Ablex.

Zecker, L.B., Schutz, K., & Barbour, K. (August, 2006). *Developmental Biliteracy: Supporting the Growth of Young Readers and Writers in a Dual-Language Program*. Budapest: International Reading Association World Congress on Reading.

Zepeda, M., Castro, D.C., & Cronin, S. (2011). Preparing early childhood teachers to work with young dual language learners. *Child Development Perspectives, 5*(1), 10–14.

5 Migrant and Refugee Children

Karen Monkman and Larissa Mulholland

Introduction

Early childhood education (ECE) programs have helped newcomer children acclimate to life in the U.S. for more than a century. In the late 19th and 20th centuries, settlement houses such as Hull House in Chicago offered ECE programs for im/migrant children and newcomer programs for adults (Lissak, 1989). Thus, as a country, we have long recognized the value of education for incorporating new residents into our social fabric. Early childhood programs provide child care for working families, as well. Thus, these ECE programs are often the earliest sustained contact im/migrant families have with social institutions in the U.S. As such, ECE educators are important resources in families' cultural transition processes of learning the customs of the country and acculturating to their new nation (Crosnoe & Ansari, 2015; Maher & Smith, 2014; Tadessee, Hoot & Watson-Thompson, 2009). When ECE programs sensitively respect the cultures of the families through interactions and program design, children's long-term academic success is facilitated (Magnuson, Lahaie & Waldfogel, 2006; Tobin, Arzubiaga & Adair, 2013)

Im/migrants are extremely diverse, coming from many countries with different cultures, languages, socio-economic status and ethnicities. Prior family-life experiences influence im/migrants' adaption to education in the U.S.; however, experiences in their countries of origin and the circumstances of their migration vary widely. For example, many im/migrants leave their countries and arrive in the U.S. under very different conditions than refugees and asylum seekers. Some im/migrants settle in traditional im/migrant communities in cities such as Los Angeles and New York and therefore have drastically different experiences than those in rural areas and small cities where communities may have little experience with newcomers. Im/migrant experiences, particularly the variations of life experience and complexities inherent in the migration process, may not be well understood by their teachers. The intention of this chapter is to enrich our understandings of these influential experiences so that our classroom practices can be informed by that deeper knowledge.

Despite great differences among im/migrants, common to the im/migrant experience is cultural change. Families leave their homes and must adapt culturally and raise their children in a foreign society with unfamiliar customs, ways of thinking, and laws. Even when the circumstances of migration are not as traumatic as they are for many refugees and asylum seekers, the immigration experience can be stressful, and the stress can be long-lasting. Upon arrival in the U.S., many im/migrant groups also face racism, poverty, and discrimination for the first time (Tobin et al., 2013; Crosby & Dunbar, 2012). Such experiences exacerbate the processes of adaptation and acculturation, and may be particularly challenging for young children. Moreover, many im/migrants' cultural and linguistic assets differ from the implicit expectations in U.S. schools and society; this cultural dissonance may not be well understood by their teachers or local communities. Because ECE programs are often the first involvement im/migrant families have with U.S. social institutions, ECE teachers are particularly influential in helping newcomers adjust to U.S. social institutions and their expectations (Crosnoe & Ansari, 2015), assuming that they know how to help. The number of children with im/migrant parents—both native born children and im/migrant children—has been rising in recent decades. As of 2011, more than one in four U.S. children up to the age of eight had at least one foreign-born parent (Park & McHugh, 2014). Early childhood educators are now and will be into the future in a unique position to positively support im/migrant families' adaptation experiences.

Debates about how best to offer ECE and newcomer programs continue today. Arguments are infused with ideological assumptions about immigration and im/migrants (see Tobin et al., 2013). When im/migrants are perceived negatively, educational strategies are based in a deficit perspective with families and their children needing remediation so they can be successful citizens. This view makes families feel diminished and intruded upon rather than welcomed and valued. When im/migrants are perceived to be an asset to our multicultural society, we build educational programs that acknowledge their assets, consequently creating a healthy link with home as well as a positive school experience. In the latter instance, ECE programs can provide secure care for children from working families and opportunities for English language development, socialization, and acculturation. Such programs socialize young children through opportunities for informal communication in play and game activities, bridging home and school.

To successfully engage in the complex work of teaching the diverse population of im/migrant families in all of our communities, we must focus our attention on the importance of the impact of culture and the social processes of cultural change, and work toward acceptance and inclusion. However, we cannot model inclusivity if we do not appreciate im/migrants' lived experiences that are shaped by the migration journey. So, first we discuss the process of migration, as this is an important context to understand as we work with im/migrant families, and next we focus on some key issues impacting the provision of appropriate and positive ECE experiences for newcomer children and their families.

Paths of Migration

Migration as a social process is experienced differently by different groups of im/migrants, namely refugees, asylum seekers and other categories of im/migrants. Following Arzubiaga, Noguerón and Sullivan (2009), we "use the term *im/migrant* to denote those who have been labeled im/migrant, migrant, and refugee, including the undocumented" (p. 246). We also use the term *newcomers* to recognize the experience common to those recently arrived and adapting to a new society.

Migration

The social process of migration is both longer and more complicated than mere movement from one place to another. The term *migration* refers to international migration (moving from other countries to the U.S., for example), as well as internal migration, such as migrating within the U.S. for farm work or within the home country prior to international migration. Our focus here is primarily on international migration, which is shaped by societal connections between multiple communities in two or more countries. These connections are embedded in economic relationships between countries and among communities, as well as in social relationships of people living in multiple places. The relationships may include families split between different communities and often countries. Migration research recognizes phases (Chavez, 2013), beginning with a process of *separation* from home communities (reflecting decisions to leave, conditions that push people out of their communities, e.g., lack of jobs or violence, and conditions that pull people to new locations). The next phase is *transition*—moving from home to host countries. The final phase is *incorporation* or *integration* (becoming part of the host country's social fabric). This process, especially the third phase, often spans decades, and is closely intertwined with changes in cultural identity. Additionally, some migration patterns are not linear, with return migration, cyclical, and temporary patterns increasingly recognized (Massey, Alarcón, Durand & González, 1987). Some im/migrants create *transnational* lives, i.e. lives lived in multiple spaces (Levitt & Waters, 2002). Boundaries among the three phases of migration are often blurred and fluid (Brettell, 2015).

National and international policies impact the process of migration, particularly who migrates and whether they have legal documentation. Changes in U.S. immigration policies in 1965 opened the door to people from areas beyond Europe, which had until then been the historical origin of most im/migrants (Gjelton, 2016). Since then, the result is greater diversity among im/migrants and, therefore, U.S. society. However, these changes came with quotas, leading to long wait times for visa applicants from certain countries, including the Philippines and Mexico. Some applicants wait about 20 years to legally reunite their families, resulting in children growing up without their parents. For this reason, among others, some make the difficult decision to migrate without documentation. Because of the risk involved, this is usually done under dire circumstances, such as violence or extreme poverty due to a lack of economic possibilities in their homeland.

The 1951 Geneva Convention, which the U.S. committed to, created a pathway for refugees and asylum seekers fleeing life-threatening conditions. In addition to undergoing the long-term adaptation process shared by all im/migrants, refugees and asylum seekers have also experienced violence, war, famine, political persecution, and the like, which leave lasting scars. Many refugees spend years in transition, often in refugee camps, waiting to find a country that will accept them. The journeys are not easy. Often there are gaps in children's—and sometimes parents'—educations as schooling is frequently not available or of poor quality. More recently, U.S. policy decisions to detain asylum seekers, including children, fleeing domestic and gang violence in Central America, as well as separating children and parents, added a new set of challenges for the long-term well-being of children and families (Healy, 2018; Ferguson, 2018).

Who Are Our Newcomers? Paths to the U.S.

With about 47 million im/migrants, the U.S. has the largest number of im/migrants of any country. However, only 14% of the population in the U.S. is foreign-born. In several Persian Gulf countries as much as 75% of the population is foreign-born. The foreign-born represent 28% of the population in Australia and 22% in Canada (Connor, 2018). While our percentage is lower, the public perception often assumes it is much higher.

Circumstances under which im/migrants migrate create very different experiences of migration. The term *refugee* applies to people fleeing their countries to escape war, persecution, and violence. Refugees must have a credible fear of persecution or torture and receive no help from their home countries (UNHCR, 2015). About 8% of the world's international migrants are refugees, totaling about 16 million worldwide in 2016 (Connor, 2018). Migrants apply for refugee status before migrating, often while living in refugee camps. Once a country accepts individuals as refugees, they migrate and are granted permission to live and work in their new host country. Decisions about who is considered a refugee are internationally determined, as well as subject to national political priorities. The U.S. government prioritizes particular groups for example, accepting opponents to communist regimes in their countries as a strategy to promote democracy.

Major flows of refugees began as a consequence of World War II with those fleeing Nazi persecution. Since then, other flows of refugees have come to the U.S. from Cuba (1960s), Vietnam (after 1975), Soviet states (after 1989), and Somalia (after 2004). About three million refugees have been resettled in the U.S. since 1980 (Krogstad & Radford, 2017). Like im/migrants broadly, refugees have become increasingly diverse ethnically and culturally. Currently, over half of refugees come to the U.S. from Somalia, the Democratic Republic of Congo, Myanmar, Iraq, and Syria (Igielnik & Krogstad, 2017).

Asylum seekers, like refugees, are fleeing dangerous conditions in their home-lands. However, while refugees obtain refugee status before arriving in the U.S., usually when in refugee camps, asylum seekers apply for asylum only upon arriv-ing at the U.S. border, where their cases are then processed. In 2016, 20,455 people were granted asylum, yet there were 180,617 applications. In compari-son, nearly 85,000 refugees entered the U.S. in 2016 (Mossaad & Baugh, 2018).

Most *migrant workers* in the U.S. (another category of im/migrants) are farm-workers who follow seasonal agricultural work. This tradition began in earnest with the Bracero Program (1946–1964) when the U.S. recruited workers from Mexico, which resulted in Mexican villages' dependence on remittances and U.S. farmers' reliance on migrant agricultural workers. An estimated three mil-lion migrant and seasonal farmworkers are thought to be in the U.S., nearly three-quarters of whom were born elsewhere (NCFH, 2012). Some migrant workers return to their home countries in the winter, but others migrate for work in the U.S. year-round. Most migrant workers—about 57%—are parents (USDOL-ETA, 2016). Children of migrant/seasonal farmworkers either live apart from one or more parents, which enables more educational stability, or move frequently during the school year to be with their parents. The U.S. Office of Migrant Education and specific states support the education of migra-tory children through various programs seeking to counteract the schooling interruptions caused by seasonal migration. The Binational Migrant Education Initiative (BMEI) promotes educational continuity between Mexico and the U.S. primarily with states along the border, to support students who move back and forth following their parents' migratory trajectory (USDOE, 2018).

The majority of im/migrants are neither refugees nor asylum seekers; they migrate through the visa system. Qualification for a U.S. visa is usually based on jobs without sufficient numbers of workers, or having close family in U.S. The U.S. government allots the same number of visas to each country, regard-less of its population size. However, the highest numbers of visa applications come from Mexico, India, China, and the Philippines—all countries with fairly large populations. The backlog for visa applicants from these countries is long—often 20 years or more. The backlog creates difficult choices for many families, especially those who are already divided across national boundaries. They must decide whether to wait for a visa and not be with their family or forgo working in the U.S. to support their families, or to seek other avenues to entry. Entering without documentation is generally a last resort; it is difficult and dangerous and fear of deportation and separation from each other causes enormous and harmful stress for im/migrant parents and children in the U.S.

Migration means not just a change in location but also in identity, as new-comers learn to adapt and participate in a new society and cultural spaces (Souto-Manning, 2007). Experiences of economic and political uncertainty, violence, hunger, and other challenges before migration can be traumatic and hard to overcome. Experiences of discrimination within the U.S. and fear of deportation make it difficult to adjust to life in a new country. Many families' language and cultural strengths, as well as experiences before and after im/migration, diverge from school expectations that reflect dominant Anglo middle-class culture.

These differences can lead to misunderstanding, complicating the relationship between im/migrants and school. But education plays a key role in im/migrant children's process of learning English and becoming culturally at home in the U.S. so we, as educators, need to know how best to support them.

Recognizing Assets and Cultural Influences

We know already that high quality ECE is linked to children's long-term academic success, particularly for children who experience poverty and whose first language is not English (Magnuson, Ruhm & Waldfogel, 2004). Thus, many of our usual teaching practices with young children should also be useful in educating im/migrant children (Magnuson, Lahaie & Waldfogel, 2006; Tobin et al., 2013) as high-quality ECE classrooms foster all children's active learning, holistic development, and meaningful relationships (Copple & Bredekamp, 2009). High-quality ECE classrooms also build on the cultural and linguistic resources of the children and their families, and are sensitive to the particular experiences and perspectives of im/migrants and newcomers. However, im/migrants' experiences are not the same as the experiences of other U.S. minority groups, so adapting our approaches to their lived experience is recommended.

To accurately understand im/migrant children's behaviors, assess their abilities and needs, and, ultimately, foster their healthy integration, effective educators adopt culturally sensitive, strengths-based approaches. This means that while we strive not to underestimate the stresses of migration and settling in—especially considering today's increasingly hostile attitudes toward and punitive policies around immigration—we also recognize the strengths families bring and how home cultures contribute to children's well-being and success.

Strengths, for many im/migrant families, might include not only multiple languages but also knowledge of the world that is more nuanced than that of many U.S. citizens (because of their experience in multiple regions of the world) and rich experience in cultures unfamiliar to U.S. educators. Regardless of the circumstances of their migration, families demonstrate enormous resilience and ingenuity in the face of change few of us can imagine. Families strive to make a good life for their children in unfamiliar contexts and often under challenging conditions. Im/migrant families tend to have high marriage and employment rates, with strong kinship networks (Crosby & Dunbar, 2012; Hernandez, 2004). Research suggests strong family structure may promote higher self-esteem in children of im/migrants than children with native-born parents. Im/migrant children are widely regarded by teachers as having better self-regulation and behavior (Crosnoe, 2006; Crosby & Dunbar, 2012). All of these qualities relate to higher academic success (McClelland, Cameron, Connor, Farris, Jewkes & Morrison, 2007). These findings lead to the "im/migrant paradox" in which children of im/migrants, many of whom face significant challenges, are more resilient and have more positive outlooks than the population at large, resulting in more successful academic and lifetime outcomes than groups facing similar challenges such as racism, poverty and limited parental English fluency and education (Marks, Ejesi, & Garcia Coll, 2014, p. 59). This paradoxical success largely depends on their *acculturation* processes and development of *bilingual* and *bicultural* identities.

Acculturation differs significantly from assimilation. Whereas assimilation has historically meant the price of im/migrants' success is the loss of their primary language and culture, acculturation means im/migrants maintain their language and culture while taking on a new language and culture, i.e. they become bilingual and bicultural. When early childhood programs and families adopt an assimilationist perspective, they view family and school cultures as oppositional—children must choose between home and school cultures— which is an unfair and untenable position for children. Acculturation supports biculturalism, which allows people to embrace both cultures simultaneously. Bilingualism and biculturalism not only result in stronger family connections and higher self-esteem, they also promote children's long-term academic success and protect against some of the harmful consequences of poverty and prejudice (Arzubiaga et al., 2009; Mosselson, 2006). Indeed, the more discrimination newcomer children face, the greater the protective impact of biculturalism (Portes & Rivas, 2011). Therefore, it is critical for early childhood programs to foster bicultural development, which is based in an understanding of culture and cultural change processes.

Culture is about meaning systems—the basis of our sense making—that underly how people live their lives and share a group identity. Culture involves the values people hold, which shape the ways they parent. Practices families engage in around feeding, expressing affection, and educating and disciplining children are cultural and impact children's behavior, identity and development, including how they interact with adults and peers (Derman-Sparks & Edwards, 2010; Rogoff, 2001). Cultural practices and values make sense to those within the cultural group and should not be judged by outsiders who do not understand their sense-making. Culture is also dynamic and always changing. As people acculturate, their sense-of-self changes.

Key to understanding culture is being aware of our own culture and our underlying meaning systems. When we use our own cultural lenses to make sense of others and decide what is "normal" we often make incorrect assumptions. This means as teachers, we too should allow ourselves to face cultural dissonance and also adapt when collaborating with families whose cultures differ from our own. In our society today, we should strive to respect the broad and complex diversity within and across im/migrant groups. Even within ethnic and nationality groups, cultural understandings vary as they are shaped and reshaped by experiences and social spaces, influenced by age, gender, class, etc. Therefore, it is best not to make assumptions about culture, people or groups (Tobin et al., 2013), but to seek understanding from the families and children we serve.

In the next section, we discuss several strategies for supporting young im/migrant children. We do not focus on the very important strategies discussed widely and more generally for minoritized groups and language learners in the U.S., even though those strategies are also useful with im/migrant children; these include bilingual and dual language education and many approaches to multicultural education, culturally relevant teaching, and anti-bias education (see Banks, 2017; Derman-Sparks & Edwards, 2010; Genishi & Goodwin, 2008; Saracho & Spodek, 2010; Wong Fillmore, 1991; Garcia & Markos, 2015). We instead focus on several strategies that relate specifically to im/migrant children and their families. This is not a complete set of such practices however; it is a starting point in thinking about how to better support im/migrant children.

ECE Practices to Support Im/migrant Children

Since language is a fundamental component of culture, including gestures, words and all aspects of communication, best ECE practice for young im/migrant children is anchored in culturally responsive bicultural and bilingual practice. Many young im/migrant children do not speak English and may also be unfamiliar with classroom expectations and routines; therefore, the teacher's role demands cultural sensitivity to the specific experiences of im/migrant children. Often, young im/migrant children have never been away from family. So, while they struggle with separation from family, they also face the stress of cultural dissonance and an unfamiliar language. In this new social group situation, it can be hard for them to predict what will happen, or to understand what teachers and other children say or expect. It is also difficult for them to convey their needs or feelings (Haines, Summers, Turnbull, Turnbull, & Palmer, 2015). Thus, they are likely to feel overwhelmed (Igoa, 1995). Being unable to communicate can feel very isolating. Stress may show up as disruptive behavior, aggression, emotional upset or avoidance of interactions with classmates and teachers. Additionally, some young im/migrant children may lack the knowledge and skills expected as markers of school readiness, such as counting or emergent literacy (Magnuson, Lahaie, & Waldfogel, 2006). Therefore, to facilitate child learning and language development for young im/migrants, we would do well to understand their histories and perspectives, including their strengths, especially when those differ from our school readiness expectations, so we can start where they are and build effective bridges to learning and be more inclusive.

Two broad areas to consider promoting children's cultural adaptation and inclusion in our classrooms require that we learn from families and understand their perspectives and priorities, thereby developing a more nuanced appreciation for diversity and building bridges between home and school (Yahya & Wood, 2017). The first area involves making connections between children's home and school experiences. The second broad set of practices involves providing opportunities for children to be active members of the classroom, develop agency and form friendships (Maher & Smith, 2014). To do this well, newcomers' cultures must have a central place in the mainstream cultural space of the classroom; classrooms should be places where everyone can feel at home. Mosselson (2006) explains: "understanding the concerns and processes in play for [newcomer children] helps educators to see [them] more fully … in terms of their individual experiences rather than in terms of expectations of adaptation to the mainstream" (p. 27).

Building Relationships with Families

Trusting and respectful relationships between ECE educators and families are important for supporting all children's adjustment to school (Copple & Bredekamp, 2009) but especially important when working with young newcomers. Good relationships are the foundation for connecting home and school and are essential to learning about children's culture and experiences (Donnelly, 2010; Tadessee, 2014; Hoot, 2011; Hurley, Medici, Stewart, & Cohen, 2014). However, building relationships takes time and language and cultural differences can make the process challenging (Strekalova-Hughes & Wang, 2017).

Communication with im/migrant families is both essential and difficult, especially when teachers and im/migrants do not speak a common language. While interpreters may be found (e.g. through organizations that work with im/migrant groups or family or community members more fluent in English), using interpreters also brings challenges. Professional interpreters rarely have a background in child development or education, so they may translate information inaccurately. Friends, family or community members often paraphrase, leave out important content, or offer their own commentary instead of interpreting. Sometimes older children interpret, which can support their confidence and self-esteem (Orellana, Dorner, & Pulido, 2003), but also disrupt parent-child relations by putting the child in a position of power and parents in a position dependent on their children (Wong Fillmore, 1991).

Communication extends beyond language; it is profoundly cultural. Many behaviors assumed to be normal are not universal. Everyday acts such as greetings and body language differ across cultures. Interpreters can serve as cultural brokers, helping educators to understand some of the subtler but critical aspects of communication. They can explain some widely held cultural norms such as how formal or informal interactions should be, and how to address different family members. Interpretation is a skilled practice prioritizing cultural meaning, rather than literally translating individual words. Also, translation of written documents should be done with care. School documents are imbued with cultural understandings often taken for granted, and can be confusing or intimidating to people not familiar with them. Some im/migrants also have limited reading skills, depending on their personal histories. Finally, it is important to think through information requests, avoiding sensitive topics such as immigration or citizenship status. These questions may create distrust or anxiety.

Questions about family history or migration experience can also be stressful triggers for refugees or asylum seekers who may not be ready to share traumatic experiences with teachers.

Im/migrant parents and ECE teachers in the U.S often have quite different perspectives about education (Tobin et al., 2013). Parents want their children to learn English and do well in school, which can mean they prefer the focus to be on English instruction and traditional academics rather than play or project-based learning. Teachers, on the other hand, tend to be committed to play-based ECE curricula, and so are often torn. Teachers want to be culturally responsive yet their "willingness ... to be culturally responsive [is often] trumped by their commitment to their notions of best practice, which [in Tobin et al.'s (2013) research] centered on the principles of constructivism, learning through play, and resisting a pushed-down academic curriculum" (p.12). Similarly, im/migrant parents often expect a clear distinction between teachers' and parents' roles and responsibilities. It may seem odd to families when they are asked by teachers to do academic activities with their children as they may see academics as the work of schools. In the same way, they may not welcome teachers encroaching on their home life as in, for example, home visits. The way parent involvement and family-school relations are understood and dictated by U.S. schools blur the lines between what parents and teachers are expected to do. While some families may welcome family-school collaboration, others find these expectations confusing, ambiguous, and unwelcome. Thus, strong collaborations with families are nuanced, individualized for families, and evolving as families acculturate to their early childhood programs and U.S. society.

We can ease transitions for families by explaining the rationale for developmentally appropriate practice, play-based curricula, and the advantages of bilingual development (Tadessee et al., 2009). Rather than dictating *how* families should engage in and contribute to their children's education, we can recognize and support the ways families already do those things, though these might look quite different from schools' traditional narrow definition of parent engagement based in dominant norms and assumptions (Lopez, 2001). This requires teachers to see beyond the social norms expected in schools, to recognize other ways that families are engaged. When we find common ground and establish shared goals, their ways and ours can complement rather than contradict each other to contribute to children's bicultural identities.

Im/migrant parents are navigating and raising children in settings very different than those they grew up in (Tobin et al., 2013) and face many anxieties as their children start school. Teachers can help in this process by establishing ourselves as allies and adjusting our practices so they make sense to newcomers. We can help families to understand expectations and policies, as well as their rights, as they navigate the educational system. Unfamiliar with U.S. norms and laws, im/migrant parents often worry that their parenting practices will be judged negatively and fear their children may be taken away from them, making them wary of teachers (Tadessee, 2014). Teachers can lessen their anxiety by valuing their parenting practices, and by helping them know the laws and policies that may affect them.

Undocumented im/migrant parents, or parents of undocumented children, fear entering their children in early childhood settings may heighten the risk of deportation. Teachers can explain the sensitive locations policy (Ulrich, 2018), which requires government agents be turned away from schools and child care centers unless they have a warrant. When educators are allies, parents are more willing to engage with them. However, to be a good ally one needs to be informed and knowledgeable. This requires listening deeply to families sharing their own ways of thinking about their experiences and what they want for their children (Tobin et al., 2013). In today's environment, being vigilant with regard to immigration practices in our communities, and seeking alliances with community organizations when necessary is most likely to meaningfully support parents concerned about im/migration status. Furthermore, it is critical for teachers to understand that all children in the U.S. have a right to education, regardless of their migration status (Plyler v. Doe, 1982).

Many families walk the fine line between supporting their children's inclusion in U.S. society while maintaining their cultural heritage (Tobin et al., 2013); we can also be allies in supporting biculturalism by respecting family cultural practices. When we find ways to balance home and school culture, we are more likely to engage children. In the school environment we can promote children's friendships, challenge bias, and foster bicultural and bilingual development. When we do so, families can more easily trust the classroom will be an emotionally and culturally safe place for their children. This in turn helps children feel safer in the classroom so they can integrate more easily as full members of the classroom community.

Supporting Bicultural and Transnational Identities in the Classroom

As early childhood educators, we know home language and culture are integral to bicultural development and im/migrant families' lived experience and cultural knowledge (González, Moll, & Amanti, 2005). Children experiencing stress, the kind coming with entrance to a foreign, often incomprehensible setting, can be reticent to engage in activities or with others. Culturally responsive classrooms lay the foundations of children's bicultural and bilingual identities when they incorporate children's language and culture as part of daily classroom life. Teachers create opportunities for children's cultural practices and perspectives to emerge in play and learning by including artifacts such as toys, clothing and household items, books and technology reflective of the cultures represented, and by allowing for ways of doing things not necessarily reflective of U.S. cultural norms. Artifacts can become learning and teaching materials as they can encourage children to enact their experiences in play, and in the primary years, share their customs and background knowledge from their lived experiences. It is important, however, that these approaches should not be superficial or based on stereotypes.

Because children need to feel safe socially and emotionally in order to engage in the classroom, our first responsibility to children of im/migrants is to help them develop a sense of security and control. Classrooms structured around a regular schedule, predictable routines, and consistent expectations benefit all children but are especially important for im/migrant children. Clear and consistent communication about the expectations, routines, and schedule fosters young children's self-regulation. Using multiple means to supplement oral directions, such as pictures of the daily sequence of events or a bell or various available technologies to indicate that it is time to clean up, not only helps children to prepare for transitions and function more independently, but also helps them to understand rules that might otherwise seem arbitrary or ambiguous. These practices also help them to learn English (Hurley et al., 2014).

Ways that educators engage children in conversation about their lives are too often limited to life experience in the local community. Newcomer children have often left family members behind, so questions that assume that grand-parents or both parents are present locally can be misguided. While sometimes newcomer children and families do not want to talk about their migration experiences, sometimes they do; when they do, it is important to not assume that their life experiences are only in the local community. Im/migrants often observe that people in the U.S. do not seem interested in their lives outside the local community or in the past; this creates feelings of invisibility. Knowing how to show interest, without prying, is important in conveying to newcomers that they have a place in our classrooms and schools.

Similarly, many im/migrants' sense of self is transnational—the scope of their lives extends beyond the local community and across national borders; the frame of reference is much broader than for most Americans. Children further develop their bicultural and transnational identities in the classroom when provided with opportunities to bring and share their home culture and, if they choose, their migration experiences, in the classroom in ways that become integral to life in the classroom. Classrooms are microcosms of mainstream society, so inclusion means broadening that culture and scope of life to be more inclusive. Integrating newcomer children's home language and culture in the classroom is not merely a means of supporting their emotional comfort and understanding, it is also important in terms of giving them opportunities to positively express themselves and share and build on their prior experiences as they engage with other children and with teachers. It is important, however, to not make a spectacle of their difference and to have non-newcomer children share their lives in ways that make these shared activities equally valued. (Care should be taken to not value the mainstream cultures more than the others as this creates a hierarchy of social life in the classroom.) In this way friendships are built on equal footing. Friendships with children are important for all children's overall development and their confidence in themselves as young scholars and as residents in the U.S. who feel a sense of belonging, being and becoming (Maher & Smith, 2014, p. 28). The approach to early education with a focus on bicultural and bilingual development, and allowing for transnational forms of identity, provides a foundation for self-esteem that underlies later identification with and sense of belonging in schools (Yahya & Wood, 2017). Our practice can, thus, secure a firm foundation for young children beginning their educational lives in the U.S. system.

Conclusion

While there are many challenges newcomer children face in adapting to the early childhood classroom, they also bring many strengths teachers can build upon not only to support their transition, but also to enrich the classroom community overall. When teachers examine their own cultural beliefs and assumptions, they are better able to adapt their classroom practices to provide opportunities for children to share and celebrate their languages and cultures in the classroom in meaningful ways, which helps children lay a strong foundation for bicultural identities. Thus, teachers play a critical role in supporting the success and resilience of children from im/migrant families. In the process, teachers also create more inclusive classrooms, promoting understanding, respect and dialogue for all children as they prepare them for life in a diverse and democratic society. Nevertheless, there are no pre-packaged strategies for working with newcomers where one size fits all. Getting to know and understand people on their terms provides a meaningful foundation on which we work with families and children to build a shared vision of the future honoring everyone's perspectives in our complex and changing environment. Our practice serves young im/migrant children well when we recognize how migration, culture, language, discrimination, and poverty affect children's experiences before they enter our care in our educational settings. It is only with a much deeper understanding of prior life experiences in their families' journeys that we form valued relationships to foster newcomer children's learning and school success.

References

Arzubiaga, A.E., Noguerón, C., & Sullivan, A.L. (2009). The education of children in im/migrant families. *Review of Research in Education*, *3*, 246–271.

Banks, J.A. (2017). *Cultural Diversity and Education: Foundations, Curriculum, and Teaching* (6th ed.). New York: Routledge.

Brettell, C.B. (2015). Theorizing migration in anthropology: The cultural, social, and phenomenological dimensions of movement. In C.B. Brettell & J.F. Hollifield (Eds.), *Migration theory: Talking Across Disciplines* (3rd ed., pp. 148–197). New York: Routledge.

Chavez, L.R. (2013). *Shadowed Lives: Undocumented Immigrants in American Society* (3rd ed.). Belmont, CA: Wadsworth.

Connor, P. (2018). Most displaced Syrians are in the Middle East, and about a million are in Europe. *FacTank: News in the Numbers*, January 29; Pew Research Center. Retrieved from: http://www.pewresearch.org/fact-tank/2018/01/29/where-displaced-syrians-have-resettled/

Copple, C., & Bredekamp, S. (Eds.) (2009). *Developmentally Appropriate Practice in Early Childhood Programs Serving Children from Birth Through Age 8* (3rd ed.). Washington, DC: National Association for the Education of Young Children.

Crosby, D.A., & Dunbar, A.S. (2012). *Patterns and Predictors of School Readiness and Early Childhood Success Among Young Children in Black Immigrant Families.* Washington, DC: Migration Policy Institute.

Crosnoe, R. (2006). *Mexican Roots, American Schools: Helping Mexican Immigrant Children Succeed.* Palo Alto, CA: Stanford University Press.

Crosnoe, R., & Ansari, A. (2015). Latin U.S. immigrant parents and their children's teachers in U.S. early childhood education programmes. *International Journal of Psychology, 50*(6), 431–439.

Derman-Sparks, L., & Edwards, J.O. (2010). *Anti-Bias Education for Young Children and Ourselves.* Washington, DC: NAEYC.

Donnelly, P. (2010). Starting school in Ireland: The experience of young children from the refugee community. In M.M. Clark & S. Tucker (Eds.), *Early Childhoods in a Changing World* (pp. 21–31). Sterling, VA: Trentham Books.

Ferguson, S. (2018). Separating migrant children from their families is wrong. UNICEF USA, June 18. Retrieved from: https://www.unicefusa.org/stories/separating-migrant-children-their-families-wrong/34425

Garcia, E.E., & Markos, A.M. (2015) Early Childhood Education and Dual Language Learners. In W.E. Wright, B. Sovicheth, & O. Garcia (Eds.). *The Handbook of Bilingual and Multicultural Education* (Ch. 18, pp. 301–318). Hoboken, NJ: Wiley.

Genishi, C., & Goodwin, A.L. (Eds.). (2008). *Diversities in Early Childhood Education: Rethinking and Doing.* New York: Routledge.

Gjelten, T. (2016). *A Nation of Nations: A Great American Immigration Story.* New York: Simon & Schuster.

González, N., Moll, L., & Amanti, C. (Eds.) (2005). *Funds of Knowledge: Theorizing Practices in Households, Communities and Classrooms.* New York: Routledge.

Haines, S.J. III, Summer, J.A., Turnbull, A.P., Turnbull III, H.R., & Palmer, S. (2015). Fostering Habib's engagement and self-regulation: A case study of a child from a refugee family at Home and Preschool. *Topics in Early Childhood Special Education, 35*(1), 28–39.

Healy, M. (2018). The long-lasting health effects of separating children from their parents at the U.S. border. *Los Angeles Times,* June 20, Science Now section. Retrieved from: http://www.latimes.com/science/sciencenow/la-sci-sn-separating-children-psychology-20180620-story.html

Hernandez, D.J. (2004). Demographic change and the life circumstances of immigrants. *Future of Children, 14*(2), 16–47.

Hoot, J. (2011). Working with very young refugee children in our schools: Implications for the world's teachers. *Procedia Social and Behavioral Sciences, 15,* 1751–1755.

Hurley, J.J., Medici, A., Stewart, E., & Cohen, Z. (2014). Supporting preschoolers and their families who are recently resettled refugees. *Multicultural Perspectives, 13*(3), 160–166.

Igielnik, R., & Krogstad, J.M. (2017). Where refugees to the U.S. come from. *FacTank: News in the Numbers,* February 3; Pew Research Center. Retrieved from: http://www.pewresearch.org/fact-tank/2017/02/03/where-refugees-to-the-u-s-come-from/

Igoa, C. (1995). *The Inner World of the Immigrant Child.* Mahwah, NJ: Lawrence Erlbaum Associates.

Krogstad, J.M., & Radford, J. (2017). Key facts about refugees to the U.S. *FacTank: News in the Numbers,* January 30; Pew Research Center. Retrieved from: http://www.pewresearch.org/fact-tank/2017/01/30/key-facts-about-refugees-to-the-u-s/)

Levitt, P., & Waters, M.C. (Eds.). (2002). *The Changing Face of Home: The Transnational Lives of the Second Generation*. New York: Russell Sage.

Lissak, R. (1989). *Pluralism and Progressives: Hull House and the New Immigrants, 1890–1919*. Chicago, IL: University of Chicago Press.

Lopez, G. (2001). The value of hard work: Lessons on parent involvement from an (im) migrant household. *Harvard Educational Review, 71*(3), 416–438.

Magnuson, K., Lahaie, C., & Waldfogel, J. (2006). Preschool and school readiness of children of immigrants. *Social Science Quarterly, 87*(5), 1241–1262.

Magnuson, K.A., Ruhm, C.J., & Waldfogel, J. (2004). Does pre-kindergarten improve school preparation and performance? National Bureau of Economic Research [NBER] Working Paper 10452. Cambridge, MA: NBER.

Maher, M., & Smith, S. (2014). Asylum seeker and refugee children belonging, being and becoming: The early childhood educator's role. *Australian Journal of Early Childhood, 39*(1), 22–29.

Marks, A.K., Ejesi, K., & Garcia-Coll, C. (2014). Understanding the U.S. immigrant paradox in childhood and adolescence. *Child Development Perspectives, 8*(2), 59–64.

Massey, D.S., Alarcón, R., Durand, J., & González, H. (1987). *Return to Aztlan: The Social Process of International Migration from Western Mexico*. Berkeley, CA: University of California Press.

McClelland, M.M., Cameron, C.E., Connor, C.M., Farris, C.L., Jewkes, A. M., & Morrison, F.J. (2007). Links between behavioral regulation and preschoolers' literacy, vocabulary, and math skills. *Developmental Psychology, 43*(4), 947–959.

Mossaad, H., & Baugh, R. (2018). Refugees and asylum: 2016. Annual flow report, January 2018. Homeland Security, Office of Immigration Statistics, Office of Strategy, Policy & Plans. Retrieved from: https://www.dhs.gov/sites/default/files/publications/Refugees_Asylees_2016.pdf

Mosselson, J. (2006). Roots and routes: A reimagining of refugee identity constructions and the implications for schooling. *Current Issues in Comparative Education, 9*(1), 20–29.

National Center for Farmworker Health, Inc. [NCFH]. (2012). Farmworker health fact sheet. Retrieved from: http://www.ncfh.org/uploads/3/8/6/8/38685499/fs-migrant_demographics.pdf

Orellana, M.F., Dorner, L., & Pulido, L. (2003). Accessing assets: Immigrant youth's work as family translators or "para-prasers". *Social Problems, 50*, 505–524.

Park, M., & McHugh, M. (2014). Immigrant parents and early childhood programs: Addressing barriers of literacy, culture, and systems knowledge. Migration Policy Institute, Washington, DC. Retrieved from: http://www.migrationpolicy.org/research/immigrant-parents-early-childhood-programs-barriers

Plyler v. Doe 457 U.S. 202, 1982.

Portes, A., & Rivas, A. (2011). The adaptation of migrant children. *The Future of Children, 21*(1), 219–246.

Rogoff, B. (2001). *The Cultural Nature of Human Development*. New York: Oxford University Press.

Saracho, O., & Spodek, B. (Eds.). (2010). *Contemporary Perspectives on Language and Cultural Diversity in Early Childhood Education*. Charlotte, NC: Information Age.

Souto-Manning, M. (2007). Immigrant families and children (re)develop identities in a new context. *Early Childhood Education Journal, 34*, 399–405.

Strekalova-Hughes, E., & Wang, C. (2017). Intercultural experiential continuum: A case study of early childhood teachers working with refugee children. *Journal of Early Childhood Education Research, 6*(1), 61–88.

Tadessee, S. (2014). Parent involvement: Perceived encouragement and barriers to African refugee parent and teacher relationships. *Childhood Education, 90*(4), 299–305.

Tadessee, S., Hoot, J., & Watson-Thompson, O. (2009). Exploring the special needs of African refugee children in U.S. schools. *Childhood Education, 85*(6), 352–356.

Tobin, J., Arzubiaga, A.E., & Adair, J.K. (2013). *Children Crossing Borders: Immigrant Parent and Teacher Perspectives on Preschool*. New York: Russell Sage Foundation.

Ulrich, R. (2018). Keeping immigrant families safe in early childhood programs. Center for Law and Social Policy [CLASP]. Retrieved from: https://www.clasp.org/blog/keeping-immigrant-families-safe-early-childhood-programs

United Nations High Commissioner for Refugees [UNHCR] (2015). *World at War: UNHCR Global Trends: Forced Displacement in 2014*. Geneva: UNHCR.

U.S. Dept. of Education [USDOE]. (2018). Binational Migrant Education Initiative [BMEI]. Retrieved from: https://www2.ed.gov/admins/tchrqual/learn/binational.html

U.S. Dept. of Labor [USDOL] Employment and Training Administration [ETA]. (2016). A Demographic and Employment Profile of U.S. Farmworkers. Findings from the National Agricultural Workers Survey (NAWS) 2013–2014. Research Report number 12, US Department of Labor, Employment and Training Administration, Office of Policy Development and Research. Retrieved from: https://www.doleta.gov/naws/pages/research/docs/NAWS_Research_Report_12.pdf

Wong Fillmore, L. (1991). When learning a second language means losing the first. *Early Childhood Research Quarterly, 6*, 323–346.

Yahya, R., & Wood, E.A. (2017). Play as third space between home and school: Bridging cultural discourses. *Journal of Early Childhood Research, 15*(3), 305–322.

6 Challenging Behaviors in the Classroom

Julie Parson Nesbitt

Jesse is an engaging six-year-old who has trouble sitting in his seat to focus on his work. When his teacher hears the snap of his pencil breaking, she knows he will quickly escalate to throwing books on the floor. During a full-scale meltdown, Jesse has overturned desks and thrown chairs across the room. D'Andre loves to color and will become very absorbed in his drawing. But when his teacher touches him lightly on the shoulder to transition to the next activity, he flinches, jumps up, and runs out of the classroom. Lining up in the hallway for recess, Kayden will fall on the floor, covering his ears and crying when a noisy group of students passes. All of these challenging behaviors in the classroom are familiar to many teachers. But understanding the reasons and finding solutions can be just as challenging.

Up to 30% of US students have challenging behaviors in school, ranging from inappropriate to violent. Teachers in cities, rural areas, and suburbs, in classrooms of kids from every social and economic background, struggle to help students with challenging behaviors. Challenging behavior impedes learning and disrupts the environment. It bothers other students, frustrates teachers, and uses up classroom time. Students who don't get the support they need to change their challenging behaviors are more likely to have learning and behavioral problems throughout their school years. Consequently, they risk social acceptance, employment opportunities, and face health issues throughout life.

Teachers are given primary responsibility for helping these students. But standard interventions often frustratingly fail. Sticker charts, time-outs, threats to lose recess, and being sent to the principal's office do not seem to stop so-called "repeaters." Strategies that seem to work, like sensory corners or one-on-one time, are not always supported by the school environment. Lacking support to help with challenging behaviors can leave teachers feeling frustrated and burned out.

Impact of Trauma on Behavior and Learning

We now know that behavioral and learning issues in school may be caused by a child's experience of early or ongoing trauma. Early trauma is much more common than most of us realize: an estimated 26% to 40% of US children experience trauma. Trauma affects children from every economic, racial/ethnic, and geographic background, but impacts some communities more than others.

We often hear the word "trauma," but what does it really mean? Trauma is usually defined in two categories: acute (a single event, usually sudden and brief, like a car crash) or chronic (ongoing over time, such as repeated abuse or homelessness). But trauma is not just an event or experience; it is how an individual responds. Trauma occurs when an individual is overwhelmed by events or repeated stressful situations, making it difficult for him or her to cope effectively. This helps explain why people experiencing similar situations may respond in very different ways: some prove resilient, while others become overwhelmed. The intensity of an event, how long it goes on, and how often it occurs are also important factors. We also need to consider the child's development stage, other protective or harmful circumstances in their lives, and even personal attributes such as temperament, and how these factors interact. Chronic trauma is more harmful and more likely to lead to negative outcomes.

A child's experience of trauma may come from physical, sexual, or emotional maltreatment; difficult circumstances at home; foster care or homelessness; prenatal alcohol or drug abuse; immigration experiences; social issues such as racism or misogyny; or even events from previous generations.

The effects of early, chronic trauma can be devastating on a child's ability to learn, behave appropriately, and interact with peers and adults. It can inhibit learning and processing information, problem solving, sequential and organizational thinking, attention, self-regulation, understanding social cues, and trusting others; while increasing impulsivity, aggression, defiance, and/or withdrawal. In the long term, children who have experienced chronic trauma are more than twice as likely to fail a grade in school, "score lower on standardized tests, have higher rates of suspension and expulsion, and are more likely to be placed in special education classrooms" (Statman-Weil, 2015, p. 1). The impact on students, teachers, schools, families, and society can be long term, costly, and significant.

How Trauma Affects the Brain

Why does trauma have such a dramatic impact on children's behavior and learning, and how have we developed this knowledge?

ACEs Study

Between 1995 and 1997, the Kaiser-Permanente health insurance company surveyed 17,000 members in largely affluent or middle-class areas of southern California. The survey asked whether and to what extent individuals had experienced specific adverse childhood circumstances, known as ACEs. The study proved groundbreaking: it documented the previously unknown extent and high rates of childhood trauma across economic groups, including

Disorder versus Distress

Disorder: A manifestation of a behavioral, psychological, or biological *dysfunction* within the individual.

Distress: *normal* human response to overwhelming stress & sustained through continued response to stress.

How can ACEs shift the frame from disorder to distress?

Figure 6.1 Adverse childhood experiences affect life. From Adverse Childhood Experiences Presentation Graphics (2016).

well-educated, affluent people; it categorized and quantified ACEs; and it gave evidence that childhood trauma creates lifelong consequences.

Adverse childhood experiences surveyed in the study included emotional, physical, and sexual abuse; neglect; violence against the mother; parental separation or divorce; substance abuse; mental illness; incarceration of a household member; and other issues ("About Adverse Childhood Experiences (ACEs)," 2016). The more ACEs experienced, the higher the probability of consequences. Consequences of early trauma include lifelong social, emotional, and cognitive problems; risky behaviors; mental and physical health problems; economic loss; and even early death. (About the CDC-Kaiser ACE Study, n.d.). The research results were used to develop a "pyramid" showing lifelong consequences of early trauma (Figure 6.1). You can test your own ACEs score here with the Adverse Early Childhood Experiences: ACEs Too High tool (https://acestoohigh.com/). The ACEs Study, as it became widely known, laid the foundation for a trauma-informed approach to education. Subsequent research has supported and expanded the ACEs study findings that chronic trauma results in childhood behavior issues and lifelong problems.

Seeing into the Brain

Also, in the 1990s, MRI and other brain-scanning techniques became much more accurate at mapping children's brain development. Using these techniques, neuroscience showed how chronic trauma physically changes the architecture of a child's developing brain. Scientists charted how changes in a child's brain caused by trauma specifically correspond to behavioral, cognitive, and social/emotional domains necessary for academic learning and behavior. Neurological research has driven the development of specific strategies to help such children, often called a trauma-informed approach.

Fortunately, children's developing brains also have the ability to repair and recover. Neuroplasticity allows new neural pathways to develop in the brain. Using strategies and interventions aligned with neuroplasticity can substantially help students' behavior and learning in the classroom. However, lack of support or aggravating conditions can create secondary issues, making the situation even worse for students, teachers, and schools.

How Trauma Changes Brain Development

Our brains develop through dynamic interaction with our environment. A parent's smile, a quiet place to sleep, and being comforted in response to crying all help an infant's brain lay a solid foundation for growth and learning. Our neurological functions are built by increasing areas that are used often, and decreasing those that are not used as often. The more a part of the brain is stimulated, the more neural pathways it develops, while under-used areas become weaker and less developed. A child who lives in a stable, safe and loving environment develops areas of the brain responding to attachment, trust, and regulation. When an infant or child experiences physical or emotional stress or trauma, the brain physically develops to respond to an unstable and threatening environment. The brain of a child who was neglected or abused actually looks different and functions in a different way. Over time, and especially during the "sensitive period" of birth through age five, the brain of someone in an unstable or unsafe environment goes on continuous high alert. Parts of the brain, such as the "flight, fright, or freeze" mode, become overdeveloped, while areas regulating impulse control and higher cognitive functions are underdeveloped. These physical changes depend on onset, intensity, frequency, and continuity of stress.

Most of us have heard the expression "fight, flight, or freeze." In a dangerous situation, our bodies automatically respond physically in order to survive. If you have ever felt a hot rush of anger overcome you when someone yelled at you, run faster than you thought possible hearing footsteps on a dark street, or felt your whole body freeze at a strange sound in the night, you understand how this feels.

In a threatening situation, the brain releases a surge of the hormones adrenalin and cortisol, called the "stress response." These hormones stimulate the body to fight hard, move fast, or freeze in order to survive the threat. The heart rate increases, and blood is directed to survival functions, along with other physiological changes.

When an infant or child experiences stress over a sustained period of time, the brain responds by maintaining this state of high alert all the time. The hormones do not "turn off" as they should when the threat has passed.

Hyper-arousal becomes the regular state of functioning, and areas of the brain regulating cognition and impulse control are bypassed. When the child's brain is in a hyper-alert state, it is not calm. The systems necessary for higher levels of thinking, responding, and organization have, in a sense, been co-opted; all the focus is on survival. Cortisol and adrenalin trigger the brain to interpret the behavior of others as threatening or rejecting, making children misread social cues, become hostile at a chance encounter, or take a helpful suggestion as criticism. The stress response leads to aggression, impulsivity, hyperactivity, disassociation, or withdrawal. In other words: fight, flight, or freeze. This response is related to a part of the brain called the amygdala.

Like a company CEO or a school principal, the brain's prefrontal cortex (PFC) is the boss of the organization and controls "executive function." Executive function is critical to success in school. It provides the ability for attention, working memory, planning, organizing, staying on task, and completing a task. It enables cognitive flexibility and mediates other cognitive functions. But early trauma and stress impair and diminish the PFC and lessen its ability to function, making it difficult to learn and behave in school.

Two other areas of the brain strongly impacted by trauma are the hippocampus and the limbic system. These areas are involved with self-regulation and impulse control, and relational skills. Resulting problems may include a need to control, a seeming lack of interest in others, anxiety, helplessness, and/or disinterest in trying or learning new things.

Trauma is not just psychological but is physically embedded in our bodies (van der Kolk, 2014). Healing from trauma is a physical process. In addition, research has shown that trauma is "epigenetic": interaction with the environment changes our genetic structures. "Nurture" and "nature" are not separate but entwined. Trauma-informed practices work neurologically and physically to change the way our brains function and help us heal.

Early trauma affects the brain in complex, dynamic, and interactive ways. A short explanation can't fully explain the way trauma impacts our ability to learn, behave, and relate to others. Ongoing research is still revealing many of the brain's secrets. But there are many things we already know.

Early and ongoing stress and trauma impairs a wide range of cognitive abilities, including working memory, retaining and processing verbal information, sequential thinking, abstract thinking, problem solving, analysis, communication skills, spontaneous speech, expressive language, ability to organize experiences, planning, goal setting, communicating one's experience to others, and cognitive flexibility. Behavior also suffers due to the impact on brain functions related to impulse control, self-regulation, attention, and the ability to understand cause-and-effect. Trauma interferes with early patterns of attachment that physically lay the brain's foundation for developing relationships. Children who have been neglected or maltreated often have difficulty interpreting social cues, understanding body language, trusting adults, developing friendships with peers, and other relational skills. Without appropriate interventions, these patterns persist throughout life.

It's important—though sometimes difficult—to remember that this behavior is *not intentional*. The student is not willfully breaking rules, ignoring the teacher, or daydreaming in class. His or her brain is responding to normal life as a threatening situation, sending signals to fight, flee, or freeze. If we keep this in mind, it is easier to respond with empathy in order to help the child and remediate the behaviors.

What Helps Students in the Classroom

Fortunately, children's brains have the ability to repair and recover due to neuroplasticity: the brain's ability to create new neural pathways. Children who have experienced trauma can grow and heal through protective factors such as warm relationships and positive interventions. Neuroplasticity is especially possible during "sensitive growth periods," especially birth to age five. Appropriate early support and intervention "can dramatically reduce the effects of early trauma" (Craig, 2016, p. 25). Many familiar and common early learning and school activities fall into this healing category: structured play, physical activity, music, art, sitting close to a teacher, and, for some children, hugs or back-rubs. However, lack of support or aggravating conditions can re-traumatize children and create secondary issues causing lifelong problems.

Classroom Strategies

Teachers often know what helps their students. Strategies we call "trauma-informed" are often familiar and even assumed. What makes them "trauma-informed" is that we now understand *why* they work based on brain neurology. Of course, not all strategies work for all children. Age, developmental stage, trauma history, environment, culture, and individual traits all affect what a child needs and what will help. These are general strategies that can be adapted as needed.

When working with students with trauma histories, the general rule (in this order) is: **Safety, Connection, Repair, Growth**.

Safety

- Make sure you, the student, other students and adults are safe.
- Your student's brain is on fire. He can't regulate his own behavior in that moment. He needs to feel safe before his behavior can change.
- Helping your student de-escalate is a physical process. Her body and brain must be calm in order to process language and respond to directions or questions.
- Use as few words as possible. Speak softly. Say, "it's okay" or "you're safe."
- Take deep breaths along with the student: say "blow out the birthday candles" or "blow up the balloon" to encourage long exhales. Deep breathing helps decrease heart rate and calm the nervous system.

- When the student is no longer physically aggressive, sit with him. If you know him well and you know it helps, give a hug, rub his back or put your hands firmly on his shoulders.
- Focus the student's attention on the present moment by using a physical object like a stuffed animal or a physical activity like pressing her palms together.
- Give the student water or a healthy snack. Children with trauma histories often have higher levels of glutamate, a neurotransmitter associated with aggression and seizures. Hydration or a healthy snack stabilizes the student's blood sugar and helps stabilize behavior. This may seem unfair to other students, but all kids have to learn that each person's needs are different.
- Offer a safe option, such as punching a pillow or throwing a nerf ball. You may feel you are enabling bad behavior, but actually you are helping fulfill a physical need in a safe way.
- Create a sensory corner that is a safe place to go; it might have pillows, a rocking chair, a weighted blanket, stuffed animals, fidgets, and a nook or cloth "snake" to hide in. Pressure on the joints, rocking, hugging, and being squeezed in a small space all give proprioceptive input that helps the child's body and brain calm down.
- Some sensory-seeking students need the sensation of a crack or snap. Chewing gum or crunching on a cracker can help a child self-regulate. To avoid food (or pencil breaking), there are many chewy and snap-able safe toys available.

Every child is different. A child who has been sexually molested may be averse to touch. Some students are "runners" while others feel safe inside a tight space. Be sure you know which response is safe and not re-traumatizing for that child.

Stability, structure, and routine are crucial. A safe, stable environment and a predictable routine help regulate the brain. Students who have experienced instability and upheaval need to know what to expect and what will come next in the day. Structure and predictability help children self-regulate and feel more in control.

- A visual chart of the daily routine using pictures helps with transitions.
- "Check-in" at the beginning of the day for signs of distress or escalation.
- Assign one "key adult" who is available to the student when needed.
- Give 10- and 5-minute heads-up alerts before and extra time for transitions.
- Set clear, appropriate limits in ways the child understands (possibly non-verbal).
- If a student can't manage limits, adapt the environment so the student can be successful.
- Alert students in advance to a change in the routine and help them prepare for changes.

Connection, Repair, Growth

The single most important help for children who have experienced trauma is the presence of a caring adult. Adult support not only serves as a protective factor, but it also encourages emotional and cognitive growth. Empathy, safety, and connection are the best ways to help students with challenging behaviors learn and succeed in school. Here are some suggestions based on a trauma-informed approach:

- Start with wherever the student is. If she is angry, start there. If she acts like a two-year-old, start there.
- Stay with the child's feelings in the moment until she is ready to move on.
- Put words and gestures to her feelings. She may not know her own feeling or be able to answer an open-ended question like "how do you feel?" Reflective thinking teaches her how to identify and articulate her own emotions. Say, "Wow, you feel THIS angry!" stretching your arms wide, or, "It must be scary to hear that loud noise" covering your ears.
- Don't explain, lecture, or appease; she literally will not hear/process what you are saying. Use only a few words. Pause; give the child time to process.
- Don't judge or blame.
- Connection is empathy.

Behavior Is Communication

A child whose brain has developed through trauma has difficulty telling you what he needs. Instead, he communicates through behavior. Whether the child is "daydreaming" or throwing chairs, ask "What is this child trying to tell me?"

Address the Root Cause

Many standard school interventions follow a behavior modification approach based on punishments and rewards. Delayed gratification or punishment, or interventions relying on cause and effect, may not work because children with trauma histories have trouble understanding sequential thinking, time, and cause and effect due to the ways their brains have developed. Your student may not be able to connect breaking a rule today with losing a field trip next week. A student may not process the idea that he is being sent out of class because he used bad words; he just thinks you are being mean to him. Although it takes more time and effort, the best way to help students change their behavior is to figure out the cause of the behavior, and what triggers it. Many times, there is a sensory reason. For example, a student who bolts from the lunch line may not be able to process different levels of noise, turning lunchroom clatter into a painful roar. She could be given noise-reducing headphones or assigned to a quieter lunch period. A student who gets aggressive could be triggered by frustration with a long worksheet of problems; sometimes covering all the problems but the one he is working on can head off the explosion.

Redirect to an Activity That Fulfills Student's Needs

Often, teachers intuit a student's needs and do exactly the right thing. A boy who is racing around the room may need a safe sensory break to release energy, like jumping jacks or a trip to the water fountain. Teachers often know their students' needs from experience, bringing antsy students to sit next to them during story time.

Use Positive Language

Tell a student what you want her to do and save "no" for safety issues. Instead of "no running," use "walking feet"; instead of "don't hit!" use "safe hands." For some students, use physical reinforcement, such as softly stroking the child's hands, or using a song with a walking rhythm.

Focus on Strengths

Use positive motivation. Build on the positive qualities you see in the student. As much as possible, remind him of his good qualities. Is he kind, funny, creative, a helper? What does the student like to do? If he likes to sing, use music to help regulate physical activity. If she likes to draw, encourage her to express her feelings through drawing.

Never Shame

Never shame a child who has experienced trauma. Shame will reinforce negative feelings and low self-esteem. It will re-traumatize children, trigger challenging behaviors, and generate negative consequences for a lifetime.

Ask: Who Is He?

Sometimes students are defined more by their diagnoses than as a whole, complex child. Looking at who the student is helps create compassion, encourage positive motivation, and build a connection between the student and teacher. Instead of asking: "What are his problems?" try asking, "Who is he?"

Use Win-Win Consequences

Use natural, immediate consequences that encourage the child to feel good about himself. Instead of being sent out of the room, the consequence could be a "helping" activity, like picking up the blocks or pushing the chairs under the table. When the student finishes the task, give him acknowledgment and praise for helping. It may feel counter-intuitive or like you are rewarding him for bad behavior. But it builds trust, self-esteem, and a sense of agency, all of which re-build neural connections in our brains. We want students to *want to be good*. Your student will be motivated by your relationship and try to do better to get your approval.

Give Structured, Safe Agency and Voice

When possible, give the student agency. Give two choices that are both acceptable. Provide a chance for a "re-do." If the student is capable, try to identify the problem together, and brainstorm together to solve the problem. Use the best means for the student to communicate—it may be through drawing or making up a rap.

Remember the Brain

Ask: "Is this behavior a 'won't' or a 'can't'?" Much behavior that seems willful is actually sensory or motor-driven. Try to re-frame behavior: Is he climbing on the table to intentionally break rules, or is he hyperactive and needs a sensory break? Is she lazy and won't finish her work, or is she over-stressed and shut down?

Daniel was constantly breaking pencils. The teacher thought he was trying to get attention and tried all kinds of punishments. Nothing worked. She finally realized that, due to his sensory needs, Daniel liked to feel the "snap" when the pencil broke. She gave him a sensory toy to "snap" and he stopped breaking his pencils.

Ella's teacher documented every time she wiggled off her mat; the other kids sat on their mats, and she should too. She was disrupting the other students and taking class time. When the teacher realized this was because of Ella's hyperactivity, she placed a mat in the back of the room defining an area where Ella could move around without disturbing others.

Bucket Theory

Imagine your student only has only one bucketful of self-regulation for the day. If she is great during math class in the morning, she has probably used up the whole bucket, and has nothing left over for language arts in the afternoon. She needs to refill her bucket. This may take a physical activity like recess, or quiet time in the sensory room. Or morning class may be all she can manage for the day. Until she refills her bucket, don't expect her to self-regulate or learn.

Sensory and Trauma-Informed Activities

- Experiential, hands-on, concrete, and multiple styles of learning
- Proprioceptive activity that puts pressure on joints such as pushing (appropriately) heavy boxes, moving chairs or tables
- Sensory input supports: fidget toys, ball seats, stretchy bands that go around chair legs to push against, beanbag chairs, rocking chairs
- Weighted vests, blankets, or weighted items designed for shoulders or laps
- Art, including play-dough, clay, finger-paint, paper-mache and other hands-on materials
- Music: singing is great for regulating the breath! So is chanting or reciting poems or raps
- Physical activity: recess, dance, and PE—especially non-competitive games
- Ripping up, tearing into strips, or crumpling pieces of paper
- Sensory corner (see above)

There are many websites with sensory tools and ideas available for teachers.

Adapt the Environment

Match your expectations to the student's ability. Students with trauma histories are not always able to comply; sometimes, we need to adapt the environment to support them. Try altering sensory triggers in the classroom, such as diminishing noise, dimming lights, reducing wall art that may be over-stimulating, and slowing down transitions. If you can't do these things for the whole classroom, create a sensory corner as described above. Use individual sensory tools, such as noise-canceling headphones, a weighted vest or blanket, or another of the many items available online.

Cultural Awareness

Cultural awareness is important for understanding a student's needs, finding the best ways to connect, and helping them repair, recover and grow. Try to learn about a students' family and culture: do they touch often or rarely? what traditions provide comfort? what is considered strength and what is considered weakness? Behavior that is non-compliant in the classroom may follow parental expectations. One teacher learned the father of an aggressive kindergarten student constantly exhorted him to fight back in order to "be a man." What seems like shyness or reluctance to participate may be due to a cultural expectation or a language issue. Building on cultural strengths can provide agency, self-esteem, and a broader perspective.

"Healing" Approaches and Alternative Practices

The term "trauma-informed" has been criticized for focusing on the problem, instead of on the solution. No one wants to be defined or stigmatized by their negative experiences. Resilience theory and positive psychology focus on moving beyond trauma and actively building holistic well-being. Approaches such as "Healing Centered Engagement" (Ginwright, n.d.) also incorporate cultural, spiritual, political, and collective resources to understand and heal trauma experiences. Some strategies focus on building a "flow": the feeling of being in a balanced, comfortable, and energized space where our bodies and minds function at their best.

- Mindfulness, yoga, Calm Classrooms™
- Deep breathing, visualization
- Therapy dogs
- Neurofeedback
- Aromatherapy
- Individual agency/giving voice: restorative justice, healing circles
- Cultural and community resources, institutions and beliefs

A Trauma-Informed School

We don't always know whether a student's behavior is due to early trauma. But we know trauma-informed strategies help stabilize behavior, nurture relationships, create calmer classrooms, and make learning possible for all students. Trauma-informed strategies can be targeted for specific students or used as a universal approach. Some school systems across the country have implemented a trauma-informed approach school-wide and even at the district level (Cole et. al., 2013). A trauma-informed approach helps prevent behaviors that cause lifelong academic and social problems. It also helps other students and teachers experiencing challenging behaviors in their classrooms.

Early learning programs and grade school classrooms are often the primary place children with trauma experiences can find the safety and support they need to grow and succeed. Interventions and supports that work are not necessarily expensive; they are often available and familiar. Teachers use them in their classrooms all the time. Some educational models, like play-based and whole-child learning, are more conducive to a trauma-informed approach than models such as direct instruction.

In many schools, educators and administrators are not given the knowledge, resources, and support needed to help their students, their classrooms and themselves. Not every school will support trauma-sensitive strategies. Many schools will not have the resources, funding, or inclination to implement the strategies discussed above. Standardized testing and "success"-based approaches can run counter to trauma-informed research. Large classroom size makes building relationships with individual students more difficult. The significant emotional work of a trauma-informed approach may feel like overload to teachers who are already stressed and overwhelmed. But even using a few strategies can help students for whom school may be the safest, most predictable part of their lives.

What Doesn't Work

Children who have experienced early trauma often react *differently* to, and may not be helped by, standard interventions. Positive change does not come from punishment or isolation; it comes from de-escalating the stress response and re-building neural pathways to support executive function. Behavioral models need to be done within a very immediate time-frame. Punitive disciplines, such as time-outs, suspension and expulsion can trigger and re-traumatize students and lead to long-term consequences.

Teacher Objections

Trauma-informed educational strategies may feel counter-intuitive and ineffective to some teachers. It may feel like students are "getting away with" bad behavior. Not punishing students may feel like giving up control and losing a tool that gets students to behave. Some of the strategies suggested, like snacks or gum, may be unfair to other students; why is a non-compliant student getting a treat but not students who are complying? This approach may also feel more appropriate for a parent, therapist, counselor or social worker than for the teacher. A teacher may wonder why this is her job, along with everything else she must do.

These feelings and objections are all valid. The thing to remember is: this is about the brain. It is not about control, rewards, or who is a "good" student. It is simply acknowledging that trauma impacts a child's brain and understanding how we can help the brain recover so students can learn.

A child whose leg is in a cast needs crutches, a ramp or elevator. Similarly, a child whose brain is shaped by chronic trauma needs cognitive, physical, and emotional scaffolding. Keeping this in mind helps with the frustration and sometimes powerless feeling of working with students with challenging behaviors, and can help teachers feel positive, successful, and rewarded.

Trauma in Larger Context

Schools can do much to help students who have experienced trauma, but schools cannot do everything. Schools don't exist in a vacuum: families, communities, and society need to be a part of the solution.

New research has shown that trauma is not just personal and individual. Trauma theory is paying more attention to the intersections between inequality, racism, and trauma. For example, Black boys are more likely than their White peers to be punished for the same behaviors (Losen, 2015). Community violence, social stress, and stigmatization have physical and psychological impacts. Homelessness, foster care, and immigration experiences affect children in the classroom. Trauma can also be passed down through generations. Slavery, the Holocaust, displacement of Native Americans, and other historical events can be embodied in intergenerational and historical trauma. Here is an interpretation of the ACEs pyramid developed by the RYSE Youth

Center that incorporates some of these new ideas: https://static1.squares-pace.com/static/58ece61644024383be911a95/t/593e579b37c58172ed513 40c/1497257886219/ACEs_social-location_2015.pdf

Children who have experienced chronic trauma need a continuum of care in their lives. There are many protective factors: supportive family members and other supportive adults; social, physical and mental health services; and cultural, religious, and community organizations.

Educational policies and school resources impact efforts to support students with trauma histories. It's difficult to nurture individual relationships in over-crowded classrooms lacking aids or support staff. A revolving door of teachers, staff, and administrators disrupts relationship-building. Sometimes schools do not feel physically safe for students or teachers. All of these issues increase stress and re-trigger trauma, impacting how students learn, behave, and grow.

Conclusion: Hope for Healing and Growth

Trauma-informed education is optimistic and hopeful. Recovery and trans-formation are possible. We have the tools and knowledge to help our students heal, learn, and grow; we just need to do the work.

Take-Aways

- Safety, Connection, Repair, Growth
- Instead of asking, "what's wrong with this student?" ask, "who is he?"
- Behavior is communication.
- Work on changing *the cause* of the behavior.
- Do not shame.
- Use a "trauma lens." Remember the brain.
- Change expectations.
- Adapt the environment to support the child, instead of expecting the child to conform to the environment.
- Connect.
- Get support for yourself.

References

About the CDC-Kaiser ACE Study. (n.d.). Retrieved 10/24/2016 from: http://www.cdc. gov/violenceprevention/acestudy/about.html

Adverse Childhood Experiences Presentation Graphics. (April 1, 2016). Retrieved 11/8/2018 from: https://www.cdc.gov/violenceprevention/acestudy/ACE_graphics.html

Bayat, M. (2015). *Addressing Challenging Behaviors and Mental Health Issues in Early Childhood.* New York and London: Rutledge University Press.

Brunzell, T., Stokes, H., & Waters, L. (2016).Trauma-informed positive education: Using positive psychology to strengthen vulnerable students. *Contemporary School Psychology, 20,* 63–83.

Cole, S., Eisner, A., Gregory, M., & Ristuccia, J., (Eds.). (2013). *Helping Traumatized Children Learn 2*: Creating and Advocating for Trauma-Sensitive Schools. Boston, MA: Massachusetts Advocates for Children and Harvard Law School.

Craig, S.E. (2016). *Trauma-Sensitive Schools: Learning Communities Transforming Children's Lives K-5.* New York City and London: Teachers College Press, Columbia University.

Ginwright, S. (n.d.). The future of healing: Shifting from trauma informed care to healing centered engagement. Retrieved 8/18/18 from: https://medium.com/@ginwright/the-future-of-healing-shifting-from-trauma-informed-care-to-healing-centered-engagement-634f557ce69c

Losen, D.J. (Ed.). (2015). *Closing the School Discipline Gap: Equitable Remedies for Excessive Exclusion.* New York: Teachers College Press.

Statman-Weil, K. (May 2015). Creating trauma sensitive classrooms. *Young Children NAEYC, 70*(2), 72–79. Retrieved 11/9/2018 from: https://www.naeyc.org/system/files/YC0515_Trauma-Sensitive_Classrooms_Statman-Weil.pdf

Van Der Kolk, B. (2014). *The Body Keeps the Score: Brain, Mind, and Body in the Healing of Trauma.* New York City: Viking Penguin.

Suggested Resources

Adverse Childhood Experiences (ACEs). (April 1, 2016). Retrieved 11/9/18 from: https://www.cdc.gov/violenceprevention/acestudy/index.html

ARC: Attachment, Regulation and Competency. (2016). Retrieved 11/9/18 from: https://arcframework.org

Bombèr, L.M. (2007). *Inside I'm Hurting: Practical Strategies for Supporting Children with Attachment Difficulties in Schools.* London: Worth Publishing Ltd.

Child Trauma Toolkit for Educators. (October 2008). The National Child Traumatic Stress Network. Retrieved 11/9/18 from: https://www.nctsn.org/resources/child-trauma-toolkit-educators

Sorrels, B. (2015). *Reaching and Teaching Children Exposed to Trauma.* Lewisville, NC: Gryphon House, Inc.

Wolpow, R., Johnson, M.M., Hertel, R., & Kincaid, S.O. (May 2016). *The Heart of Learning and Teaching: Compassion, Resilience, and Academic Success* (3rd ed.). Retrieved 11/9/18 from: http://k12.wa.us/CompassionateSchools/HeartofLearning.aspx

7 Supporting Exceptional Children and Their Families

Nancy Hashimoto

Figure 7.1 Comfort dogs in classrooms are found to be beneficial for many students.

The National Association for the Education of Young Children (NAEYC) identifies the promotion of positive relationships and community building as the first standard for Early Childhood programs (Copple & Bredekamp, 2009). For families and young children with special needs this standard is critically important. In this chapter, the parent perspective and the reasons for strong collaborative relationships emphasize the importance of creating an inclusive classroom community. The inclusive classroom fosters development and skill building in social, emotional, and cognitive areas and establishes a sense of belonging, feeling welcome, included, and valued. To build such a community, teachers need an understanding of characteristics and supports for children with special needs and twice-exceptional students. This understanding requires teachers to incorporate differentiated instruction, intentional social engagement, and promotion of the appreciation of difference. Such practices help children's engagement in learning and play, as well as facilitate individuals in making connections to their peers and the world around them (Figure 7.1).

Benefits of Inclusive Classrooms

In these classrooms a warm, nurturing environment fosters the growth and development of everyone. Welcoming communities invite all children to be included as members of the whole, allow children to participate in all the activities and conversations, and break down barriers that could prevent development and learning. For, according to Albert Bandura's social learning theory, social interactions provide learning through imitation, processing, and modeling of behaviors (Justice, Logan, Lin & Kaderavek, 2014).

Therefore, in high-quality inclusion classrooms where engagement and interaction are fostered, children's cognitive and social/emotional development, and appropriate learning outcomes, are achieved (DEC/NAEYC, 2009). It is here where children with special needs who may have cognitive or social/emotional behaviors impacting their academic performance can be successful. For here their interaction with peers and others, specialized instruction, emotional supports, and regulation, or physical or environmental support can be provided, since the inclusive classroom emphasizes interaction and engagement.

To establish inclusive classrooms, it is imperative for teachers to have sufficient, current knowledge of special needs conditions and how developmentally appropriate practice implements an effective inclusion classroom with special emphasis on the role of social interaction to promote growth (Kwon, Hong, & Jeon, 2017). Ongoing professional development regarding the latest research on special needs of young children facilitates teachers' confidence so they can demonstrate favorable attitudes toward modifying curriculum and environmental design. Understanding the importance of integrating social interactions into the curriculum will have a key influence on the confidence and competence of the children as they relate to others.

Social interaction benefits all children but has a special influence on children with developmental or neurological challenges (Justice et al., 2014). For those with special needs, making connections with peers and developing social confidence has a lasting impact (Wiebe, 2006; Odom & Diamond, 1998). The children gain academic ability, self-confidence, social connectedness, acceptance, and independence (Wiebe, 2006; Wright, Diener, & Kemp, 2013). In addition, they show greater improvement in language scores when integrated into typical classrooms (Justice et al., 2014). Students with special needs also participate and communicate more in classrooms with a higher ratio of typical peers (Odom & Diamond, 1998).

For children with autism, peer interactions can be challenging. Providing all children with facilitated interactive play and communication and finding ways to naturally incorporate play into regular instruction and activities creates space for children with autism to thrive. Play encourages typically developing students to engage with their special needs peers, provides opportunities for feedback (Kamps, Thiemann-Bourque, Cox, et al., 2015), knowledge of consequences of social choices (Bass & Mulick, 2007), develops relationships (Papacek, Chan, & Green, 2016), and allows children to practice empathy (Szumski, Smogorzewska, Grygiel, & Orlando, 2017). Practicing prosocial behavior techniques, utilizing peer buddies, and encouraging all students to engage socially with one another can also reduce perceived stigma around special needs (O'Connor, 2016).

Facilitated interactions create opportunities for all children to learn social behaviors (Lee & Lee, 2011; Myles & Simpson, 2001). The intentional inclusion of social skills in the curriculum mitigates the hidden curriculum typically assumed for children learning social behaviors appropriately through play. One of the characteristics of children with autism is their deficiency in affective interactions with others and challenges to communication (Wimpory, Hobson, & Nash, 2007). Repeated social learning opportunities with peers, facilitated by a teacher or adult, can benefit social relationships so that the student feels more connected, confident, and develops a sense of belonging. It can reduce isolation, challenging behavior and aggression while improving academic performance (Weng & Niehart, 2015b) and self-esteem (O'Connor, 2016).

Teachers may see the benefits of social engagement but do not often focus on the intentional planning of embedding and integrating social skills into the curriculum (Joseph, Rausch, & Strain, 2016). Preschool and kindergarten are opportune times to have various occasions for social interactions at different activities and playtime involving more direct instruction (Justice et al., 2014). Students with special needs see the most benefit from interactions with their typical peers, having planned opportunities fostering engagement within curricular activities, incorporating many of their IEP goals (Joseph et al., 2016; Nabors et al., 2001).

Using natural opportunities in the classroom such as circle time, free play, socio-dramatic play, snack/lunchtime, or during repetitive social routines (Wimpory et al., 2007), teachers can scaffold social skills in a predictable way to increase development and integrate social connectedness. Arranging the physical play space for smaller, more intimate interactions among peers can also be beneficial. Interactive activities, social toys, and structured play can facilitate engagement (Papacek et al., 2016). In addition to peer supports, other strategies can involve video modeling, social stories, peer grouping, and behavior skills training. No one strategy is going to work for every child, which is why it is best to vary the range of options and opportunities.

Children with special needs in an inclusive classroom benefit from the reduced barriers to social interaction and participation in the classroom community. Inclusive classrooms avoid the limitations on speech and communication, lack of social skills instruction and capacity for reciprocal engagement in conversation. Such classrooms call out for an awareness of appropriate behavior or emotions of others and do not limit interest in discussion. By contrast, not having the opportunity or ability to connect with others can leave special-needs children discouraged, lonely, unconnected, and hinder self-sufficiency and independence (Wiebe, 2006; Watson & McCathren, 2009). To avoid these stresses, inclusive classrooms promote positive peer interactions and welcome all as part of the community.

Besides the benefit to children with special needs, typically developing peers benefit with the nurturing and appreciation for diversity and inclusion in a classroom community where all members are valued participants (Odom & Diamond, 1998). Positive interaction between peers with special needs in the preschool years provides a positive foundation for a favorable view of disabilities and encourages more frequent interaction (Kwon, Hong, & Jeon, 2017). Ongoing interaction and the building of relationships with one another create a culture where familiarity with children with special needs can aid in the recognition of differences and at the same time build friendships and relationships going beyond ability or disability.

Children shape their beliefs and attitudes on the information they receive and perceive from those closest to them. Promoting positive images in the classroom, including difference in activities and in the community, reading children's books discussing difference, developing positive relationships, and personal interactions promote a positive attitude (Odom & Diamond, 1998). Similarly, incorporating children with special needs in inclusive classrooms has an encouraging effect on the attitudes and perspectives of families of typical students towards those with disabilities (Odom & Diamond, 1998), so it is beneficial for the whole family as well as the classroom community.

Supporting All Children

Besides the humane emphasis of the inclusive classroom, children with special needs have a right to the same type and quality of education available to all children. Educational programs must be accessible to all children to nurture their growth and provide access to classrooms, teachers, curriculum, activities, materials, and each other (Watson & McCathren, 2009). Under the Individuals with Disabilities Education Act (IDEA, 2004), a commitment to providing inclusive programs in the least restrictive environment is a requirement. The federal law mandates all children are eligible for free and appropriate public education if the child has been diagnosed with a disability. IDEA mandates children must receive services if the disability impacts academic performance. Statistics for the 2015–2016 school year reflect that 13 percent of all public-school students receive special education services (National Center for Education Statistics, 2018). However, those statistics capture only students diagnosed with a disability and only those attending public institutions. Thus, the actual number could be much higher.

Understanding IDEA

Enacted in law in 1975 as the Education for All Handicapped Children Act (Public Law 94-142), it guaranteed access to a free appropriate public education (FAPE) in the least restrictive environment (LRE) to each child with a disability. Now called the Individuals with Disabilities Education Act (IDEA) it also provides for early intervention services to children from birth to age five.

What Do Special Needs Look Like?

It is important to support all students in the classroom and to meet children at their ability level in order to foster their growth and development. Each child has personal strengths and struggles, and in an inclusion classroom those individual differences may be more pronounced. The most prominent disabilities present within inclusion classrooms are students with Autism Spectrum Disorders (ASD), Specific Learning Disabilities (SLD), twice-exceptional students (*2e*), and sensory processing disorders. Understanding the variety of disabilities present in an inclusion classroom is important for the teacher to support the student appropriately and understand the appropriate practices to benefit instruction and services.

Autism Spectrum Disorders

Autism Spectrum Disorders (ASD) are neurodevelopmental disorders characterized by core deficits in social communication, interaction functioning, and restrictive and repetitive patterns of behavior or interests (Dyches, Wilder, Sudweeks, Obiakor, & Algozzine, 2004; Kreiser & White, 2014). The Diagnostic and Statistical Manual of Mental Disorders, 5th edition (DSM-V) indicates individuals with autism may have symptoms impairing social interaction, which cannot be explained by another disability, and have levels of severity that replace previous diagnoses such as autism, Asperger's, and pervasive persistent disorder-not otherwise specified (PPD-NOS) which all now come under the umbrella of ASD (American Psychiatric Association, 2013). It is not a disability apparent at birth, does not have physical or biological identifiers, and is a lifelong condition.

ASD encompasses a wide spectrum of behaviors with similar core markers (Croen, Grether, Hoogstrate, & Selvin, 2002), but there is no single reliable diagnostic characteristic, complicating the diagnosis process because it is based on clinical evaluation and not genetic information (Thomas et al., 2012). Some individuals may be non-verbal and others may be highly verbal (but with communication limitations); others may have sensory issues or self-stimulating behaviors. No two cases of autism present the same combination of symptoms, making diagnosis extraordinarily difficult. Additionally, the symptoms can be similar phenotypic markers that can be used to identify a variety of etiologies, and individuals may have multiple conditions which are mixed with autism (called *comorbidity*), such as ADHD, sensory processing disorder, etc. (Mandell, Ittenbach, Levy, & Pinto-Martin, 2007; Overton, Fielding, & Alba, 2007; Kreiser & White, 2014; Thomas et al., 2012). The diagnosis of autism must be ruled out before a judgment can be made if the child has ADHD or Obsessive Compulsive Disorder (Mandell et al., 2007).

Early diagnosis is important because it provides families with education about ASD and allows for access to treatment. It also helps families to face the challenges associated with autism and access to therapy that will be beneficial to both the child and the family as a whole. Parenting a child with autism can be very stressful and not understanding why your child may be behaving a certain way, not responding to you, having obsessive interests, or not engaging with other children, creates a stressful family dynamic and puts added pressure to explain the actions (or inactions) of the child. Parents have reported "extreme difficulties in dealing with challenging behaviors, teaching their child to communicate, teaching basic life skills, guarding their child from danger, and preparing their child for adult life" (Dyches, Wilder, Sudweeks, Obiakor, Algozzine, 2004, p. 211). Children receiving treatment earlier can lead to improved outcomes and enhance the quality of their lives (Begeer et al., 2013; Ennis-Cole, Durodove, & Harris, 2013; Daley, 2004; Shattuck & Grosse, 2007). Early intervention can ameliorate negative behaviors before they become ingrained and can be beneficial for parental mental health (Daley, 2004). Shattuck and Grosse (2007) also point out that early diagnosis can offer important knowledge about genetic information for family planning of additional siblings given the biological prevalence since most children are not diagnosed with ASD until after age four.

However, reasons for delayed diagnosis include families not understanding the behaviors and signs, limited availability of appointments with professionals, and the cost of and access to health care benefits. Delays could also be due to the masking of disability traits by other attributes such as giftedness, unwillingness by professionals or parents to ascribe a label, denial of the disability, access to health care, presentation being different in each child, no standard measurement or assessment tool, and evaluation tools not being culturally or gender sensitive (Shattuck & Gross, 2007).

The occurrence of ASD is one in 59 children (one in 37 boys and one in 151 girls), and comprises up to 9% of children with special needs (CDC, 2018). The prevalence has been steadily on the rise over the last 12 years with an increase of 289.5% during that time (CDC, 2018). It is four times more common in boys than in girls and occurs in all racial, ethnic, and socioeconomic groups. Many children with ASD are likely to have a second diagnosis (*comorbid*) of a developmental disability or specific learning disability (SLD). The comorbid diagnosis of other non-ASD developmental diagnoses (psychological, neurologic, or genetic) occurs in up to 83% of children with ASD (CDC, 2018). A majority of children with ASD also struggle with sensory processing issues which can interfere with their social connectedness, participation, and acceptance by their peers and society as a whole. Though not a marker for ASD, the high co-occurrence of sensory processing challenges can be seen as an indicator by families and professionals to seek diagnosis for access to treatment.

Sensory Processing Disorders

Children with sensory issues may have acute sensitivity in auditory noises, touch, taste, or smell, or they seek stimulation of the senses. Students may react to loud noises, harsh smells, be selective eaters, or may chew on their shirts, flap their hands, or spin in circles. They may also perform repetitive behaviors in an effort to self-regulate and calm themselves (Case-Smith, Weaver, & Fristad, 2015). Estimates range from 45% to 95% of children with autism spectrum disorder may have sensory processing disorders (Case-Smith et al., 2015; Matsushima & Kato, 2013). Sensory processing disorders can inhibit social interaction and cognitive functioning (Matsushima & Kato, 2013) because the brain is engaged in sensory challenges which may supersede all other functions.

Understanding the sensitivities of children in the classroom and planning ahead can help to avoid triggers causing meltdowns. Teachers can proactively intervene by modifying the classroom environment to limit stimulation or control the environment (Matsushima & Kato, 2013). This can mean lowering the brightness of the classroom, using fabric to cover or hide areas that look busy for reduced visual interest, providing movement breaks throughout the day, allowing fidgeting, and providing a quiet space where a child can retreat if feeling overstimulated. Even something as simple as changing the color of worksheet paper to a less bright contrast can help. If your school has an Occupational Therapist, work with that professional for additional techniques and strategies.

Twice-Exceptional

Twice-exceptional children are often overlooked or ignored because they are unidentified, misdiagnosed, or misunderstood (Leggett, Shea & Wilson, 2010). Known also as *2e* students, twice-exceptional individuals possess both a disability and giftedness. Often one quality can mask another, which can make identification difficult (Park, Dimitrov, & Park, 2018; Leggett et al., 2010; Neumeister, Yssel, & Burney, 2013; Reis, Baun, & Burke, 2014; Baldwin, Omdal, & Pereles, 2015) or can balance one another so that they appear typical (Leggett et al., 2010). Additionally, there is no test or path to diagnosis for *2e* students and they are often identified and receive services for the disability while their gifted qualities are ignored (Dare & Nowicki, 2015). Such a delay can cause a student to be bored, unruly, disruptive, or challenging because they have lost interest or desire stimulation. Often *2e* students are the puzzling ones, out of the norm, and atypical. They might be seen as lazy, inattentive or capricious but they're also creative, capable, inquisitive, and knowledgeable (Omdal, 2015).

Many teachers are unaware of the existence of twice-exceptional students (Dare & Nowicki, 2015), which can include a variety of combinations of disabilities and gifted qualities and presents a paradox often causing doubt among educators (Foley-Nicpon, Assouline, & Colangelo, 2013). This multifaceted nature can present challenges to providing appropriate, quality instruction for *2e* children (Besnoy et al., 2015). It is unknown how many *2e* students there really are because so many are undiagnosed or misdiagnosed (Lee & Ritchotte, 2018) or they fly under the radar. Nor are IQ tests the best measurement of identification because such instruments do not assess all areas of giftedness or intelligence (Dare & Nowicki, 2015). Parents may be the best resource for initial identification of *2e* students because they may be the first to recognize their gifts as well as their challenges (Neumeister et al., 2013).

Encouraging parental involvement and support correlates to improved academic performance (Neumeister et al., 2013) and motivation and in turn builds resilient and constructive coping tactics in the family (Weng & Niehart, 2015b). Empowering parents and encouraging positive attitudes toward their children and situations, use of praise, strengthening intelligence areas, and building confidence help parents in building resilience qualities within the family.

Both sides of a *2e* child need to be addressed, including challenging their gifted abilities. Under IDEA they are eligible for services for their disability but there is no federal funding or mandate for gifted services. Their talents should be developed and strengthened to cultivate depth and advancement in their abilities and creativity. Focusing on stretch activities to challenge critical thinking, giving choice in activities, and supporting growth through creative problem solving will help *2e* students with enriched growth opportunities (Omdal, 2015).

The risk for not addressing the needs of *2e* students is more than combatting boredom in the classroom. Students have shown that they struggle academically, suffer depression and self-esteem issues, and face anxiety because they are not challenged, or they struggle in their disability area(s). Utilizing a strengths-based approach has the best overall potential for development in *2e* students (Baum, Schader, & Hebert, 2014). Encouraging positive self-esteem as well as positive behavior helps encourage abilities in talent areas, and providing opportunities for creativity, analytical and problem-solving skills (Neumeister et al, 2013), self-regulation development, and practice in social connectedness (Wang & Neuhart, 2015b) will have beneficial effects. The development of a positive self-perception will produce a longlasting improvement in academic ability (Wang & Neuhart, 2015a).

Specific Learning Disabilities

Another group of children requiring special attention is those that struggle with a variety of special needs, including specific learning disabilities (SLD). These children face challenges in learning due to psychological processes that impede their ability to speak, read, write, spell, pay attention, control behavior, or process and understand information. Examples of learning disabilities may include dyslexia (difficulty with reading), dyscalculia (difficulty with math), or dysgraphia (difficulty with writing). As many as 35% of all students with special education services are diagnosed with an SLD (Learning Disabilities of America, 2018; NCES, 2018). In some cases, these disabilities are apparent and easily recognizable, but many children go undiagnosed because of circumstances in how the disability may present itself in that child, that there may be more than one learning difference present, that the child may be both gifted and have a disability or disorder, or other causes.

The variety of special needs present in an inclusion classroom means the teachers must practice individualized instruction. Preparing the classroom and the curriculum to incorporate a vast complex of various special needs can be challenging. An approach to meet this challenge is differentiated instruction providing an avenue to address each child individually, with appropriate challenges, and engagement of all students.

Differentiated Instruction

Differentiated instruction approaches curriculum and the mode of instruction by allowing multiple, accessible opportunities for learning for all (Patterson, Connolly, & Ritter, 2009). Differentiated instruction promotes diverse strategies for learning similar concepts, such as small groups, student-led coaching, student roles in instruction assistance, activity choices, and peer-to-peer partners (Wiebe, 2006; Nabors, Willoughby, Leff, & McMenamin, 2001). There are no set rules for the implementation of differentiated instruction, since it is meant to serve particular individuals within a group (Ernest, Thompson, Heckaman, Hull, & Yates, 2011). However, the benefit of differentiated instruction is that each individual student succeeds based on analysis of their own needs and level and preferred learning style; they are challenged appropriately, and the variety of strategies makes learning active, promoting interest and engagement (Ernest et al., 2011).

Using sociodramatic play allows for collaboration between peers in developing storylines, resolving conflict, assigning characters and roles, and problem solving (Wright et al., 2013). Each child can take a turn as writer, director, creative director, storyteller, costume designer, and actor, adding to the allowance for exploring each role as a part of differentiated instruction and promoting within the classroom the diversity of thought, action, and creativity. These activities can also help students feel supported, build self-esteem and self-determination, and feel that they are validated members of the community (Wright et al., 2013).

Similarly, moving classroom activities to the playground or other alternative setting allows for out-of-the-box thinking in both the realms of social interaction and differentiated instruction, especially for children with special needs (Nabors et al., 2001). The alternative setting breaks down barriers and allows for more natural communication. Moving activities such as water tables, dramatic play, music, or blocks outdoors allows for a variety of interactions for different needs, interests, and ages (Nabors et al., 2001). Allowing children to have the freedom to be able to select activities according to interest and ability is in accordance with developmentally appropriate practice and is beneficial for development (Odom & Diamond, 1998). The freedom of choice empowers them and results in confidence building, engagement in learning, empowerment, and perseverance (Earnest et al., 2011).

Practicing differential instruction in the classroom requires teachers to be intentional about building the social dynamics, as students may need specific direction on how to communicate, how to use materials at their developmental level (Wiebe, 2006; Nabors et al., 2001), what words to use, and how to have a proper reciprocal communication exchange. These teacher practices use explicit integration of social interaction throughout the day and within activities, not just for set academic subjects or circle time (Copple & Bredekamp, 2009; Joseph et al., 2016). The supports put into place for children with special needs are similarly beneficial for typical children since the focus is on strengthening individual capacity. (Joseph et al., 2016). In the differentiated classroom teachers provide support for the individual and the many.

The many may struggle with transitioning from one activity to another. Using a visual schedule can be helpful because children know what to expect and when. If an individual resists change, strategies to employ include going to the child and sitting with them, getting involved in what they're doing and discussing it, and allowing extra time to complete the transition when necessary. When there is a natural break, work on wrapping it up, continuing the conversation into the next activity. Though individualization can be difficult to do with large classrooms, this necessary step for the child who has trouble transitioning teaches an important skill for future classroom success. Such teaching helps them to find that natural break, thus empowering them.

So, an inclusive classroom encourages community building among peers and employs differentiated instruction. Engaging with the family and developing interactive communication benefits all involved. Understanding the situation of the family provides the teacher with perspective on challenges and issues that can impact that communication. Every family situation has unique qualities but there are common experiences among families with children with special needs.

Parent Experiences

Some parents may hesitate to get a diagnosis or to talk about it because the diagnosis of a disability carries with it a stigma. No parent wants their child to be negatively separated from other children or to be looked down upon by a label. Parents may even hide the diagnosis from friends, family, or strangers because they don't want their child or their family to be put into an unfavorable category. Parents themselves can also feel shame about the diagnosis because they can be made to feel (by professionals, by family, by others) that they are the cause of the disability and thus it imposes shame and blame on them. Helping parents to understand the nature and causes of disability, how special services can be offered to their child, support groups of other parents, and other resources available to them can be very helpful and reassuring.

There is a tremendous need for appropriate resources for parents. Understanding how best to advocate for their child requires that parents know the relevant laws, developmental appropriateness and characteristics, the IEP process and regulations, presentation of developmental challenges, and local support groups and resources. Helping their child grow and develop appropriately can be a very daunting undertaking. Parents are under a great deal of stress and attending to the needs of their child can be exhausting and emotionally draining. Parents motivated and with access to resources have more potential to be successful advocates (Neumeister et al., 2013).

Parenting is difficult and challenging in the best of circumstances. Parenting a child with special needs adds additional stresses and layers of emotions to an already complex and demanding responsibility. The daily struggles that parents face include coordinating therapy sessions, being attentive to sensory issues and situations, dealing with and working through meltdowns (reactions to environmental triggers or sensory overloads), negotiating medical issues and diagnosis, advocating at school for services or IEP issues, and challenges with costs associated with therapy and medical needs. Parents of children with autism have reported high stress levels related to parenting, and there is often a greater burden and responsibility on the mother (Sharabi & Marom-Golan, 2017).

In addition, parents of special-needs children often feel isolated and discouraged. They can feel left out of regular activities that children engage in because there are safety issues, sensory challenges, supervision concerns, or behavioral problems. Parents can feel that activities, camps, and even day-to-day functions can be stressful or unattainable. They also may not be able to celebrate typical milestones in the way that other families are able to, and constant comparisons can lead to depression and further isolation. Finding social groups with other special-needs parents, activities exclusively for the disabled, and support from families facing similar changes can help emotionally encourage and uplift parents and aid in the sharing of resources and opportunities. Teachers can facilitate this by providing referrals and resource information, establishing trust and collaboration with the family.

Family Collaboration

Family collaboration with teachers and advocacy in their child's education, social interactions, and support services can be critical to the child's success (Park et al., 2018). Collaboration for the benefit of the whole family shows respect, acknowledgment, and value for all those involved (Besnoy et al., 2015). However, there are often barriers to family involvement. From the beginning, families may struggle to understand and find appropriate resources for children with special needs. Having access to information, knowing how to identify differences and who to turn to for assistance, getting access and funding for services, knowing what to advocate for and when, and understanding federal laws and rights can be challenging.

Families may look to educators for advice and information about effective strategies for their child, legal issues, and resources (Besnoy et al., 2015). This may or may not be the educator's strength, despite their training, level of professional development, or years of experience. Knowing how to help families advocate for their children is an essential quality for teachers to earn trust from the family. Teachers must also understand how to assess and challenge students, communicate with parents appropriately, and offer additional resources.

Parents often assume teachers have knowledge about policies and best practice for all children's needs due to their formal training. In fact, parents may be more informed about legal rights and characteristics common in a specific disability area, especially if they have taken initiative to learn about their child's needs to become better advocates (Besnoy et al., 2015). Teachers can help by being emotional supports with positive encouragement and direction on how to help a child achieve their best potential (Neumeister et al., 2013). Parents can play a critical role in academic development outside of the school by providing enriching activities (e.g., literacy, early math, social-emotional skills) and interacting with the child at home (Rispoli, Hawley, & Clinton, 2018).

Additional life circumstances can present challenges and barriers to family involvement both inside and outside of school. The socio-economic status of the family (e.g., working multiple jobs or third-shift jobs), being a working parent, the conditions and safety of the neighborhood, ethnicity and race (e.g., power dynamics, expectations), and mental or physical health status can be important factors (Rispoli et al., 2018). Family perception of the outreach of the school (friendliness, communication, support, etc.) can differ based on the barriers above including income, race, and disability.

Set the stage and build communication properly from the start. Send out a welcome letter inviting families to a meeting or open house before school starts. Give parents a questionnaire to ask about the child's preferences, challenges, and needs, as well as any concerns from the family. Continue the conversation on a weekly, if not daily, basis. Parents want to know what their child has been involved with that day, interactions with other children, and if there were any struggles or difficulties. To an overstressed teacher this can present challenges, but either utilizing technology (e.g., apps or text messages) or a simple half-sheet of paper with prefilled responses that just need to be circled and a short note about how the day went will be much appreciated by the family.

Conclusion

Children with special needs must have access to quality educational programs with proper and appropriate supports and interactions. They should be welcomed into a classroom as members of the community, engage with other children, and receive instruction appropriate to their developmental level. Teachers serve children with special needs by being prepared with the latest research on disabilities and appropriate techniques and curricular modifications. Of special importance for all children is the creation of inclusive environments promoting socialization among peers. Planning for differential instruction and building social skills into all areas of the curriculum ensures optimal learning for each child. Finally, of critical importance is the encouragement and facilitation of family involvement both in and outside of the classroom, and collaboration between parents and teachers. Each of these important elements benefits special-needs children, their social-emotional wellbeing, their future success, the development of their typical peers, their families, the teaching staff and support personnel, and the education profession. Providing quality education and supports for all children builds community, facilitates healthy development, and enriches the quality of life for all individuals.

Resources

Autism Speaks 100 day kit
https://www.autismspeaks.org/family-services/tool-kits/100-day-kit

Council for Exceptional Children Resources for Families
https://www.cec.sped.org/Tools-and-Resources/For-Families

DEC Resources
http://www.dec-sped.org/resources

Exceptional Parent
https://www.eparent.com/

IEP Process
https://www.parentcenterhub.org/pa12/

Learning Disabilities of America
https://ldaamerica.org/types-of-learning-disabilities/

NAEYC Resources for Families
https://www.naeyc.org/our-work/for-families

National Association of Parents with Children in Special Education (NAPCSE)
http://www.napcse.org/

Web Resources for Parents
https://www.masters-in-special-education.com/50-great-websites-for-parents-of-children-with-special-needs/

References

American Psychiatric Association. (2013). *Diagnostic and Statistical Manual of Mental Disorders: DSM-5*(5th ed.). Arlington, VA: American Psychiatric Association.

Baldwin, L., Omdal, S.O., & Pereles, D. (2015). Beyond stereotypes: Understanding, recognizing, and working with twice-exceptional learners. *Teaching Exceptional Children, 47*(4), 216–225.

Bass, J.D., & Mulick, J.A. (2007). Social play skill enhancement of children with autism using peers and siblings as therapists. *Psychology in the Schools, 44*(7), 727–735.

Baum, S.M., Schader, R.M., & Hébert, T.P. (2014). Through a different lens: Reflecting on a strengths-based, talent-focused approach for twice-exceptional learners. *Gifted Child Quarterly, 58*(4), 311–327.

Begeer, S., Gevers, C., Clifford, P., Verhoeve, M., Kat, K., Hoddenbach, E., & Boer, F. (2011). Theory of mind training in children with autism: A randomized controlled trial. *Journal of Autism and Developmental Disorders, 41*(8), 997–1006.

Besnoy, K.D., Swoszowski, N.C., Newman, J.L., Floyd, A., Jones, P., & Byrne, C. (2015). The advocacy experiences of parents of elementary age, twice-exceptional children. *Gifted Child Quarterly, 59*(2), 108–123.

Case-Smith, J., Weaver, L., & Fristad, M. (2015). A systematic review of sensory processing interventions for children with autism spectrum disorders. *Autism: The International Journal of Research and Practice, 19*(2), 133–148.

Centers for Disease Control and Prevention. (2018). Autism Spectrum Disorder. Retrieved from: https://www.cdc.gov/ncbddd/autism/data.html

Copple, C., Bredekamp, S., & National Association for the Education of Young Children. (2009). *Developmentally Appropriate Practice in Early Childhood Programs Serving Children from Birth Through Age 8.* Washington, DC: National Association for the Education of Young Children.

Croen, L., Grether, J., Hoogstrate, J., & Selvin, S. (2002). The changing prevalence of autism in California. *Journal of Autism and Developmental Disorders, 32*(3), 207–215.

Daley, T.C. (2004). From symptom recognition to diagnosis: Children with autism in urban India. *Social Science & Medicine, 58*(7), 1323–1335.

Dare, L., & Nowicki, E.A. (2015). Twice-exceptionality: Parents' perspectives on 2ème identification. *Roeper Review, 37*(4), 208–218.

DEC/NAEYC. (2009). Early childhood inclusion: A summary. Chapel Hill, NC: The University of North Carolina, FPG Child Development Institute.

Dyches, T.T., Wilder, L.K., Sudweeks, R.R., Obiakor, F.E., & Algozzine, B. (2004). Multicultural issues in autism. *Journal of Autism and Developmental Disorders, 34*(2), 211–222.

Ennis-Cole, D., Durodoye, B.A., & Harris, H.L. (2013). The impact of culture on autism diagnosis and treatment: Considerations for counselors and other professionals. *Family Journal, 21*(3), 279–287.

Ernest, J.M., Thompson, S.E., Heckaman, K.A., Hull, K., & Yates, J. (2011). Effects and social validity of differentiated instruction on student outcomes for special educators. *Journal of the International Association of Special Education, 12*(1), 33–41.

Foley-Nicpon, M., Assouline, S.G., & Colangelo, N. (2013). Twice-exceptional learners: Who needs to know what? *Gifted Child Quarterly, 57*(3), 169–180.

Individuals with Disabilities Education Act, 20 U.S.C. § 1400 (2004).

Joseph, J.D., Rausch, A., & Strain, P.S. (2018). Social competence and young children with special needs: Debunking "mythconceptions". *Young Exceptional Children, 21*(1), 48–60.

Justice, L.M., Logan, J.A.R., Lin, T.-J., & Kaderavek, J.N. (2014). Peer effects in Early Childhood education: Testing the assumptions of special-education inclusion. *Psychological Science, 25*(9), 1722–1729.

Kamps, D., Thiemann-Bourque, K., Cox, S., Heitzman-Powell, L., Schwartz, I., Rosenberg, N., & Mason, R. (2015). A comprehensive peer network intervention to prove social communication of children with autism spectrum disorders: A randomized trial in kindergarten and first grade. *Journal of Autism and Developmental Disorders, 45*(6), 1809–1824.

Kreiser, N.L., & White, S.W. (2014). ASD in females: Are we overstating the gender difference in diagnosis?. *Clinical Child and Family Psychology Review, 17*(1), 67–84.

Kwon, K., Hong, S., & Jeon, H. (2017). Classroom readiness for successful inclusion: Teacher factors and preschool children's experience with and attitudes toward peers with disabilities. *Journal of Research in Childhood Education, 31*(3), 360–378.

Learning Disabilities of America. (2018). Retrieved from: https://ldaamerica.org/types-of-learning-disabilities/

Lee, S.H., & Lee, L.W. (2015). Promoting snack time interactions of children with autism in a Malaysian preschool. *Topics in Early Childhood Special Education*, *35*(2), 89–101.

Lee, C.-W., & Ritchotte, J.A. (2018). Seeing and supporting twice-exceptional learners. *Educational Forum*, *82*(1), 68–84.

Leggett, D.G., Shea, I., & Wilson, J.A. (2010). Advocating for twice-exceptional students: An ethical obligation. *Research in the Schools*, *17*(2), 1–10.

Mandell, D., Ittenbach, R., Levy, S., & Pinto-Martin, J. (2007). Disparities in diagnoses received prior to a diagnosis of autism spectrum disorder. *Journal of Autism and Developmental Disorders*, *37*(9), 1795–1802.

Matsushima, K., & Kato, T. (2013). Social interaction and atypical sensory processing in children with autism spectrum disorders. *Hong Kong Journal of Occupational Therapy*, *23*(2), 89–96.

Myles, B., & Simpson, R. (2001). Understanding the hidden curriculum. *Intervention in School and Clinic*, *36*(5), 279–286.

Nabors, L., Willoughby, J., Leff, S., & McMenamin, S. (2001). Promoting inclusion for young children with special needs on playgrounds. *Journal of Developmental and Physical Disabilities*, *13*(2), 170–190.

National Center for Education Statistics. (2018). https://nces.ed.gov/programs/coe/indicator_cgg.asp

Neumeister, K.S., Yssel, N., & Burney, V.H. (2013). The influence of primary caregivers in fostering success in twice-exceptional children. *Gifted Child Quarterly*, *57*(4), 263–274.

O'Connor, E. (2016). The use of 'Circle of friends' strategy to improve social interactions and social acceptance: A case study of a child with Asperger's syndrome and other associated needs. *Support for Learning*, *31*(2), 138–147.

Odom, S.L., & Diamond, K.E. (1998). Inclusion of young children with special needs in early childhood education: The research base. *Early Childhood Research Quarterly*, *13*(1), 3–25.

Omdal, S. (2015). Twice exceptionality from a practitioner's perspective. *Gifted Child Today*, *38* (4), 246–248.

Overton, T., Fielding, C., & Alba, R. (2007). Differential diagnosis of Hispanic children referred for autism spectrum disorders: Complex issues. *Journal of Autism and Developmental Disorders*, *37*(10), 1996–2007.

Papacek, A.M., Chai, Z., & Green, K.B. (2016). Play and social interaction strategies for young children with autism spectrum disorder in inclusive preschool settings. *Young Exceptional Children*, *19*(3), 3–17.

Park, M.-H., Dimitrov, D.M., & Park, D.-Y. (2018). Effects of background variables of Early Childhood teachers on their concerns about inclusion: The mediation role of confidence in teaching. *Journal of Research in Childhood Education*, *32*(2), 165–180.

Patterson, J.L., Connolly, M.C., & Ritter, S.A. (2009). Restructuring the inclusion classroom to facilitate differentiated instruction. *Middle School Journal (j3)*, *41*(1), 46–52.

Reis, S.M., Baum, S.M., & Burke, E. (2014). An operational definition of twice-exceptional learners: Implications and applications. *Gifted Child Quarterly*, *58*(3), 217–230.

Rispoli, K.M., Hawley, L.R., Clinton, M.C. (2018). Family background and parent–school interactions in parent involvement for at-risk preschool children with disabilities. *The Journal of Special Education*, *52*(1), 39–49.

Sharabi, A., & Marom-Golan, D. (2017). Social support, education levels, and parents' involvement: A comparison between mothers and fathers of young children with autism spectrum disorder. *Topics in Early Childhood Special Education, 38*(1), 54–64.

Shattuck, P.T., & Grosse, S.D (2007). Issues related to the diagnosis and treatment of autism spectrum disorders. *Mental Retardation and Developmental Disabilities Research Reviews, 13*(2), 129–135.

Szumski, G., Smogorzewska, J., Grygiel, P., & Orlando, A.-M. (2017). Examining the effectiveness of naturalistic social skills training in developing social skills and theory of mind in preschoolers with ASD. *Journal of Autism and Developmental Disorders*, 1–16.

Thomas, P., Zahorodny, W., Peng, B., Kim, S., Jani, N., Halperin, W., & Brimacombe, M. (2012). The association of autism diagnosis with socioeconomic status. *Autism : The International Journal of Research and Practice, 16*(2), 201–213.

Wang, W.C., & Neihart, M. (2015a). Academic self-concept and academic self-efficacy: Self-beliefs enable academic achievement of twice-exceptional students. *Roeper Review, 37*(2), 63–73.

Wang, W.C., & Neihart, M. (2015b). How do supports from parents, teachers, and peers influence academic achievement of twice-exceptional students. *Gifted Child Today, 38*(3), 148–159.

Watson, A., & McCathren, R. (2009). Including children with special needs: Are you and your Early Childhood program ready? *Young Children, 64*(2), 20–26.

Wiebe, B.R.A. (2006). Inclusion, power, and community: Teachers and students interpret the language of community in an inclusion classroom. *American Educational Research Journal, 43*(3), 489–529.

Wimpory, D.C., Hobson, R.P., & Nash, S. (2007). What facilitates social engagement in preschool children with autism? *Journal of Autism and Developmental Disorders, 37*, 3, 564–573.

Wright, C., Diener, M.L., & Kemp, J.L. (2013). Storytelling dramas as a community building activity in an Early Childhood classroom. *Early Childhood Education Journal, 41*, 3, 197–210.

8 Changing Curricular Trends in Early Childhood Education
Addressing the Needs of All Children

Dominic F. Gullo

Figure 8.1 Integrating the arts and exploration in the curriculum.

The landscape of early childhood education (ECED) is both dynamic and evolving. Changes in the ECED landscape are occurring both within the United States and around the world. These changes affect all aspects of ECED:

- the ways we view children and their development;
- program structure;
- curriculum development and its content; and
- instructional strategies and teaching methods.

These adjustments to thinking and practice are driven by trends that emanate from multiple sources. One of the major contributors to these changes are the ever-changing demographic trends among children who attend early childhood programs. The diversity of family, economic, cultural, and linguistic circumstances in which children live have implications for how they develop, their approaches to learning, and how they perceive themselves in social situations with other children and adults. These, in turn, impact early childhood programs where children develop and learn (Figure 8.1).

A one-size-fits-all model of early childhood curriculum is no longer efficacious or appropriate. Classroom teachers and other early childhood education professionals must be aware of the present-day trends affecting early childhood curriculum and teaching. They must be knowledgeable and skillful in using strategies to differentiate learning opportunities for children from all demographic groups, so that each child can optimally benefit. This chapter will focus on strategies teachers can use to ensure all children's development and learning needs are met. Areas of emphasis in this chapter include:

- a discussion of current trends in early childhood education demographics affecting current views of children, curriculum, and teaching;
- effective approaches for engaging in developmentally responsive teaching while addressing early learning standards;
- effective strategies for increasing exploratory learning in early childhood settings;
- effective ways to integrate the arts into the early childhood curriculum while maintaining sufficient focus on math and literacy.

Integrated throughout this chapter, as each topic is discussed, will be an emphasis on changing curricular trends. The ways in which curriculum development, curriculum use, instructional strategies, and accountability are affected by today's social and political influences on ECED.

Evolving Landscape of Early Childhood Education

In this section, several elements of the changing landscape of ECED and development are considered. Changing demographic trends among children and families who participate in early education programs are examined.

Early Childhood Demographics Are Changing

The diverse experiences children have within their family, economic, cultural, and linguistic milieus have significant consequences that affect actual and perceived developmental trajectories and characteristics of children. In addition, the diverse types of family, economic, cultural, and linguistic circumstances children experience have significant implications for the evolution of early childhood programs where they develop and learn. Both the number of early childhood programs accessible to children and families and the number of children participating in these programs have increased over the years. The result is that children come from a great variety of experiential and educational environments. In turn, this becomes progressively significant for children's early schooling. The question must be posed, how are the changing demographics of children and their families affecting the early childhood landscape in the United States?

The number of children who are attending early childhood programs who are culturally and/or linguistically diverse has increased significantly. Per the Center for Public Education (2012), between the year 2000 and 2010, the Hispanic population in the United States grew by 43%; the Asian population during that same period grew by 43%; the African-American population by 12.3%, and the non-Hispanic White population by 4.9%. It is estimated that 45% of children under the age of five in the U.S are minorities. At the same time, the growth of the numbers of children in early childhood programs during the last decade who are English language learners (ELL) has increased in some parts of the U.S. by 300 to 400%. In many parts of the country, more than 50% of children who are enrolled in prekindergarten programs come from families who do not speak English at home (Espinosa, 2008) and nearly 29% of all children in the U.S. speak a language other than English at home (Center for Public Education, 2012).

Second, the characteristics of children who attend early childhood programs are increasingly disparate due to their varied experiential backgrounds. Experiential diversity results from children having vastly different kinds of experiences inside and outside the school experience. These differing experiences have the potential to influence children's school readiness potential and/or academic performance trajectories once in school. Key reasons why children may be experientially diverse stem from the cultural and/or linguistic diversity among them.

Another factor contributing to the diversity of children attending early childhood programs is socioeconomic status (SES). Data show that over 50% of children in early childhood programs are eligible for free and reduced lunch; 48% of children under the age of six live in low-income families; 25% of these children live in extreme poverty (Jiang, Y., Elono, M., & Skinner, C., 2015). Consequently, children who live in homes lacking economic resources frequently begin school appreciably behind their higher income age- and grade-mates. Lack of economic resources can have an effect on children's out-of-home experiences (e.g., going to the library, going to the zoo, going to cultural events) as well as having high-quality, developmentally appropriate toys or other learning materials. Lack of experiences and materials such as these have been shown to cause learning disparities (Bransford, Brown, & Cocking, 2004). These academic and developmental disparities are commonly sustained beyond the early grades unless far-reaching and comprehensive intervention focuses on child, family, and community. In addition, it is increasingly likely that children who reside in poverty are likely to suffer inadequate health care, inconsistent childcare, stressed caregivers, and unreliable or inadequate housing (National Education Association, 2016).

Third, there are increasing numbers of young children who live in homes with diverse family structures. The Center for Public Education (2012) indicates that the percentage of births to unmarried mothers rose from 26.6% in 1990 to 40.6% in 2008. Concomitantly, the percentage of young children who reside with both parents dropped from 69% in 2000 to 64% in 2012.

This number appeared to stabilize in 2015 at 65% (Child Trends, 2016). Data show that children living with no biological parents or in single-parent homes are less likely to display self-control and are more likely to face aggravated parenting, a measure of stress associated with caring for children. Great consequence is placed on quality parenting in the early childhood years. This is evidenced by increased parent opportunities for educational advancement, intervention, home visits, and parent training (Harvard Family Research Project, 2006).

Finally, there are increases in the number of children entering school at wider-ranging levels of school "readiness." This is primarily due to their having varied program experiences prior to entering the primary grades (e.g., prekindergarten vs no prekindergarten, academic focus vs socialization focus, structured curriculum vs unstructured experiences). Between the years 1990 and 2000, the percentage of three- to five-year-old children in preprimary programs increased from 59% to 64% (NCES, 2015). To date, there have been no measurable increases.

Unfortunately, the picture of preprimary and primary education and care in the United States is not straightforward as it seems at first glance. What do we mean by preprimary programs? What do we mean by prekindergarten programs? Per the National Center for Educational Statistics (NCES, 2015), preprimary programs include kindergarten, preschool, and nursery school. This definition does not account for the number of children who are in childcare programs. The percentages of three- and four-year-old children in childcare programs are 33% and 56%, respectively. The quality of childcare programs is often unknown. Children's "readiness" and performance levels are frequently determined by whether they are enrolled in preprimary or prekindergarten programs. The quality and focus of these programs is an added influence on school readiness and performance.

ECED program foci differ greatly. Some programs emphasize socialization, while others emphasize academics. While most programs have elements of both, the balance between socialization and academics may differ greatly. Adding to this complexity is that some of the children attend programs for a full day while others attend for a half day. The percentage of children attending full-day programs increased from 36% to 60% between 1990 and 2013.

The dynamic nature of changing demographics, whether related to race, immigration status, family structure, community composition, parental income and education, or the quality and nature of early childhood programing, combine to reinforce the need for greater social integration and a more equitable use of resources. This opportunity and challenge provide context when considering other trends and practices in early childhood education.

Engaging in Developmentally Responsive Teaching

"The failure to adequately prepare teachers who can educate all children has been identified as evidence of pedagogical, instructional and conceptual problems in teacher preparation" (Ray, Bowman, & Robbins, 2006, p. 3).

The authors emphasize that the word "all" in this quote is the operative word, making the task of preparing highly qualified early childhood teachers even more challenging as child demographics become more complex and diverse. In the book *Children of 2020: Creating a better tomorrow*, the authors provide a persuasive argument that high-quality early childhood education is increasingly imperative for the fulfillment of the "American Dream" (Washington & Andrews, 2010). According to the authors, there are three reasons for this:

1. Early education and care systems are the first educators of children outside the home and the first social system to identify children's strengths and potential as contributors to the common good of society;
2. Early education and care programs are often the first experiences that children have interacting with individuals from different cultures, religions, languages, and family backgrounds. How these experiences are dealt with will have a great impact on our nation as it rapidly becomes more and more diverse.
3. Early education and care of high quality lay the foundation for children's developing ideas of freedom and democracy through daily routines and through the educational process itself. Each child's value is confirmed through the process of being provided with choices, through the process of being listened to, and through the process by which they are supported in the learning and care environments.

Inservice and preservice teacher preparation and development is an important part of ensuring that the experiences children receive in early childhood programs are of high quality (Haslip & Gullo, 2018). This is an especially significant issue given the changes emanating from the ever-changing early childhood landscape described and discussed above. Therefore, teacher preparation and professional development should ensure that inservice and preservice teachers have:

1. A strong foundation in both typical and atypical child development. An understanding of atypical development should include an awareness of the ways in which social, political, and physical environments can affect developmental trajectories in children. For example, how do the SES, cultural, and linguistic backgrounds of children affect the kinds of experiences that children will have and ultimately affect their construction of knowledge, problem-solving ability, and learning potential?
2. More depth of understanding within each curriculum content area so that appropriate cross-curriculum connections can be made. This should also include an awareness and understanding of related national, state, and local standards. By having this depth of knowledge, early childhood teachers can create learning environments that are meaningful to children, optimize each child's learning potential, and still address early learning standards.

3. An understanding and appreciation for the cultural, linguistic, and socioec-onomic differences among children. This will increase teachers' appropri-ate responses to children's unique strengths. For example, early childhood professionals need to know the impact of these for understanding assess-ment outcomes and to use assessment data to design and make informed and appropriate modifications in children's learning opportunities.

4. An understanding of the implications related to risk, resiliency, and pro-tective factors that may influence children's learning potential. This has the potential of increasing the likelihood that teachers will recognize the abili-ties in each child, therefore leading to teachers having high expectations for all children, creating opportunities for all children to be engaged in caring relationships, and have opportunities to contribute and participate in meaningful ways.

5. An expanded focus on extended field and clinical experiences beginning early and including guided observation, exploration and assisting in teach-ing, active participation, and student teaching that encompasses all the grade and developmental levels represented in early childhood education. This will give early childhood professionals an opportunity to see, first-hand, both typical and atypical developmental trajectories across the early childhood spectrum.

Adequate early childhood teacher preparation is key to early childhood pro-fessionals developing proficiency in creating curricula, teaching, and assess-ing children who come from diverse family and community backgrounds. Adhering to pedagogy that aligns with children's developmental needs and abilities is indispensable. A critical feature of the early childhood curriculum and teaching landscape is a learning environment rich in both exploratory and play-based experiences embedded within a context of concrete activities fol-lowing children's interests (Graue, Whyte, & Karabon, 2015). When teachers and other early childhood professionals consider individual children's strengths, needs, backgrounds, and experiences, the learning experiences developed and provided for them will adhere to certain tenets. This has the effect of increas-ing the likelihood children will optimally benefit from the learning experience.

Optimal learning is achieved by all children when they have opportunities to learn through hands-on experiences of their choosing. Teachers should struc-ture the learning environment with multiple and varied activities to achieve the targeted learning outcomes for children so any and all available activities children choose will lead to desired goals. Within these learning opportuni-ties, children should be given multiple opportunities to test their ideas, test the materials, test their relationships and test themselves. Since children who participate in early childhood programs come from such diverse backgrounds, they require opportunities to "try things out" in non-standard and often in unconventional ways.

Children should be given opportunities to explore their fears and anxieties as well as learn from their mistakes. "Awareness of self and others" has been valued as a key outcome of early childhood education (Graue et al., 2015, p. 13). The more children gain confidence in themselves, and share in the safety of learning through "trial-and-error," the greater the likelihood children will see the potential open to them within the classroom and other learning contexts. During these times, children's concepts, skills, attitudes, dispositions, and achievements are extended.

Developmentally appropriate practice. A key element of developmentally responsive teaching is learning experiences that are relevant to the life experiences of children who are engaged in learning within these environments. While the ECED landscape is ever changing, certain early childhood principles remain constant. The core elements embodied in what early childhood professionals have come to know as "developmentally appropriate practice" address the concerns of providing optimal developmental and learning experiences for all children (NAEYC, 2009). There are three core considerations embodied in developmentally appropriate practice.

First, early learning experiences should reflect what is known about the age-related characteristics of child development and learning. The assumption here is that at any specific age, there are certain typically common traits characterizing children's development and learning. Being cognizant of this permits one to make general age-related predications about what types of experiences are most likely to promote optimal learning and development. This includes recognizing what kind of learning content is appropriate, what kinds of learning materials are appropriate, what kinds of learning environments are appropriate, and what kinds of instructional strategies are appropriate. Child development knowledge helps teachers and others understand what kinds of learning opportunities are appropriate and what kinds of learning opportunities are not appropriate for children at a given age.

Second, early learning experiences should reflect what is unique about children as individuals. Each child brings to the learning environment different experiences, different expectations, different ways of knowing and understanding, and different approaches to learning. It is incumbent upon early childhood educators to become familiar with each child so appropriate modifications and adaptations can be made to reinforce the appropriateness of individual learning opportunities. While it is true that all children of a specific age share common developmental traits because of their age, at the same time these children are unique because of their individual backgrounds and experiences. A "one-size-fits-all" approach to curriculum and teaching is not appropriate. Assessment plays an important role in helping early childhood professionals understand the unique qualities of each child. It is important that assessment strategies are grounded in naturalistic methods engaging children in "real-life" learning experiences. Children should be assessed as they are engaged in learning activities within the curriculum.

Third, early learning experiences should reflect what is known about the social, cultural, and linguistic milieus in which children live and develop. Understanding these elements will help early childhood professionals become cognizant about the values, expectations, and behavioral conventions that are important elements in each child's life. By knowing these, early childhood professionals can ensure learning and development experiences are meaningful, relevant, and respectful for each child and his or her family.

Engaging all children where they are developmentally and experientially is a significant step in the process of meeting the educational and developmental needs of all young children; it becomes even more significant while teaching classrooms of children who are culturally, linguistically, and/or socioeconomically diverse. According to the National Association for the Education of Young Children (2009), "Learning and development are most likely to occur when new experiences build on what a child already knows and is able to do and when those learning experiences also entail the child stretching a reasonable amount in acquiring new skills, abilities, or knowledge" (p. 10). Effective teaching does not happen by chance, rather it is an intentional process. The ever-changing landscape of early childhood education makes it imperative that early childhood professionals have a comprehensive and current understanding of the children that are represented in their schools and classrooms.

Early learning standards and developmentally responsive teaching. The Common Core State Standards shape the scope and sequence of K-3 curricula, as well as the instructional strategies, materials, and environments used (Evenson et al., 2013). The challenge for early childhood practitioners is meeting the standards while maintaining developmentally responsive classrooms and teaching practices (NAEYC, 2015).

The temptation is to address all the standards. This may cause some teachers to discard more developmentally appropriate teaching and learning methods. Standards can and should be integrated into all child-centered approaches to teaching and learning, such as emergent curriculum, Big Ideas, or project-based learning. There seems to be an assumption that only a teacher-centered instructional approach can address the learning standard(s) efficaciously. As such, this approach is thought to be of equal worth to child-centered, developmentally responsive teaching. This may cause administrators and/or educators to disregard more experiential and child-centered approaches so long as the state standards are addressed and met.

Standards are, however, essential for evaluation of learning objectives within and across programs. They are also essential for measuring individual child growth and progress. Well-written standards can encourage better pedagogy. The Common Core State Standards, as well as the Next Generation Science Standards, are facilitating improved pedagogy for later grades compared to many past practices. Enforcing *pedagogical standards* will create more consistently meaningful and appropriate experiences for young children (Biggam & Hyson, 2014). Systems of accountability evolve to ensure that meaningful and integrative pedagogy properly balances the enforcement of learning standards (Haslip & Gullo, 2018).

Learning standards are stratified into separate and discrete curricular areas including language and literacy, math, science, as well as social and emotional competencies. In a landscape where standards influence the public conversation about the content and practice of education, the absence of *holistic standards* and unequal accountability for different developmental and teaching domains leads directly to the neglect of important educational priorities. Serious development and enforcement of authentically comprehensive standards will require all stakeholders to embrace the principle of holistic well-being already represented in community-school models and integrated service-delivery partnerships. It is little wonder a direct result of standards being developed for and applied to select curriculum areas, the remaining become less visible in curriculum foci; namely the arts, social studies, and social-emotional learning.

A trend influencing the landscape of early childhood is exploratory learning and the arts are being gradually displaced by the academic preparation of young children. As this trend becomes more pervasive, literacy and numeracy standards are emphasized and the number of resource teachers (e.g., art, music) are reduced and education budgets are tightened. The following two sections will focus on the importance of increasing exploratory learning and the arts into the early childhood curriculum. The focus will be on how the arts and exploratory learning benefit children who come from diverse backgrounds.

Increasing Exploratory Learning Opportunities

Exploratory learning opportunities are important for children for many reasons. These kinds of learning experiences are particularly significant within learning environments for a diverse group of learners. Exploratory play is important because it provides children with many and varied learning opportunities (KEAP, 2007, pp. 3–4):

- making choices and decisions;
- using one's own ideas and imagination;
- experimenting;
- trying out new behaviors and practicing old ones;
- practicing skills and learning new ones;
- adapting or transforming knowledge, attitudes, and skills;
- following an interest or line of inquiry;
- making mistakes;
- demonstrating one's competence in many areas of development;
- setting one's own goals;
- using symbols;
- making sense of puzzling situations, events or equipment;
- becoming and being confident and enjoying challenges;
- learning how to be a "player" for life in a high-tech, post-industrial society.

Exploration comes spontaneously and naturally for most children. Early childhood practitioners should plan and equip learning environments to be challenging and a place where children's exploration can be supported and extended.

To facilitate exploratory learning in early childhood settings, the role of the teacher and the role of the student need to be re-defined. In the conventional sense, teachers are the keepers of information. Equally so, teachers are the dispensers of information; dispensing the information to students according to a preset schedule, at a predetermined rate, in order to address and meet particular learning standards. Also, teachers, or in many cases prescriptive curricula, dictate the learning content. Teachers need to move from these positions to becoming the orchestrators of learning (Greenberg, 2014).

Students' roles should also be redefined. Children should become co-constructors of knowledge and learning. There should be a balance of teacher-directed activities and student-initiated activities. Teachers become guides and mentors, sources and resources, and most of all facilitators of a culture of learning that is shared equally by students and teachers alike. The benefits of exploration are maximized when teachers are purposive and plan for exploratory learning. They need to:

- determine specific goals for learning outcomes;
- individualize learning opportunities for children based on children's developmental capacities, strengths, and past experiences;
- build upon what children already know;
- provide enough time during the day for children to engage in meaningful exploration for the purpose of gaining knowledge and/or skills;
- integrate exploratory learning opportunities throughout the day.

When children are engaged in exploratory learning they can remain flexible while responding to events and changing situations. They are also able to adapt and "think on their feet." They become skilled at adjusting what they are doing in response to a changing scene. Exploratory learning best takes place in settings that are familiar to children. Through this process, they share experiences and their understandings with others, both other children as well as adults (McLeod, 2012). Exploration of one's environment is a universal human trait that serves both natural and biological functions (Elkind, 2004).

Integrating the Arts into the Curriculum

Despite evidence demonstrating that the arts can have long-lasting beneficial effects on children's academic achievement and development, there has been a continual decline in arts education in the early years of schooling (National Endowment for the Arts, 2011). The arts are defined as instruction in music, the visual arts, dance or drama/theatre and the process of producing such creative works" (Parsad & Spiegelman, 2012). The U.S. Department of Education completed studies of public school art education access in 1994, 1999 and 2009. There are notable differences in art instruction between public elementary schools depending on average family income. There was a decline among all elementary schools in providing dance and drama/theatre instruction, from 20% of schools in 1999 to just 3 to 4% of schools by 2009 (Parsad & Spiegelman, 2012).

When surveys report high frequencies of *access* to arts education without documenting changes in weekly minutes devoted to its *instruction,* potentially substantial trends are hidden. Minutes devoted to arts and music show broad declines in the few metropolitan and state areas where surveys have been conducted (Rabkin et.al., 2011). Schools have cut the amount of time children attend regularly scheduled music and arts classes in order to increase classroom time devoted to literacy and math. After transitions to and from the music teacher, the number of minutes devoted to instruction in music (K-3) is often just 30 minutes once a week (as compared to 450 minutes per week for literacy). This decline in time spent on arts instruction occurred concomitantly as accountability shifted wholly to testable subjects.

Other indicators of a more exploratory, artistically stimulating and creative environment include participation in arts-related field trips and related school-community partnerships. Per the most recent survey of this information, the U.S. Department of Education reports that 61% of all public elementary schools provided arts-related field trips in the form of trips to concerts, plays, and museums. Simultaneously, 42% of schools had a partnership with a cultural or community organization potentially related to the arts (Parsad & Spiegelman, 2012). These numbers illustrate that only about half of public elementary school students receive any creative stimulation from outside the classroom. For this half, unfortunately, such opportunities are usually infrequent. This results in half of all public elementary school children not experiencing arts-related enrichment opportunities at all.

The amount of arts instruction children receive has been shown to be an important indicator of long-term positive outcomes. Children from low socioeconomic backgrounds who experience active involvement in arts learning perform better in high-school academics, have higher college attendance rates and grades, and have a higher likelihood of maintaining adult employment (Catterall, 2009). Causal connections between music training in childhood and cognitive and neural functions for older people have also been explored. Four or more years of music training is associated with increased neural processing of speech in older age (White-Schwoch et al., 2013).

Early childhood teacher preparation programs are compelled to cut rather than add courses in the creative and expressive arts. For the most part, this is due to increasing budgetary constraints narrowing the university curriculum (Oliff et al., 2013). Additionally, it is due to the "need" to align more closely with academic-oriented teacher preparation. As arts courses in teacher licensure programs are eliminated or significantly reduced in number, administrators may propose that creative expression be integrated into other classes. However, trying to integrate creative expression in other courses in the curriculum may not be efficacious in improving pre-service teachers' skills to integrate arts into early grades pedagogy. At the PK – 12 level, appeals for such integration may be used to justify or excuse elimination of "discrete courses in the visual arts, music, dance, and theatre taught by certified arts educators" (Education Policy and Leadership Center, 2012, p. 9).

Providing arts-related experiences to young children across the prekinder-garten through grade 3 continuum can be inexpensive and feasible. To make this happen, teachers must feel competent and prepared to integrate the arts across the curriculum. When simple methods such as the use of drama, song, rhythm instruments, and how to use art supplies have not been modeled and demonstrated for pre-service teachers, graduates of these licensure programs are unprepared to enhance literacy, STEM, and social/emotional learning through the integration of art, music, drama and creative activities. Or to enhance creative expression for its own sake, for that matter. Lacking knowledge and skills of how to manage the arts, new teachers are often remiss in providing the experiences for young children that are most developmentally appropriate and essential for holistic brain development.

As was discussed in the previous section, children's opportunities to participate in play-based and exploratory learning experiences have likewise been reduced (Nicolopoulou, 2010). As with the arts, play-based, exploratory and project-based approaches follow their own pedagogies and require targeted teacher preparation and training. Facilitating a high-quality exploratory learning environment, by mastering the project-based learning cycle, for example, is a skill needing several years of careful refinement and support among a collaborative team of teachers. These approaches allow for playful initiative and expression across the curriculum. Yet discovery-based environments have been difficult to maintain among in-service teachers because the schedule has become defined and structured by subject area. This hinders integrated approaches and often leads to a reliance on direct instruction which evidence suggests is less effective than discovery-based methods (Dean & Kuhn, 2007).

According to Silverstein and Layne (2010), "arts integration is an approach to teaching in which students construct and demonstrate understanding through an art form" (p. 5). In order to make this happen, one must first and foremost identify the art connections. This is the most critical step in planning for and creating an arts integrated curriculum. The connection is created by identifying a specific art focus, such as music, movement, visual arts, dramatics, or creative storytelling. Next, this focus is connected to either a curriculum area (science, math, literacy, social studies). The specific knowledge and/or skills that the student is to learn in order to meet a particular standard should be specified. "Arts integration requires that objectives are met in both the art form and the other subject areas" (Silverstein & Layne, 2010, p. 22).

According to Crawford (2004), there are six vital reasons for integrating the arts into the early childhood curriculum. By integrating the arts into the curriculum, you:

Make curriculum content more accessible. Teachers may recognize that a child is better at talking than writing, better at drawing than at solving math problems, or better at visual arts than at doing science experiments. Teachers can use children's artistic strengths and likes to help them successfully engage in curriculum activities. For example, the child who likes oral story-telling better than creative writing can use their story-telling skills as a bridge to the actual writing of a story.

Encourage joyful and active learning. When children are engaged in activities related to the arts, they are active and they are learning. When children are engaged in activities related to the arts, they are having fun and they are learning. A skillful teacher will be able to make the connections between the arts activities and curriculum and help the child see the connections. If children are active and they are having fun while learning, they will persist in those activities and increase their opportunities for learning.

Help children make and express connections to curriculum content. It is true that children are less likely to learn something in which they have no interest. For many children, particularly younger children, the arts provide a meaningful context for learning. The arts provide a personal connection to the child and their interests. The arts help children care about new information that is presented to them and make meaning from it.

Help children understand and express abstract concepts.

Many of our strongest neural networks are formed by actual experience. Without the concrete experience of a subject, the representation or symbol may have little meaning, no matter how much someone explains it to you.

(Wolfe, 2001, pp. 137–8)

This quote highlights the importance of how effective learning moves from what one knows to what one does not know; from what is personal and familiar to the abstract. The arts help students make these learning leaps with self-confidence.

Stimulate higher-order thinking processes. We want to encourage three types of thinking in our children: attending, discerning, and inventing. Attending and discerning are analytical skills, which involve paying attention, accurately relating information, scrutinizing information, and detecting the relationships among the realities explored. Inventing, on the other hand, takes students one step beyond. Here they build upon what they have previously known and learned so that they can use this information to build new knowledge. The arts provide students with the tools that they need to develop the intellectual capacity for analyzing from multiple perspectives.

Build community and help children develop collaborative skills. The arts provide a natural conduit for working collaboratively to create a "product" that is the result of negotiation and mutual understanding. This process creates a learning environment that results in satisfaction for all children, regardless of their individual backgrounds.

Considering the changing curricular trends in early childhood education, the final section of the chapter will offer a challenge. The challenge is, considering all of the changing curricular trends facing early childhood professionals today, how do we address the needs of all children while maintaining pedagogical integrity?

The Challenge: Addressing the Needs of All Children

Today's early childhood education landscape is a challenging one due to the various required curricular standards coupled with the diversity of children served. In order to meet these challenges head-on, there are a number of considerations on which we should both reflect and take action (Masters, 2015).

The learning needs of children. As previously discussed, there is an assumption that children who are of the same age are similar in both their development and learning abilities. In reality, particularly at the beginning of the school year, children's development and achievement levels are varied. Due to the diverse nature of developmental levels and achievement potential among children of similar ages, they often have vastly differing learning needs. In order to address these needs, appropriate and high-quality assessments are needed. As a teacher gets to know each student through these assessments, he or she can:

- establish where children are in their developmental trajectories;
- determine where individual children are in their learning trajectories;
- identify children's distinctive strengths and talents; and
- assist children in meeting their unique learning and development needs.

Differentiating Curriculum and Teaching. A one-size-fits-all curriculum is not appropriate. Children from different socioeconomic, cultural, and/or linguistic groups require different learning experiences for optimal learning to occur. The problem is that children can disengage if their learning experiences do not match their learning levels or interests. To address this, teachers need to meet all children where they are in terms of their levels of learning and development and provide individualized and directed curriculum and teaching.

High and appropriate expectations for all children. It is not uncommon for teachers and others to shape their assumptions about children's abilities based on background characteristics such as socioeconomic status, gender, family structure, or cultural experiences. Expectations are set high, low, or somewhere in between depending on what characteristics or combination of characteristics a child has, along with accompanying assumptions that one has of individuals with those characteristics. All children need learning opportunities that are attainable, yet will challenge them to reach beyond where they are. It is important that we have expectations for all students to achieve outstanding progress regardless of their starting points and final levels of attainment.

Building teacher capacity. The difficult task for all early childhood educators is to establish an understanding of their children's learning and development levels, while executing individualized and targeted teaching. Individualized and targeted teaching focuses on addressing the learning needs of all children. This type of teaching requires teachers to use assessment to assist in identifying the learning capacity and needs of each individual child. Assessment information is used to design learning opportunities that appropriately challenge children while at the same time extending their reach. In order for teachers to achieve this, they must have a thorough understanding of the children that they teach and the material that they are teaching to these children. They must know how to meet the learning needs of each child; those who may be ahead of the rest of the class as well as those who may be achieving at a level below most of the children in the class.

The More Things Change the More They Stay the Same

This chapter focused on the changes in early childhood curriculum trends and the presumed reasons for them. It is imperative for early childhood professionals to recognize and address these changes, but at the same time recognize there are other elements within the early childhood framework that do not change. This dichotomy often results in early childhood professions being faced with a dilemma. How do we address the dynamic features of the early childhood environment while recognizing there are aspects that are static?

As early childhood professionals, we must recognize:

- Performance expectations for young children and teachers have changed due to the fact that more children than ever attend some type of early childhood program before they enter kindergarten.
- State and national academic standards for early childhood education are becoming more widespread and are not holistic in their focus.
- Formal academic teacher-directed instruction has overshadowed the need for children's active learning based on socialization, imagination, and creativity.
- An emergent and integrated early childhood curriculum has given way to a narrowly defined curriculum where the emphasis is on content-oriented and skill-based instruction and learning that can be directly measured.
- There may be inappropriate use of assessment in early childhood resulting in:
  - high-stakes testing;
  - a narrowing of the curriculum (teaching to the test);
  - inappropriate ability grouping of children.
- Often, today's early childhood curriculum and instruction have:
  - less focus on child development;
  - more focus on ability groupings;
  - less focus on differentiated instruction;
  - more focus on whole group instruction.

At the same time, early childhood professionals must recognize and take into account that:

- the fundamental developmental characteristics of young children have not changed;
- the ways in which young children construct knowledge have not changed;
- the ways in which young children problem-solve have not changed;
- the ways young children socially interact with others have not changed;
- not all young children of the same age are at the same developmental level;
- not all young children share the same life experiences;
- not all young children learn at the same rate or in the same way.

As early childhood professionals, we *must* take into account the dynamic nature of the early childhood education experience that results from changing demographics and social and political landscapes. At the same time, we *must* take into account the relatively static nature of child development that affects how children at specific ages benefit from these early childhood experiences. It is imperative that we balance "the more things change" with "the more they stay the same." The idea of responding to changing trends in the field is not new. In fact, it's been a mainstay of the profession for decades. As Paula Jorde Bloom said over 30 years ago:

> Historically the field of early childhood education has always been closely tied to changes in society. Like a barometer, early childhood programs respond to change in the social, political, and economic climates...But early childhood education does more than merely respond to societal changes, and may in fact serve as an important agent of change.
>
> (Jorde, 1986, p. 171)

References

Biggam, S.C., & Hyson, M.C. (2014). The common core state standards and developmentally appropriate practices: Creating a relationship. In C. Copple, S. Bredekamp, D. Koralek & K. Charner (Eds.), *Developmentally Appropriate Practice: Focus on Kindergarteners* (pp. 95–112). Washington, DC: NAEYC.

Bransford, J.D., Brown, A.L., & Cocking, R.R. (2004). *How People Learn: Brain, Mind, Experience and School*. Washington, DC: National Academy Press. Retrieved from: http://www.csun.edu/~SB4310/How%20People%20Learn.pdf

Catterall, J.S. (2009). *Doing Well and Doing Good by Doing Art: A 12-Year National Study of Education in the Visual and Performing Arts*. Los Angeles, CA: I-Group Books.

Center for Public Education. (2012). *The United States of Education: The Changing Demographics of the United States and Their Schools*. Alexandria, VA: Center for Public Education. Retrieved from: http://www.centerforpubliceducation.org/The-United-State-of-education-The-changing-demographics-of-the -United-States-and-their-schools.html

Child Trends Databank. (2015). Family structure. Retrieved from: http://www.childtrends.org/?indicators=family-structure

Crawford, L. (2004). *Lively Learning: Using the Arts to Teach the K-8 Curriculum*. Greenfield, MA: Northeast Foundation for Children.

Dean Jr, D., & Kuhn, D. (2007). Direct instruction vs. discovery: The long view. *Science Education, 91*(3), 384–397.

Education Policy and Leadership Center. (2012). *Creating Pennsylvania's Future Through the Arts and Education*. Harrisburg, PA: Education Policy and Leadership Center. Retrieved from: http://www.eplc.org/wp-content/uploads/2012/03/Creating_PAs_Future_New Color_final.pdf.

Elkind, D. (2004). Thanks for the memory: The lasting value of true play. In D. Koralek (Ed.), *Spotlight on Young Children and Play* (pp. 36–41). Washington, DC: NAEYC.

Espinosa, L.M. (2008). *Challenging Common Myths About Young English Language Learners*. New York: Foundations for Child Development.

Evenson, A., McIver, M., Ryan, S., & Schwols, A. (2013). *Common Core Standards for Elementary Grades K-2 Math & English Language Arts: A Quick-Start Guide*. ASCD.

Graue, M.E., Whyte, K.L., & Karabon, A.E. (2015). The power of improvisational teaching. *Teaching and Teacher Education, 48*, 13–21.

Greenberg, J. (2014). *Teaching Children to Think: Meeting the Demands of the 21st Century*. Toronto: Hanen Early Learning Program.

Harvard Family Research Project. (2006). *Family Involvement Makes a Difference* (Spring 2006), 1–8.

Haslip, M., & Gullo, D.F. (2018). The changing landscape of early childhood education: Implications for policy and practice. *Early Childhood Education Journal, 46*(3), 249–264.

Jiang, Y., Elono, M., & Skinner, C. (2015). *Basic Facts About Low-Income Children: Children 6 Through 11 Years, 2014*. New York: National Center for Children in Poverty.

Jorde, P. (1986). Early childhood education: Issues and trends. *The Educational Forum, 50*(2), 171–181.

Kernow Education Arts Partnership – KEAP. (2007). *Effective Practice: Play and Exploration*. Redruth: Crown. Retrieved from: http://www.keap.org.uk/documents/eyfs_ep_play_ exploration.pdf

McLeod, S.A. (2012). Zone of proximal development. Retrieved from: https://www. simplypsychology.org/Zone-of-Proximal-Development.html

Masters, G. (2015 March). *Addressing the Needs of All Children*. Paper presented at the International Conference on Giftedness and Talent Development, Brisbane, Australia.

National Association for the Education of Young Children. (2009). *Developmentally Appropriate Practice in Early Childhood Programs Serving Children from Birth Through Age 8 – Position Statement*. Washington, DC: National Association for the Education of Young Children.

National Association for the Education of Young Children. (2015). *Developmentally Appropriate Practice and the Common Core State Standards: Framing the Issues*. Washington, DC: National Association for the Education of Young Children.

National Center for Educational Statistics. (2015). *The Condition of Education 2015 (NCES 2015–144), Preprimary Enrollment*. Washington, DC: National Center for Educational Statistics. Retrieved from: https://nces.ed.gov/fastfacts/display.asp?id=516

National Endowment for the Arts. (2011). *Arts Education in America: What the Declines Mean for Arts Participation*. Washington, DC: National Endowment for the Arts.

National Education Association. (2016). *Backgrounder: Students from Poverty*. Washington, DC: National Education Association.

Nicolopoulou, A. (2010). The alarming disappearance of play from early childhood education. *Human Development, 53*(1), 1–4.

Oliff, P., Palacios, V., Johnson, I., & Leachman, M. (2013). Recent deep state higher education cuts may harm students and the economy for years to come. Center on Budget and Policy Priorities.

Parsad, B., & Spiegelman, M. (2012). Arts Education in Public Elementary and Secondary Schools: 1999–2000 and 2009–10 (NCES 2012–014). National Center for Education Statistics, Institute of Education Sciences, U.S. Department of Education. Washington, DC.

Rabkin, N., Reynolds, M., Hedberg, E.C., & Selby, J. (2011). *Teaching Artists and the Future of Education: A Report on the Teaching Artist Research Project: Executive Summary.* NORC at the University of Chicago.

Ray, A., Bowman, B., & Robbins, J. (2006). *Preparing Early Childhood Teachers to Successfully Educate ALL Children: The Contribution of Four-Year Undergraduate Teacher Preparation Programs.* Report to the Foundation for Child Development. Chicago, IL: Erikson Institute. Retrieved from: http://fcd-us.org/sites/default/files/TeacherPreparationPrograms.pdf

Silverstein, L.B., & Layne, S. (2010). *Laying the Foundation: Defining Arts Integration.* Washington, DC: The John F. Kennedy Center for the Performing Arts.

Washington, V., & Andrews, J.D. (2010). *Children of 2020: Creating a Better Tomorrow.* Washington, DC: National Association for the Education of Young Children.

White-Schwoch, T., Carr, K.W., Anderson, S., Strait, D.L., & Kraus, N. (2013). Older adults benefit from music training early in life: Biological evidence for long-term training-driven plasticity. *The Journal of Neuroscience, 33*(45), 17667–17674.

Wolfe, P. (2001). *Brain Matters: Translating Research into Classroom Practice.* Alexandria, VA: Association for Supervision and Curriculum Development.

9 Playful Learning

Bridget Amory

The value of play in helping our children thrive in their childhood learning environment will help support the increasingly complex needs of our children as they enter formal school experiences. Play has become an exception versus a norm in our Common Core classrooms. A classroom grounded in play provides young children with learning opportunities measuring greater outcomes than any nationally identified standard. If we are truly committed to educating our children, we need to become reacquainted with play and its many values. In this chapter we will explore the benefits of play, share strategies to encourage engagement in play, and justify play opportunities for all students.

What Is Play?

In this era of education where accountability and rigor have become the norm, we educators often find ourselves grappling with evolving practices. Increased focus on data, standards-based direct instruction, and high-stakes assessments are just a few of the critical focus areas we must consider. One such victim of accountability demands and calls for increased rigor is the practice of play in our classrooms. The absence of play in our curricula is not just the victim of our zealous approach of using numbers to represent accountability in education, but also our society as a whole. What is more, when you ask a child "What is play?" the answer is certain to be different based upon who you ask. For one, play is practicing a musical instrument, while for another it is a play practiced within a game of organized youth football or basketball. For yet another, it could be gaming in a virtual world with others who are only known by their avatars. The definitions of play are as diverse as the children we teach. Play is often considered a vague term within the world of education, especially in the classroom context. However, there is a common theme found among both formal research and informal understandings:

- "Play is fun when you play with the kitchen toy. I like play." – Makenzie, 4 years old
- "Fun and exciting. You do it with a friend and you have fun with them." – Emily, 6 years old

- "Playing is doing something active and fun like playing Monopoly or Candyland or outside with a frisbee." – Reed, 7 years old
- "It's when people are active and having fun." – Weston, 9 years old
- "Play is a timeless diversion tactic. A momentary release from reality." – Ashby, 17 years old
- "Play is often talked about as if it was a relief from serious learning. But for children, play is serious learning. Play is really the work of childhood." – Fred Rogers (quoted by Heidi Moore, 2014)

After reviewing the statements above, are you able to identify the common theme? Perhaps engagement? Enjoyment? Take a moment and think about your own learning. Reflect upon how you learn best. Ask yourself the following questions:

- What type of learning experiences provide me with meaningful learning?
- What type of learning experiences do I recall more than another?
- Am I able to identify what it is that sets that learning experience apart from another?

Upon reflection, are you able to see the connection between the found theme and your personal learning experiences? Play means different things at different ages, stages, and personalities. Play can be simple and complex. It involves talking, exploring, challenging, nurturing, sharing, thinking, risk taking, having choices, relaxing, daydreaming, imagining, trying, running, measuring, building, singing, being yourself, friendships, taking risks, freedom … learning.

So …

Why is it, when we know our greatest learning happens whenever there is a high level of engagement and enjoyment, that we do not continue to seek and provide such opportunities for children? Instead, we find ourselves shifting our focus onto the standards and rigor required in our current era of education. We have overwhelming evidence of the value of learning through play, yet we do not seek avenues to integrate standards and rigor through play. We continue to see a decline in child-centered, play-based early childhood classrooms and a rise in the number of classrooms that rely instead on standardized teacher-led direct instruction. As educators, how are we allowing this to happen? And perhaps more importantly, what can we do moving forward to have positive learning experiences through play while convincing key policy makers to support play-based programming? Perhaps beginning with the notion of why play is important is the perfect place to start.

Why Play?

The old adage warning against a life of "all work and no play" actually may be true. Our children and families are arriving at school with greater needs. These needs tend to range from identified complex developmental delays to a lack of social skills or even a lack of fine motor skills. Whatever the deficit, we need to continue to plan and program with them in mind.

With the growing need for mental health supports among our school-age populations, we need to continue exploring avenues to help prevent and equip our children with the skills they need. Teaching children how to collaborate and reason will further develop their internal locus of control. Providing opportunities to empower our children to hone the skills they need to help establish a sense of control over their own learning will ultimately facilitate the development of their own lives. Thus, helping them reach their full potential while directing them away from greater mental health needs such as anxiety and depression is where our educational attention needs to be. There have even been suggestions that America's schoolchildren need a Childhood Humane Association to ensure they are given regular access to breaks from work and more opportunities for play (Ohanian, 2002). The incomparable value of play in the early childhood classroom has been well documented through a variety of methods, from personal testimonials to rigorous behavioral research studies to medical investigations into brain development, cognition, and social development. In a recent article published in *Young Children* about brain science and play, it is reported that "Decades of research suggest just that. In particular, free play and guided play—together known as *playful learning*—are pedagogical tools through which children can learn in joyful and conceptually rich ways" (Hassinger-Das, Hirsh-Pasek, & Golinkoff, 2017).

Think for a moment about the type of colleagues you would like to work with. Perhaps you would like to work with those who collaborate, create, inspire, investigate, reason, problem solve? Where do you suppose one learns those skills? In over 20 years of education I have yet to see those skills develop in a child as a result of standardized testing and standards-based instruction. However, I have seen those skills as a direct result of allowing students to go about their learning through play. Play with learning materials. Play with one another. Play with the environment in which they are surrounded. Early childhood educator and writer Vivian Paley has dedicated her career to examining children's play. She believes play is the natural mode of learning which allows children to construct meaning in their worlds which can be carried into their adult lives. She believes play, indeed, is the work of children (Paley, 2004).

Children who are provided with the opportunity to actively explore their learning environment have the chance to engage in rich learning experiences through their senses in a natural way.

> Developmental theory, which has had little influence in education beyond early childhood, is quite clear on this point: "To understand is to invent," in Piaget's (1973) words. Young children learn the most important things

not by being told but by constructing knowledge for themselves in interaction with the physical world and with other children – and the way they
do this is by playing.

(Jones and Reynolds, 1992)

If you close your eyes and think back to some of your own early learning
experiences, I suspect you can almost smell a new pack of crayons or glue.
You might even be able to feel the smooth pink eraser, the surface of a desk
or the weight of a backpack you carried to school. Perhaps you sampled a taste
of Play-Doh on your tongue. You might be able to hear the chatter of voices.
You may even be able to hear the tub of learning materials crash to the floor
when a classmate spills them out to explore. The power of our senses is deeply
entwined with our ability to learn and construct knowledge. Using our senses
in learning is best done through play. Seeing. Smelling. Touching. Tasting.
Hearing.

The knowledge, skills, abilities, and understandings children develop
through meaningful, child-directed play-based learning experiences lay the
solid foundation for all learning that comes after, including but by no means
limited to later formal schooling. Children construct knowledge through play.
As early learning opportunities provide the ultimate scaffolding of one experience upon another, one could deduct that by supporting play in our early
childhood classrooms we are indeed laying the critical foundation for rigor and
standards to later be built upon.

Engaging in Play

Play is a child's context for learning. Through play, children practice and
experiment with their learning both independently as well as with their peers.
Creating an environment that supports playful learning is the first step in helping to engage in play. This means providing purposeful learning materials and
modeling play strategies connected to content and ensuring a classroom schedule provides opportunities for exploration.

The physical layout of learning materials and ease of accessibility is critical to promoting engagement. Working to ensure a good flow of traffic
throughout the learning environment means setting up shelves, tables, books,
and learning displays in a way that promotes socialization and movement.
Providing materials in an organized manner also not only helps with engagement but also helps to communicate expectations and order throughout
the classroom. Low shelves help promote the materials children can have
access to and higher shelves can be reserved for materials that are tempo-
rarily unavailable. Play does not have to be an expensive endeavor in an
early childhood classroom either. Cardboard boxes can be painted or covered in paper to create color-coded organizational bins for learning materials. Recycled cups, cans, or jars can be decorated and used to help sort and

organize learning materials. Yard sales and second-hand shops are great places to pick up additional manipulatives such as game pieces, playing cards, dress up items, or gently used toys.

Creating classroom signs or signals to help communicate which materials are available is highly encouraged. Perhaps a stoplight system of red, yellow, green can be incorporated or even the use of roadway signs that help to bring environmental print to the classroom. No matter what materials you decide to use throughout your classroom, creating a learning environment that is inviting to young children and encourages their exploration is critical to engaging them. The next step in engaging children with play is to model how you expect them to engage with the classroom materials. During the first few days in a new learning environment it is imperative that a teacher guide the children through the procedures and expectations of how to access learning materials. Even guiding the children through how to wash their hands by following step-by-step directions will help pay off in the long run. As a principal, I recall a teacher walking the children through how to use the classroom paper towel dispenser to ensure they did not waste extra towels when drying their hands. I believe that classroom of children also learned to flush the classroom toilet by pushing on the lever with their foot instead of their hand! Modeling expectations with materials in the learning environment is one critical area for teachers to focus on. Equally as important, is the ability to model how to play in the established learning environment. When a child chooses to play school, they have a chance to exercise leadership, communicate verbally and non-verbally, organize, maybe even write or draw. When a child chooses to play in a restaurant, they may choose to write or draw a menu, take orders, process payments, and perhaps even create a meal. One of my favorite moments as a building principal was when I was observing a Kindergarten teacher who exemplifies what it means to model play. This particular observation involved the teacher collecting anecdotal notes on her students during their free play time. Some of her students had individualized educational plans and their social skills were being monitored and data collected during this time. As she moved through the classroom making notes, she would stop and ask children guiding questions. She was cautious not to interrupt or to distract them from their play but engage them in dialogue about their play. As she neared the classroom housekeeping center she watched a student work to wrap a box in holiday paper. It was close to the holiday season and the housekeeping center now included some string lights, a variety of boxes, various wrapping paper scraps, gift tags, bows, scissors, and tape. When the student was finished wrapping the box, well, sort of finished wrapping the box, he presented it to her. She smiled and thanked him for the gift. There was an awkward pause and she waited and looked at him. He continued to look at her and finally asked her to open the box. She asked if she should wait until the holiday, but he insisted she open it right then. She agreed and began to carefully unwrap the box. When she opened it she found it empty inside. Without pausing, she held out the box and covered her mouth in awe. She smiled and thanked the child profusely for the beautiful necklace he had given her. She hugged him and proceeded to take the pretend necklace out of the box and asked him for assistance in putting it on, so she could wear it all afternoon. The child eagerly helped her fasten the imaginary necklace as he beamed with pride. Not only was she able to capture data on how this student was progressing with fine motor and communication skills, she was also able to capture a moment where his self-esteem grew beyond a measurable data point.

Play provides incredibly rich learning opportunities to help support children's later success and build their self-esteem. Enticing children to play is not typically a challenge. More often we find ourselves asking our children not to play. However, in the event you find a reluctant player, be sure to give the player space and time. A reluctant player may need to observe and assess before engaging. The player may need to build confidence before being comfortable engaging. This is an opportune time to model play. If the player continues to remain hesitant, pairing this player with another peer may prove successful. In a Pre-Kindergarten classroom there was a young English language learner who was hesitant to engage in any of the learning centers. Nearly all of the autumn season, he wandered throughout the classroom keeping a keen eye on those around him as they busily carried on. It was not until the teacher found books in his native language that he began to participate and join another English language learner at the classroom listening center. Each week the teacher diligently changed the story or songs to reflect the instructional theme in the classroom. After the holiday season had passed, the teacher decided to leave a variety of stories and songs in the listening center. As the children began to select their play areas, the teacher was surprised to see many of the children eager to participate at the listening center. Much to this teacher's surprise, the English learner had decided to play the popular song *Feliz Navidad* over and over again. It was not until the teacher began to notice more and more children beginning to gravitate toward the listening center, that she realized the English language learner was giggling and carrying on with his classmates singing "fleas on a dog" which, one can only imagine, provided fine entertainment.

One of the greatest measures of student learning can be observed through play. Teachers who utilize a variety of instructional strategies throughout their classroom will be successful in maximizing the achievement of their students. Teachers need to "play to" their students' strengths and weaknesses, which can be done in a variety of ways. It is important for teachers to first assess where they have success. A keen sense of observation as children complete various tasks and activities will speak to this. Learning what students are good and not so good at enables one to use the skills they are strong at to enhance the skills they need to work on (Figure 9.1).

Figure 9.1 Children playing school. Photo by Sara Croce.

Connecting Play with Standards

Look at the picture. Does it depict young children playing school as modeled for them, or perhaps is that SAT prep? What do you suppose motivated a young girl to use a flashcard with her younger brother? Perhaps it was her new schoolhouse doll set she received for her sixth birthday or perhaps she is trying to teach her younger brother one of the sight words she needed to master in Kindergarten before heading to the First Grade. Either way, looking for opportunities to connect play with the standards-based instructional movement in this era of accountability in education will be key to helping support play-based instructional opportunities in early childhood. Play should be the anchor for the curricula for young children. Wolfgang and Wolfgang (1992) share that "The child must learn by being free to work and play in a well-designed classroom full of rich variety of materials, with a teacher and same-age level peers." Early childhood educators need to help facilitate a play-based curriculum in a way that helps to stretch their children's understandings and build upon their current knowledge. Integrated thematic units of instruction are critical in helping this reality come to life—not just thematic units with lesson plan after lesson plan, but ones that include learning centers rich with learning materials connected to the themes. For example, while learning about the autumn season, a discovery table full of various autumn leaves, acorns, seeds, and bark can allow children to explore the various textures, smells, and signs of the season. In another part of the classroom, providing coloring crayons, paper, and leaves for rubbing autumn pictures to life is another opportunity to engage in learning. Examining the textures and symmetrical patterns found in nature can be naturally discovered through playing with the materials. Providing children with magnifying glasses to examine the patterns and materials to try to replicate them will help reinforce their fine motor skills and ability to attend to detail. Providing rich pieces of literature in support of an autumn theme will provide critical vocabulary and images to help shape the children's understandings.

Connecting play opportunities to learning standards can prove to be a challenge for some early childhood educators. Teachers know that explorative practice in communication skills through play support the development of language, literacy, and vocabulary skills in children; however, implementing play opportunities in a mandated curriculum can be tricky. Math concepts such as engineering, measurements, geometry, and even architecture can be developed through the exploration and building of materials. Providing opportunities for children to play in the outdoors is also of incredible value, helping to support and encourage cognitive and social development skills critical to the development of the whole child. Typically, children who have been afforded frequent breaks are able to better stay on-task, collaborate with their peers, tend to be more physically fit, and potentially have improved recall and memory performance. Even engaging children with a game such as "I Spy" can help encourage math and vocabulary skills. Encouraging conversations that include asking the child to describe an item by giving its shape, color, or size in the form of clues engages them and helps them practice and sharpen their problem-solving skills. Practicing persistence in completing the task further helps them to develop as well.

Fitting Play into the Required Assessment Systems

Play is how children naturally learn and it is also the way in which adults learn about children. Supporting an early childhood classroom rich in opportunities for play also provides educators with rich opportunities to gather assessment information about their students. Anecdotal notes, photographs, and student work all serve as tools to document the progress a child is making socially, emotionally, and academically toward the expected standards. Student assessment data can be tracked in a variety of ways. As an administrator I have seen data collection in the form of old-fashioned notes on a clipboard, notepads, index cards, and sticky notes within files, to electronic data collection. Regardless of how you intend to document the knowledge, skills, and dispositions of children, it is imperative to step back and observe children playing. Educators need to use their senses in observation as our children do in play, observing children's actions, decisions, expressions, interactions, reactions, and deliberations not only with the learning materials they have available to them, but also how they play with one another.

It is important that early childhood educators are keen observers of their children's play and are able to adapt and update the learning materials according to the observed needs. Whether they are updating the materials to match an instructional theme in the classroom or they are updating a 25-piece puzzle to a 50-piece puzzle, it is important that early childhood educators continue to help provide children with access to learning materials that support their exploration and engagement.

A caution about documenting play … One afternoon I was hosting a parent for a teacher conference after a long day at the end of the first week in the Kindergarten classroom. The parent was concerned about their child's adjustment to Kindergarten as they had recently moved and were not totally settled into their home yet. There was concern about how the chaos at home could potentially negatively impact the transition. I patiently tried to reassure the parent. While we reviewed samples of her child's work and chatted about how her child was adjusting to Kindergarten, her child happily moved about the classroom, free to explore the classroom materials without his peers present. As the conference began wrapping up, I announced to the child it was time to clean up for the other children when we returned to school the following week. The child quickly complied and began to return materials to the classroom dollhouse where he had been playing. As I was helping to direct the parent to the classroom door, together we approached the child and found the dollhouse was indeed intact with all materials having been returned. Much to our surprise, there were two of the adult dollhouse figures entangled with one another in the upstairs master bedroom of the classroom dollhouse. The parent blushed and quickly took her child by the hand excusing themselves from the classroom. We never discussed the incident as, on occasion, some observations are better left off the data dashboard.

Justifying Play

If you are an early childhood educator teaching in an environment where the justification of play is required, it is important you help reinforce the following information with the necessary stakeholders. Let's take a look at the conversation between a Kindergarten teacher and her school administrator as they discuss a recent classroom observation:

ADMINISTRATOR: Thank you for the observation in your classroom yesterday. It was wonderful to see the children active in their learning centers during that time. Could you tell me about what you planned for your students?

TEACHER: Well, yes, thank you for coming in. I am always eager to share my classroom and gain feedback. I have been using "Shapes" as a theme in my classroom this year to help reinforce some of the Kindergarten skills and to help manage my classroom. Each of our learning centers is labeled with a shape such as a circle, square, triangle, etc. I have also included a "Connections … What are we doing?" message into the label of each learning center. This helps my guests to understand what my children are working on in their learning centers. The Shapes theme has helped to reinforce my classroom community message too. We talk about how we all come in different shapes but all fit together to work, learn and grow together. So, we have been working on our "Winter" theme. With limited outdoor time due to the weather, I have been trying to incorporate a variety of activities into our learning centers to help bring the classroom to life. I am sure you could tell we have A LOT of energy in our classroom! We have been reading the text *Stranger in the Woods: A Photographic Fantasy* by Jean Stoick and Carl R. Sams II. I absolutely love this book. It allows the children, through photography, to experience a bit of a winter wonderland and see how animals live during the winter months. It has also allowed for us to discuss the curiosity of animals that can also be seen in the children. Elements of the story can be found in each of our learning centers.

ADMINISTRATOR: Wow! Can you tell me a bit more about how you have decided to expand on the instructional theme? Tell me how you are incorporating the learning standards.

TEACHER: During our Professional Learning Community (PLC) meeting, our Kindergarten team discussed how we could bring the story alive for our children. We really have a lot of energy in our classrooms at this time of the year so we brainstormed how we could extend the learning opportunities to incorporate more hands-on learning, independence, and play.

ADMINISTRATOR: Could you tell me about the lesson plans you created to support your learning centers?

TEACHER: Of course. Here are my lesson plans.

Kindergarten Learning Centers

Theme: *Winter*

Text Selection Focus: *Stranger in the Woods: A Photographic Fantasy by Jean Stoick and Carl R. Sams II*

Learning Center	Connections … What Are We Doing?	Standards http://www.corestandards.org/ http://www.nextgenscience.org/	Activities and Resources
Literacy Center	**Developing language skills** **Sequencing events** **Taking care of books** **Creating our own stories** **Gathering information,** **Enjoying quiet moments** **Using our imaginations** **Learning sight words** **Using word attack skills** **Recognizing word chunks** **Learning to comprehend what we read**	CCSS.ELA-LITERACY.RL.K.5 Recognize common types of texts (e.g., storybooks, poems). CCSS.ELA-LITERACY.RI.K.4 With prompting and support, ask and answer questions about unknown words in a text. CCSS.ELA-LITERACY.RI.K.10 Actively engage in group reading activities with purpose and understanding. CCSS.ELA-LITERACY.RF.K.4 Read emergent-reader texts with purpose and understanding.	**Winter books:** The Mitten by Jan Brett Snow by Uri Shulevits The Snowy Day by Ezra Jack Keats Bear Can't Sleep by Karma Wilson, Jane Chapman Bear Snores On by Karma Wilson, Jane Chapman A Loud Winter's Nap by Katy Hudson Animals in Winter by Henrietta Bancroft and Richard G. Van Gelder Let it Snow by Maryann Cocca-Leffler The Itsy Bitsy Snowman by Jeffery Burton, Sanja Rescek **Winter vocabulary:** Winter, raincoat, white, clouds, sweater, hibernating, rain, coat, tree, wind, hat, tree, quilt, snow, scarf, storm, boots, fireplace, cold, mittens, warm, snowflake, socks, skates, icicle, umbrella, sled, snowman, grey, gray, jacket, skiing
Writing Center	**Using our fine motor skills** **Developing our language skills** **Learning hand-eye coordination** **Putting thoughts into words** **Learning that print has meaning**	CCSS.ELA-LITERACY.SL.K.5 Add drawings or other visual displays to descriptions as desired to provide additional detail. CCSS.ELA-LITERACY.L.K.1.A Print many upper- and lowercase letters. CCSS.ELA-LITERACY.L.K.1.F Produce and expand complete sentences in shared language activities. CCSS.ELA-LITERACY.L.K.2.D Spell simple words phonetically, drawing on knowledge of sound-letter relationships.	Writing about winter with vocabulary (listed above) Stamping vocabulary words

Listening Center	**Developing language skills** **Enhancing pre-reading skills** **Learning to follow directions** **Working independently** **Gathering information** **Connecting stories to pictures**	CCSS.ELA-LITERACY.RL.K.10 Actively engage in group reading activities with purpose and understanding. CCSS.ELA-LITERACY.RI.K.9 With prompting and support, identify basic similarities in and differences between two texts on the same topic (e.g., in illustrations, descriptions, or procedures). CCSS.ELA-LITERACY.RI.K.10 Actively engage in group reading activities with purpose and understanding. CCSS.ELA-LITERACY.RF.K.1.A Follow words from left to right, top to bottom, and page by page. CCSS.ELA-LITERACY.RF.K.1.B Recognize that spoken words are represented in written language by specific sequences of letters. CCSS.ELA-LITERACY.RF.K.1.C Understand that words are separated by spaces in print.	Stranger in the Woods The Mitten Walking in a Winter Wonderland
Dramatic Play / Home Center	**Cooperating with others** **Using language skills** **Verbalizing ideas** **Understanding emotions** **Observation others** **Using fine and gross motor skills** **Acting out real situations** **Prating social skills** **Role playing** **Advancing language development** **Using our imaginations**	CCSS.ELA-LITERACY.RL.K.3 With prompting and support, describe the connection between two individuals, events, ideas, or pieces of information in a text. CCSS.ELA-LITERACY.SL.K.6 Speak audibly and express thoughts, feelings, and ideas clearly. CCSS.ELA-LITERACY.L.K.6 Use words and phrases acquired through conversations, reading and being read to, and responding to texts. CCSS.ELA-LITERACY.RL.K.9 With prompting and support, compare and contrast the adventures and experiences of characters in familiar stories. K-ESS3-2. Ask questions to obtain information about the purpose of weather forecasting to prepare for, and respond to, severe weather.	Items to help build a "stranger" (snowman) Prepare for a winter snow storm Puppets to help re-create the story in sequence or create another story

(Continued)

Learning Center	Connections ... What Are We Doing?	Standards http://www.corestandards.org/ http://www.nextgenscience.org/	Activities and Resources
Building Center	**Developing manipulative skills** **Expressing creative ideas** **Enhancing hand-eye coordination** **Expanding our imaginations** **Understanding tools** **Learning how things fit together** **Learning to plan and organize**	K-LS1-1. Use observations to describe patterns of what plants and animals (including humans) need to survive. K-ESS3-1. Use a model to represent the relationship between the needs of different plans and animals (including humans) and the places they live. K-ESS2-1. Use and share observations of local weather conditions to describe patterns over time. K-ESS3-2. Ask questions to obtain information about the purpose of weather forecasting to prepare for, and respond to, severe weather.	Building an igloo with "ice cubes" Building a winter shelter
Social Studies Center	**Understand directions** **Use and read maps** **Learn about Earth and its landforms** **Recognize community helpers** **Learn about our community** **Learn about other cultures** **Learn about character education** Practice respect for others **Learn about life skills**		Closed
Creative Arts Center	**Expanding creativity** **Increasing communication skills** **Improving eye-hand coordination, Exercising fine motor skills**	CCSS.ELA-LITERACY.RL.K.7 With prompting and support, describe the relationship between illustrations and the story in which they appear (e.g., what moment in a story an illustration depicts). CCSS.ELA-LITERACY.SL.K.5 Add drawings or other visual displays to descriptions as desired to provide additional detail. K-ESS3-1. Use a model to represent the relationship between the needs of different plans and animals (including humans) and the places they live.	Creating your own winter scene with paint, crayons, and dough Designing your own stranger in the woods with the various materials in the problem-solving box Play dough will be available for students to create their own winter scene

	Center	Skills	Standards	Notes
⬤	Sand and Water Center	**Enjoying sensory experience** **Experimenting** **Discovering** **Refining our observational skills** **Measuring** **Weighing** **Enhancing our fine motor skills**	CCSS.ELA-LITERACY.RF.K.4 Read emergent-reader texts with purpose and understanding. CCSS.ELA-LITERACY.SL.K.6 Speak audibly and express thoughts, feelings, and ideas clearly. CCSS.ELA-LITERACY.L.K.6 Use words and phrases acquired through conversations, reading and being read to, and responding to texts. K-ESS2-1. Use and share observations of local weather conditions to describe patterns over time.	Observing solids, liquids, and gases with ice Winter vocabulary words and winter items are buried in the "snow" (listed above) Text selection: All About Winter Weather by Kathryn Clay and The Shortest Day: Celebrating the Winter Solstice by Wendy Pfeffer
⬟	Play Dough Center	**Advancing our fine motor skills** **Toning our manipulative skills** **Using our imaginations** **Putting ideas into shapes** **Developing artistic skills**	N/A	Closed
▮	Math Center	**Learning new ideas** **Increasing language and cognitive skills** **Enhancing hand-eye coordination** **Developing fine motor skills** **Learning to estimate** **Classifying and sorting** **Counting and comparing** **Recognizing patterns and shapes**	CCSS.MATH.CONTENT.K.CC.A.1 Count to 100 by ones and by tens. CCSS.MATH.CONTENT.K.CC.A.3 Write numbers from 0 to 20. Represent a number of objects with a written numeral 0-20 (with 0 representing a count of no objects). CCSS.MATH.CONTENT.K.CC.B.5 Count to answer "how many?" questions about as many as 20 things arranged in a line, a rectangular array, or a circle, or as many as 10 things in a scattered configuration; given a number from 1-20, count out that many objects. CCSS.MATH.CONTENT.K.OA.A.1 Represent addition and subtraction with objects, fingers, mental images, drawings[1], sounds (e.g., claps), acting out situations, verbal explanations, expressions, or equations. CCSS.MATH.CONTENT.K.OA.A.2 Solve addition and subtraction word problems, and add and subtract within 10, e.g., by using objects or drawings to represent the problem. CCSS.ELA-LITERACY.RF.K.4 Read emergent-reader texts with purpose and understanding.	Students will use "snowballs" (pom-poms) as math manipulatives and tweezers to transfer them into sorting containers aligned to the various math flash cards including numbers 0-50 and simple addition and subtraction through 20. Text selection: Ten on the Sled by Kim Norman Math number cards and +, − cards

(Continued)

Learning Center	Connections ... What Are We Doing?	Standards http://www.corestandards.org/ http://www.nextgenscience.org/	Activities and Resources
Technology Center	**Developing fine-motor skills** **Enhancing pre-writing skills** **Advancing pre-reading skills** **Covering math and concepts** **Using the computer as a tool** **Learning how a mouse works** **Understanding computer functions** **Observing cause and effect**	CCSS.ELA-LITERACY.L.K.2.DSpell simple words phonetically, drawing on knowledge of sound-letter relationships. CCSS.ELA-LITERACY.L.K.4.AIdentify new meanings for familiar words and apply them accurately (e.g., knowing *duck* is a bird and learning the verb to *duck*). CCSS.ELA-LITERACY.L.K.6Use words and phrases acquired through conversations, reading and being read to, and responding to texts. CCSS.ELA-LITERACY.W.K.6With guidance and support from adults, explore a variety of digital tools to produce and publish writing, including in collaboration with peers.	Interactive games on classroom smartboard to match vocabulary words to images and sequence events
Snack Center	**Using our fine motor skills** **Learning to follow instructions** **Improving our self-help skills** **Developing self-control** **Sharing** **Helping others** **Understanding health and nutrition**	CCSS.MATH.CONTENT.K.G.B.5Model shapes in the world by building shapes from components (e.g., sticks and clay balls) and drawing shapes. Focus on circles Discuss lines	Create a snowman out of banana slices, pretzel sticks, and mini chocolate chips. ★*Note: Allergies are dear / no peanuts*

Connections ... What Are We Doing? can be found at:
https://www.abcteach.com/directory/teaching-extras-classroom-signs-pre-school-primary-signs-what-we-are-doing-signs-795-2-2

ADMINISTRATOR: Tell me more about what your role is during the learning center time in your classroom.

TEACHER: Well, outside of providing my students with independence and opportunities for movement, I am trying to assess my students and connect with some of them to gather important progress data.

ADMINISTRATOR: Tell me more about what it is you are trying to assess.

TEACHER: Well, here are my anecdotal notes. You can see I keep a system of notes for each student.

 Learning Centers' Anecdotal Notes

Student	Date 2/1	Anecdotal Notes
#1		*Interacting positively with peers at listening center/strength in taking turns and appears engaged in texts at the Literacy Center*
		Joined peers at Dramatic Play center to use puppets
#2		*n/a*
#3 *★IEP accommodations / speech only*		*Student remained at the Literacy Center with intense focus flipping through the various texts. Pointed out illustrations to peers in the center but often returned the book to the shelf upside down or sideways. Note: Need to reinforce left to right, front to back, and proper care of books*
		Are needs greater than speech? Language?
#4		*Intense focus at writing center.*
		Worked to create personal winter story.
		Discussed with student how to publish work to share with others.
#5		*Lots of energy today. Could not decide which center to work at and wandered throughout the classroom before being redirected to work in the Technology Center to support movement.*
		Seven prompts to remain at center during 30-minute window
#6		*n/a*
#7 *★IEP accommodations*		*Student demonstrated great success in manipulating the tweezers to move the snowballs from one container to the next. Student tongue was out while manipulating tweezer / Observe again to add to data collection for goal*
		Student also appeared to be cooperating with others while at learning center despite being incredibly focused on skill.
#8		*Absent*
#9		*Successfully matched vocabulary cards to visuals*
		Shared between literacy and writing center to help classmate write winter story

(Continued)

Student	Date 2/1	Anecdotal Notes
#10		Began at Creative Arts Center but left after nobody would play with the play dough
		Moved to Dramatic Play Center and "bossed" around peers with puppets to retell winter story
		Peers responded favorably
#11		n/a
#12		Listening Center
		Followed text intently
		When I circulated the room, pointed to illustrations in the text and smiled
#13		Remained in Dramatic Play Center entire time.
		Enjoyed puppets and responded to peer who provided direction
		Pet the puppets with affection
#14		Chose the math center and lined up snowballs in rows of 1, 2, 3 ...
		Intense focus with tweezers
		Recounted snowballs
#15		Skimmed books at Literacy Center
		Appeared to enjoy quiet time
		Beginning to read independently with fluency. Note: increase text Lexile level next week
#16		n/a
#17		Student began at Building Center
★IEP accommodations		Asked to student to review sight words with me / Scored 30/65
		Progress!
#18		Began at Building Center to build igloo. Quiet and intense.
		Visited Dramatic Play center but did not remain once peer began to provide direction
		Returned to Building Center to build new structure
#19		Began at Writing Center / stamped vocabulary words / used example cards as model
		Shifted to Creative Arts Center to create winter scene to accompany vocabulary words
#20		Absent – Remember to request medical note
#21		Creative Arts Center: Created winter scene of animal tracks in the snow
		Worked intensely
		Used play dough while waiting for paint to dry
#22		Selected the Building Center
		Engaged the entire time building various structures
		Interacted with peers appropriately

It helps me with determining what needs to be followed up on, what can be included as data for an Individualized Education Plan (IEP), and general student progress. For example, look at Student #3. She currently receives support through a speech-only IEP, but I am beginning to see a pattern of some additional concerns regarding language processing. I will continue to monitor and may ask our Speech Pathologist to come in for an additional observation. Student #20 has missed quite a few days of school this year due to issues with asthma. I have been working with the family to help provide support, including having them connected with our school nurse to help develop a medical plan. I think this last round of cold winter air has just not worked in our favor. You can also see Student #15 has really taken off with their independent reading. I am super excited! I am going to have to be certain to increase my classroom library with additional texts to continue to support him.

ADMINISTRATOR: Tell me how you are communicating student progress with the students as well as with families?

TEACHER: Outside of our formal reporting procedures, I use our daily communication log to indicate student performance and write notes home as needed. I try to keep it very positive between home and school. With the students, I am certain to move throughout the learning centers and provide feedback. Sometimes I find I am prompting them, such as when I found Student #5 was bouncing everywhere. I really had to redirect her to remain in one area. Student #7 was intently focused on completing the math activities in the Math Center and I tried to gently encourage her during her work. I love how she worked so seriously to complete the task.

ADMINISTRATOR: I am curious about how you determine which centers will be open and which ones will be closed.

TEACHER: Honestly, it comes down to the materials I have available, the connections I am able to make to the curriculum, and how many I can manage at one time. It is only me and 22 students so I try to plan for activities that I can maintain comfortably while still providing developmentally appropriate activities for my students. I am really pleased with my student growth this year and believe it is in part due to providing them with the opportunity to interact and play in their learning environment.

ADMINISTRATOR: Well, thank you for your efforts. It is interesting to see the way you have woven the instructional standards into your classroom and I could not help but notice the busyness and excitement about learning while visiting. I look forward to seeing continued progress and growth in your classroom.

TEACHER: Thank you!

It important that stakeholders understand an early childhood classroom rooted in rich play opportunities for children can be busy and noisy. The classrooms can even be messy. But we know life is noisy. And life can even be messy. We are, however, trying to help prepare our children for life. Therefore, it is imperative that stakeholders understand the critical skills young children learn and practice through play will continue to help shape their academic success throughout their lifetime. The goal is to help foster a life-long love of learning. Dr. Peter Gray, a research professor at Boston College, pointed out in his research, "Children's freedom to play and explore on their own, independent of direct adult guidance and direction, has declined greatly in recent decades. Free play and exploration are, historically, the means by which children learn to solve their own problems, control their own lives, develop their own interests, and become competent in pursuit of their own interests" (Gray, P. 2018, August 1).

Early childhood educators are conducting this research every day in their classrooms. They are living and breathing the very work cited above. They are even cheering on the numerous pediatricians prescribing play to children and their families. When a family comes to a pediatrician's office or a speech therapist with concerns about their child's communication skills, one of the first interventions to help support the development of language, literacy, and vocabulary skills can be found and supported through conversations held during play. In the case of potential concerns, providing structured play to encourage and require use of language could be in order. Even play to observe areas of strength and weakness could be in order. Either way, our early childhood educators need to continue to be on the team of researchers and pediatricians who help support play and the overall healthy development of young children. In the words of Friedrick Froebel, the German educator who was founder of the Kindergarten and has been considered one of the most influential educational reformers of the 19th century: "Play is the highest expression of human development in childhood; for it alone is the free expression of what is in a child's soul" (Froebel Web, 2018).

Celebrating Play

When you ask a child what they are doing, they often respond "Just playing." What they do not necessarily realize is that while they might be "just playing" they are indeed learning in their play. They are also learning how to learn. This self-awareness is essential to their later development as a learner. We need to remember to not underestimate the value of play. Our children learn and develop cognitive skills, physical abilities, vocabulary, social skills, literacy skills, and even foster personal health by helping to reduce stress. All of these outcomes can be accomplished through incorporating play in the curriculum.

Play can be simple and complex. However, putting it simply, play is joyful. Play can provide an outlet not only for children but also for adults. Be sure to make time for play. Build on your own experiences with play and remember our children are not built to sit still or keep their hands to themselves. They need to be moving, exploring and engaging with the world around them, using all of their senses. In the words of Alan Watts, *"This is the real secret of life—to be completely engaged with what you are doing in the here and now. And instead of calling it work, realize it is play"* (Alan Watts, 2018).

References

Froebel Web. (2018). Froebel quotes. Retrieved from: http://www.froebelweb.org/web7001.html. Accessed on March 13, 2019.

Gray, P. (2018, August 1). Kids need play and recess. Their mental health may depend on it. [web log comment]. Retrieved from: http://blogs.edweek.org/edweek/finding_common_ground/2018/08/the_existential_mental_health_crisis_in_k-12_education_the_need_for_play_and_recess.html?cmp=eml-enl-eu-news2&M=58566331&U=993465

Hassinger-Das, B., Hirsh-Pasek, K., & Michnick Golinkoff, R. (May 2017). The case of brain science and guided play: A developing story. *Young Children, 72.* Retrieved from: https://www.naeyc.org/resources/pubs/yc/may2017

Jones, E., & Reynolds, G. (1992). *The Plays the Thing . . . Teacher's Roles in Children's Play.* New York: Columbia Press.

Next Generation Science Standards. (2018). Next generation standards for science: Kindergarten introduction. Retrieved from: http://www.nextgenscience.org/

Ohanian, S. (2002). *What Happened to Recess and Why are Our Children Struggling in Kindergarten?* New York: McGraw Hill.

Paley, V.G. (2004). *A Child's Work: The Importance of Fantasy Play.* Chicago, IL: The University of Chicago Press.

Rogers, Fred quoted by Moore, Heidi (2014). Why play is the work of childhood. *Blog Early Childhood Education Research and Studies Social-Emotional Learning.* Latrobe, PA: Fred Rogers Center. Retrieved from: http://www.fredrogerscenter.org/2014/09/why-play-is-the-work-of-childhood/. Accessed on March 13, 2019.

Watts, A. (2018). This Is the Real Secret Of Life – to Be Completely Engaged with Everything You Are Doing in the Here and Now: ALAN WATTS Quotes Designer Notebook Published online at Amazon by Perfect Papers (a collection of quotes by Alan Watts).

Wolfgang, C.H., & Wolfgang, M.E. (1992). *School for Young Children: Developmentally Appropriate Practice.* Needham Heights, MA: Allyn and Bacon.

10 Technology for Teachers and Learners

Sarah Bright

Figure 10.1 Teachers play an important role in introducing children to technology and ensuring that the experiences are interactive, engaging, and language-rich.

Technology is one of the most ubiquitous features of the early education classroom, but it is also one of its most contentious. The term "technology" has an enormous range of applications that reflect its wide-ranging uses and roles. A 2017 report by the Early Childhood STEM Working Group defined technology broadly, as "anything human-made that is used to solve a problem or fulfill a desire ... an object, a system, or a process that results in the modification of the natural world to meet human needs and wants" (p. 8). This expansive definition includes everything from a pencil to a robot. Even after narrowing the term within the school setting, technology incorporates tools and applications as diverse as microscopes, assessment software, and 3D printers.

In speaking with early childhood educators about their views on technology, I found a wide variety of understandings, assumptions, and opinions on the appropriate place for tech in their classrooms. Most teachers I spoke with celebrated its usefulness and efficiency while noting some areas of concern or shortcomings. One teacher argued that technology makes students lazy and impatient, like the pampered medieval kings and queens who had everything done for them. A friend and colleague who has taught outside of the mainstream classroom—in special needs, gifted, and dual-language classes—had a more complicated and nuanced view of technology's place in schools. She appreciated its uses and benefits while recognizing its limitations for her students. Her understanding and concerns clearly portrayed the complexity of technology's role in early education settings (Figure 10.1).

Technology is found in every area of the education process, and it's not going away any time soon. There is at least one computer for every five students in U.S. public schools, which spend more than $3 billion per year on digital content alone (Herold, 2016). Technology is used to assess students in both informal and high-stakes settings, to supplement and even replace in-person instruction, to deliver content, to provide access to research methods and materials, and to allow students to create, organize, and share their work.

The topic of how technology should be appropriately and effectively used is endlessly debated and seldom agreed upon. Supporters of technology argue that it can successfully benchmark, teach, scaffold, build connections, and empower educators to access and share content (Siegle, Amspaugh, & Mitchell, 2017, pp. 356-7; Wang, 2010, p. 383). It can increase hand-eye coordination, promote superior language skills, and assist in emotional development by enabling children to master skills and self-expression (Bers, 2006, p. 203; Paciga & Donohue, 2017, p. 20). Technology can enable differentiation by allowing teachers to support multiple levels and types of learners without needing to create a multitude of lessons and curricular materials. It can support problem-solving skills, simplify complex tasks, facilitate experimentation, and compare theories and experiences with others (Wang, p. 388). Technology can, in short, simplify teachers' jobs and expand the reach of their classrooms.

Detractors of technology cite a multitude of negative impacts, including sleep interruption, behavioral issues, focus and attention problems, decreased academic performance, impaired socialization and language development, and an increase in childhood obesity (Brody, 2015; Roman, 2015). They argue that technology displaces time spent with developmentally appropriate materials, outdoor time, and physical activity, and has a negative impact on imaginative play (Donohue, 2015, pp. 25–26). Critics of technology view it as a distraction and a deterrent from the most important aspects of learning.

What does the academic and medical research say on the topic? The Fred Rogers Center for Early Learning and Children's Media at Saint Vincent College and the National Association for the Education of Young Children (NAEYC) created a joint position statement in 2012 that examined the effective uses of technology and interactive media in early childhood programs, identifying the limitations and concerns surrounding it and making recommendations for its best use.

In 2017, the Fred Rogers Center and the Technology in Early Childhood Center at Erikson Institute revisited the position statement, considering the issues again and updating it (Paciga & Donohue, 2017). Both statements argued that technology and interactive media are effective, powerful, and positive educational tools when used in appropriate settings and with recommended limitations (Donohue, 2015, p. 22). The rule of thumb, the authors argue, is to look at the "child, content, and context" when using technology. They recommend that educators and caregivers consider issues such as the age, interests, and needs of the children. Is the content age-appropriate and educationally meaningful? How, where, and for how long will the technology be used? (Donohue, 2015, p. 2, from the 2012 NAEYC and Fred Rogers framework)

Several groups recommend important limitations on children's technology use. The American Academy of Pediatrics (2016) calls for no screen time for children under 18 months, only high-quality programming watched with an adult for children aged 18–24 months, and one hour per day of high-quality programming, with co-viewing, for children aged two to five (Paciga & Donohue, 2017, p. 19). They urge that screen time used with preschool children should focus on adult-child relationships through such uses as "viewing digital photos, participating in Skype interactions with loved ones, co-viewing e-books, and engaging with some interactive apps" (Fred Rogers Center & NAYEC, 2012, p. 5). Several studies cite the negative impacts of passive media experiences rather than active engagement and interactions (U.S. Department of Education and U.S. Department of Health and Human Services, 2016, p. 10). Donohue and Schomburg (2017) urge educators to find a balance in using technology with non-technical activities, cautioning that technology should not replace play in the outdoor or imaginative worlds, and it should not displace "creativity, curiosity and wonder, solitary and shared experiences" (p. 76). They argue that families should limit screen time and technology use during meals and family times and for an hour before bedtime.

Educators and administrators play a vital role in implementing guidelines and limits on technology use in the school setting. The 2012 joint position statement of the NAEYC and the Fred Rogers Center called on educators to provide guidance to the field: "Educators must be knowledgeable and prepared to make informed decisions about how and when to appropriately select, use, integrate, and evaluate technology media to meet the cognitive, social, emotional, physical, and linguistic needs of young children" (pp. 10–11). Educators also play an important role in helping parents make decisions on how to effectively use technology tools in the home (Chaudron, Di Gioia, & Gemo, 2018, p. 14). Preservice teacher education and professional development are vital in helping educators make informed decisions on how to appropriately select and integrate technology tools for in the early childhood classroom (Blackwell, Lauricella, Wartella, Robb, & Schomburg, 2013, p. 318; Donohue & Schomburg, 2017, p. 77).

Despite the essential role they play as gatekeepers for the world of technology, educators' attitudes towards technology are mixed, and their experience with it is inconsistent, especially in the early childhood education setting (Gray, Thomas, & Lewis, 2010). Many teachers do not have sufficient training and access to technology to feel fully qualified and comfortable with its use, while others have concerns and objections that result in them using it in only limited circumstances (Blackwell, Lauricella, & Wartella, 2014, p. 83). As a result, technology use in the early-education classroom is often limited in its scope and application; it is often used as a babysitter, a time-filler, or an alternate curriculum for students who do not fit into the main group.

As an educator, researcher, student, and mother I think about technology's uses from several different perspectives and share both the enthusiasm and concern for it that I heard from the educators I spoke with. Using my research, interviews with and observations of early childhood educators, and my own experiences, I've compiled a list of key themes regarding technology in early childhood classrooms. This list is designed to demystify technology and foster digital resilience in the face of inconsistent and often conflicting research and opinions.

Before getting to the list, I want to give a brief explanation of my definition of "technology" for the purposes of this chapter. I will borrow from the definition for interactive media from the 2012 NAEYC and Fred Rogers Center position statement to say that the technology I'll focus on includes such materials as software programs, apps, broadcast and streaming media, e-books, the Internet, and other forms of digital content designed for interactive engagement (p. 1). The term "digital literacy" refers to the use of technology to organize, understand, evaluate, or create information, and to facilitate communication with others through digital methods and tools (Paciga, Lisy, & Teale, 2013, p. 88). I will not focus on three areas of educational technology that are important tools but beyond the scope of the current discussion: learning management systems that allow educators to manage, publish, or share assignments and grades; lesson planning tools; and assessment software.

My first three themes concentrate on the place and role of technology within the educational world, examining how and where it fits within early education curricula and pedagogy.

Technology is an Inescapable Part of Education, and Educators Play a Vital Role in Helping Students Master It

Our educational system requires that students have a basic digital literacy from an early age. Beginning in kindergarten, the Common Core standards for English Language Arts requires that children "explore a variety of digital tools to produce and publish writing" (Council of Chief State Schools Offices & National Governors Association, 2010). With the implementation of the Common Core, standardized assessments are now introduced as early as kindergarten, with high-stakes testing commonly starting in 3rd grade (Barnum, 2017; Strauss, 2015). Most assessments require students to have computer fluency, including mouse skills and knowledge of how to navigate and respond to testing software, all under the stress of high-stakes pressure.

Beyond assessments, a basic fluency in technology is required in schools as a skill set so students can access the content and tools of the classroom, just as children need to learn how to use a pen or pencil for writing. A wide range of content and activities are presented in digital formats, from fiction and non-fiction books to math exercises or Social Studies reenactments and simulations, to name just a few. Reflecting the need for students to successfully master and utilize those, the International Society for Technology in Education (ISTE) recommends basic skills in technology operations and concepts by age five (NAYEC and Fred Rogers, p. 4). ISTE has seven standards for students that are designed to prepare them to "thrive in a constantly evolving technological landscape" by becoming empowered learners, digital citizens, knowledge constructors, innovative designers, computational thinkers, creative communicators, and global collaborators (ISTE, n.d.). Teachers and parents play a vital role in sharing technology tools with young children and modeling how to use the technology.

Technology Cannot Wholly Replace Print Materials or Manipulatives, but It Usefully Complements and Supplements Them

While there are digital equivalents of writing with pencils on paper or flipping through a print book, non-technical materials and manipulatives remain important in early education. Research is mixed on the superiority and effectiveness of digital writing tools compared with pens and pencils for students who are learning to write (Wollscheid, Sjaastad, & Tømte, 2015, p. 30). Studies have shown that having children learn manual writing on paper increases their letter recognition performance and development of fine motor skills (Stevenson & Just, 2014, p. 52), but there is also a positive link between children's writing with tablets and print awareness, print knowledge, and sound knowledge (Neumann, 2016, p. 62).

Technology can offer solutions that significantly complement and expand non-digital options. One example is interactive e-books, which offer unique ways to interact with a book, allowing students to revise or expand the story and manipulate the characters in ways that aren't possible with a print text. These enhancements can engage children who haven't been hooked by print texts (Paciga, 2015, p. 476), helping to build a love of reading at the vital age in the literacy process (Matteson, 2016). Digital books also offer helpful extra features, such as read-aloud, embedded dictionaries, and tools such as highlighters and annotation abilities (Brann, Gray, & Zorfass, 2014), as well as quizzes and activities to help children review the content.

The Joan Ganz Cooney Center at Sesame Workshop completed a study in which parents read a print book and an e-book with their three- to six-year-old children, then looked at the experiences of both for the two children. The study found that print books were more beneficial for developing literacy through co-reading, but e-books were more beneficial for engaging children and prompting physical interaction. The Cooney Center, as well as other research studies, cautioned that e-books' multimedia features should focus on enhancing the experiences of reading, comprehension, and engagement with the themes of the text, rather than just acting as distractions for the children (Chiong, Ree, & Takeuchi, 2012, p. 1; U.S. Department of Education, 2016, p. 9; American Academy of Pediatrics, 2016). Available through publishers, Amazon, iTunes, Android, and other platforms, interactive ebooks are offered for beloved classics from the Dr. Seuss collection to *The Very Hungry Caterpillar*, as well as for a range of beautifully designed and engaging new titles.

Instructional Technology Tools Can Help Educators Modify and Adapt Curricula and Content for Students With Diverse Educational Experiences and Backgrounds

Between 25 and 30% of preschool-age children in the United States have a parent who speaks a language other than English (Nemeth, p. 115). These dual language learners (DLLs) have unique needs in the classroom, where teachers strive to support them in their home language while also teaching them English. Technology offers flexibility by allowing teachers to differentiate curricula and content in order to make it more suited for students with a variety of language skills, experiences, and educational backgrounds. Teachers can adjust the pacing, difficulty level, and even the language of instruction of websites and apps, adding new languages to classroom labels, translating key words in books and games, and providing models for writing (NAEYC and Fred, 2012, p. 9). Visual representations, such as pictures taken on a digital camera or customizable flashcards, allow students to use pictures to show teachers what they need (Nemeth, p. 122). Apps such as Cram or StudyBlue for flashcards, or Quizlet, which also allows students and teachers to create their own quizzes, offer a range of functionality for creating customized flashcards.

Technology gives teachers opportunities to adjust instruction and bring in supplementary material to create a culturally responsive environment. Using characters that are familiar and relevant to the children's lives in their appearance, life experiences, and interactions helps children from other cultures feel accepted, appreciated, and understood (Piazza, Rao & Protacio, 2015, p. 3; Robb & Lauricella, 2015, p. 76). Providing children with an opportunity to see, hear, and read about a diversity of characters and examples in their instructional content helps children to broaden exposure to other cultures, beliefs, and experiences, developing greater sociocultural consciousness (Bennett et al., 2015, p. 245). The Association for Supervision and Curriculum Development and NAEYC offer resources on building a culturally responsive classroom, with sections on digital enhancements.

The next three themes focus on recommended restrictions and limitations of technology, including issues of access, involvement of adults with children, and passive versus active engagement with the instructional technology.

It is Vital to Consider the Availability and Accessibility of Instructional Technology Tools for Educators and Students

A key consideration in using technology in the classroom is ensuring that the technology is accessible to everyone involved. Educators should be aware of differences in students' ability to access instructional technology and ensure that they are closing the achievement gap and digital divide, rather than widening them (Donohue, 2015, pp. 25–26). While about 90% of U.S. households have a mobile device such as a tablet or smartphone (Pew Research, 2017), about 80% of households have a desktop or laptop computer, and 68% of households contain at least one tablet (Olmstead, 2017). And although about two-thirds of all homes in the United States have broadband Internet access, only about 45% of homes where the annual household income is less than $30,000 have Internet access (Pew Research Center, 2018). Preschoolers from families of lower socioeconomic status generally have a narrower range of experiences with oral language, vocabulary, and less content knowledge (Paciga, Lisy, & Teale, 2013, p. 88). These children come into the early elementary classroom with less technical experience and training than their more-affluent peers and need additional support and scaffolding when working with technology tools. Schools can expand students' access to technology by making instructional technology tools such as digital cameras, audio and video recorders, printers, and software available in the classroom and for borrowing (NAYEC and Fred Rogers, p. 4).

In addition to physical access to the technology, educators should ensure that students are able to use their features and functionality. Robb and Lauricella (2015) urge teachers to be aware of young children's gross motor skills and their limitations when it comes to using technology (p. 71). The Individuals with Disabilities Education Act (IDEA), Title II of the Americans with Disabilities Act of 1990, and Section 504 of the Rehabilitation Act of 1973 address the obligations of public and charter schools to meet the needs of students with disabilities by providing equal access to students with and without disabilities (U.S. Department of Justice and U.S Department of Education, n.d.). Accessibility features include speech-to-text components, adjustable fonts and sizes, and voice controls and inputs (Crossland, Gray, Reynolds, Wellington, & Zhou, 2016, p. 10). Teachers' roles in ensuring that the technology solutions used in classrooms meet these legal require-ments is of paramount importance.

Young Children Should Have Adults' Help and Involvement While Using Technology

Within the early education setting it is especially important for children to use instructional technology with a teacher or caregiver who helps make the tools interactive, engaging, and language-rich (Zero to Three, n.d.). Adults should co-view media with the children and play an active role, engaging children in conversations about what they're seeing—asking about details of the program and having them predict the upcoming action (Robb & Lauricella, 2015, p. 77). Children should be encouraged to be physically involved where possible—having them get up and act out a scene, dance to the music, or interact through touch-screen options, if available. If the media is a game, the adults should play with the child and discuss the rules, action, and outcomes. Finally, the supervising adults should tie the media back to real-world situations and questions, and ask the children to describe or retell the story or share their experiences using the technology (Lerner, 2016; Robb & Lauricella, 2015, p. 77).

Research shows that teacher and parent or caregiver involvement with technology brings many benefits. When adults treat media viewing as an educational experience rather than just entertainment, children are more likely to learn from it, remembering plot details and story content. Further, research has found that children learn letters and numbers from media better when caregivers watch the media with the children and ask them to describe what they see than if the teachers or caregivers simply describe it themselves to the children (Robb & Lauricella, 2015, p. 77). Adult supervision can also ensure that the setting, content, and duration of the technology use is appropriate to the child's interests and age.

Technology Should Be Used for Creation, Not Just Consumption

Creation empowers students to find and share their voice while building confidence and communication skills. To foster creative productivity, teachers should select and encourage technology experiences that allow children to create and produce, rather than passively consume (Donohue and Schomburg, 2017, p. 76). This active—rather than passive—engagement with technology is a key recommendation for technology use, as noted earlier. Making art, writing, drawing, and coding are just a few examples of creation that is possible through technology tools.

One area that is ideal for creation with technology in early grades is robotics and precoding, which offer a great range of engaging, hands-on activities that build problem-solving, critical thinking, communication, and planning and sequencing skills (Highfield, 2015, p. 151; McLennan, 2017, p. 19). Such interactive toys as Blue-Bot, Beebot, Cubetto, KIBO, and Code-A-Pillar are child-friendly robots designed to introduce children aged three to six to coding and sequencing, combining the hands-on creative construction of such manipulatives as Legos with the coding, sequencing, and problem-solving of the technology solutions. The Technology in Early Childhood Center at Erikson Institute offers an information sheet on "tangible technology tools," which includes questions that educators and parents should consider in selecting the tools and considering how and if the tools fit with the children's developmental needs. The Center also offers tips on how teachers can integrate technology into their lesson plans (Erikson Institute, 2017).

The last three themes focus on specific uses of technology that benefit students and educators by expanding the opportunities and resources of the classroom.

Technology Expands Access to Classroom Resources, Offering Low-Cost Solutions

Tightening school budgets limit early childhood centers' resources for content and activities outside of the core academic focuses. Technological innovations can provide broader academic experiences as well as adventures outside of the classroom at no additional cost beyond their technology set-up. These include virtual field trips, expanded access to literacy and reading resources, and demonstrations and experiments that facilitate guided exploration and discussion and allow students to gain content knowledge (Paciga, Lisy, & Teale, 2013, p. 88). Instructional technology can also broaden a school's access to expert advice and research by offering opportunities for children to communicate with world experts through Skype, email, Twitter, or other social media platforms.

As noted earlier, in classrooms with a diversity of languages, technology solutions offer opportunities for translation, audio pronunciations, and access to translators (NAEYC & Fred Rogers Center, 2012, p. 9). This flexibility facilitates teachers' abilities to tailor curricula and content to each child's needs, take advantage of teachable moments, and make connections (Nemeth, 2015, p. 118).

One area of tight budgets that technology tools can beautifully and inexpensively supplement is art. Google Arts and Culture gives access to a huge range of artworks, collections, and artists for free. Students can search or browse through collections of over a thousand museums throughout the world, such as the Metropolitan Museum of Art in New York or the Louvre Museum in Paris. Students can also use online resources to create art, through such applications and websites as PicCollage, which offers graphics and downloadable art pieces along with suggestions for how educators can use them. Through social media platforms, teachers can then publish and share these pieces within the classroom, school, or with families.

Technology is a Valuable Means of Creating Community Among Students and Educators

Technology can be used in the classroom to foster a sense of community among the children, between the teachers and the children's families, and among educators. As I'll discuss in my last theme, technology can build a sense of community and increased engagement between the educators and children's parents or caregivers by helping teachers welcome parents and families into the classroom family and allowing them to easily ask questions, seek advice, and share information about their child (NAEYC & Fred Rogers Center, 2012, p. 7). Within the classroom, technology can help build a community of students by helping teachers create representations of the class through the students' images or words, such as through project boards to which each child contributes a piece, adding his or her voice. By including all of the children's images and viewpoints, educators put forward a powerful image of the class as a "school family," with common threads that foster connections and give children a strong sense of belonging (Cotto, 2015, p. 219–222). Apps such as Kahoot or instant polling sites and apps allow teachers to create polls and quizzes that groups of students can compete in or share their opinions on, also fostering a sense of community.

Teachers can find a community of their own that will provide advice, assistance, and support through many online tools such as Twitter and Pinterest, or websites with shared lesson plans and curricular materials like Teachers Pay Teachers (www.teacherspayteachers.com). Through social media networks, teachers are able to make connections with other teachers who have similar circumstances and interests, finding valuable resources ranging from lesson plans to manipulatives to a sympathetic ear. Furthermore, teachers are able to access experts in their field who may give advice, encouragement, or access to additional resources to them or to their class (Armstrong, 2015, pp. 255–256).

Technology Facilitates Communication Among Students, Educators, and Families

Within the classroom, publishing tools give students the ability to create and share their voice. Apps such as BookCreator allow children to use text, images, audio, and video to create their own stories and books, which teachers can share within the classroom and with families through digital platforms. Digital cameras used within the classroom and in children's homes and neighborhoods help children describe and share details of their lives, finding similarities in shared experiences.

Outside of the classroom, technology solutions help students meet new friends and learn about people and cultures throughout the world. Examples include virtual pen pal programs in which children can learn about other students' daily life and culture, language, and connections while also supporting literacy and fostering cultural understandings (Barksdale, Watson, & Park, 2007, p. 58). In Mystery Skype, groups of students in different locations speak via Skype and guess each other's location by asking a series of questions. The contest sharpens critical thinking processes, fosters teamwork skills, and broadens students' exposure to different classes and students (Ripp, 2013, p. 30).

Technology tools can also help parents become connected to their children's teachers and classrooms, an important part of fostering the students' success (Puerling & Fowler, 2015, p. 186). Teachers can establish a connection even before the first day of school by reaching out to ask about the communication preferences, language, culture, interests, and assets of the students' families. For dual language students, Nemeth and Donohue (2015) recommend that teachers begin with a survey that has been translated into the family's native language (p. 119). Teachers can create a video or ebook to introduce themselves, the classroom, and staff, and share the class schedule electronically (Kaldor, 2015, p. 208), introducing the families and children to their classroom and staff and setting up expectations for daily routines and experiences. When using digital communication, shorter messages that are easier to understand and predominantly positive and informative, rather than overly negative or a list of rules and regulations, are preferable (Nemeth & Donohue, 2015, p. 122; Kaldor, 2015, p. 214).

Conclusion

Technology infuses every aspect of today's educational spaces, beginning with the youngest students. Despite the myriad concerns and challenges technology brings, when used with thoughtful consideration and oversight it is a valuable and exciting addition to the classroom. It provides new and broader learning opportunities, expands communication, and brings amazing adventures and experiences to the children, their families, and the educators.

The educators I spoke with felt most comfortable with the technology in their classroom when they had training, choices, and experiences to use with them. Bringing an informed view of their classroom's needs to the decisions on how, when, and where to implement technology solutions is an enormous first step. The sixth NAEYC Standard for Initial and Advanced Early Childhood Professional Preparation Programs addresses the need for teachers to be able to access, explore, and share technology and digital resources "in a safe environment," learning about technology by using technology (Donohue & Schomburg, 2015, p. 48). With that in mind, I will close with one last piece of advice: take time to play and discover technology, just as you encourage your children to. Discover the possibilities and opportunities that technology solutions offer to you, your children, and your classes' families. Share your thoughts, opinions, and questions with the broad community available to you. Find joy in creating and discovering with the wide opportunities that technology offers.

References

American Academy of Pediatrics, Council on Communications and Media. (2016). *Media and Young Minds*. Retrieved from: pediatrics.aappublications.org/content/pediatrics/early/2016/10/19/peds.2016-2591.full.pdf

Armstrong, A. (2015). Connected educator – Connected learner: The evolving roles of teachers in the 21st century and beyond. In C. Donohue (Ed.), *Technology and Digital Media in the Early Years: Tools for Teaching and Learning* (pp. 250–260). New York and Washington, DC: Routledge and the National Association for the Education of Young Children.

Barksdale, M.A., Watson, C., & Park, E.S. (2007). Pen pal letter exchanges: Taking first steps toward developing cultural understandings. *TRTR The Reading Teacher, 61*(1), 58–68.

Barnum, M. (2017, July 14). High-stakes testing may push struggling teachers to younger grades, hurting students. Retrieved 08/05/18 from: https://www.chalkbeat.org/posts/

us/2017/07/14/high-stakes-testing-may-push-struggling-teachers-to-younger-grades-hurting-students/

Bennett, S.V., Gunn, A.A., Gayle-Evans, G., Barrera, E.S., & Leung, C.B. (2018). Culturally responsive literacy practices in an early childhood community. *Early Childhood Education Journal, 46*(2), 241–248.

Bers, M.A. (2006). The role of new technologies to foster positive youth development. *Applied Developmental Science, 10*(4), 200–219.

Blackwell, C.K., Lauricella, A.R., & Wartella, E. (2014). Factors influencing digital technology use in early childhood education. *Computers & Education, 77*, 82–90.

Blackwell, C.K., Lauricella, A.R., Wartella, E., Robb, M., & Schomburg, R. (2013). Adoption and use of technology in early education: The interplay of extrinsic barriers and teacher attitudes. *Computers & Education, 69*, 310–319.

Brann, A., Gray, T., & Zorfass, J. (2014, April 29). Using multimedia to support reading instruction. Reading Rockets. Retrieved from: http://www.readingrockets.org/article/using-multimedia-support-reading-instruction

Brody, J.E. (2015, July 7). Screen addiction is taking a toll on children. *The New York Times*, p. D7.

Chaudron, S., Di Gioia, R., & Gemo, M. (2018). *Young Children (0–8) and Digital Technology: A Qualitative Study Across Europe.* Joint Research Centre, The European Commission.

Chiong, C., Ree, J., & Takeuchi, L. (2012, May 15). QuickReport: Print Books vs. E-books. The Joan Ganz Cooney Center at Sesame Workshop. Retrieved 07/16/18 from: http://joanganzcooneycenter.org/publication/quickreport-print-books-vs-e-books/

Cotto, L.M. (2015). Technology as a tool to strengthen the community. In C. Donohue (Ed.), *Technology and Digital Media in the Early Years: Tools for Teaching and Learning* (pp. 218–233). New York and Washington, DC: Routledge and the National Association for the Education of Young Children.

Council of Chief State School Offices & National Governors Association. (2010). Beginning in kindergarten, the Common Core standards for English Language Arts requires that children "explore a variety of digital tools to produce and publish writing (Common Core Standards, 2010). Washington, DC. Retrieved from: http://www.corestandards.org/ELA-Literacy/RL/2/.

Crossland, A., Gray, T., Reynolds, J., Wellington, D., & Zhou, A. (2016). *Digital Accessibility Toolkit: What Education Leaders Need to Know.* American Institutes for Research & Center of Technology and Disability.

Donohue, C. (2015). Technology and digital media as tools for teaching and learning in the digital age. In C. Donohue (Ed.), *Technology and Digital Media in the Early Years: Tools for Teaching and Learning* (pp. 21–35). New York and Washington, DC: Routledge and the National Association for the Education of Young Children.

Donohue, C., & Schomburg, R. (2017). Technology and interactive media in early childhood programs: What we've learned from five years of research, policy, and practice. *Young Children, 72*–78.

Early Childhood STEM Working Group. (2017). *Early STEM Matters: Providing High-Quality STEM Experiences for All Young Learners.* Retrieved from: http://ecstem.uchicago.edu

Gray, L., Thomas, M., & Lewis, L. (2010). Teachers' use of educational technology in US public schools: 2009 (NCES 2010-040). Washington, DC: National Center for Education Statistics, Institute for Education Sciences, U.S. Department of Education.

Herold, B. (2016, 5 February). Technology in education: An overview. Education Week. Retrieved from: https://www.edweek.org/ew/issues/technology-in-education/index.html

Highfield, K. (2015). Stepping into STEM with Young Children: Simple robotics and programming as catalysts for early learning. In C. Donohue (Ed.), *Technology and Digital Media in the Early Years: Tools for Teaching and Learning* (pp. 150–161). New York and Washington, DC: Routledge and the National Association for the Education of Young Children.

Internet/Broadband Fact Sheet. (2018, February 5). Pew Research Center. Retrieved 08/05/18 from: http://www.pewinternet.org/fact-sheet/internet-broadband/

International Society for Technology in Education. ISTE. Standards For Students. (n.d.). Retrieved 07/16/18 from: https://www.iste.org/standards/for-students

Kaldor, T. (2015). Technology as a tool to strengthen the home-school connection. In C. Donohue (Ed.), *Technology and Digital Media in the Early Years: Tools for Teaching and Learning* (pp. 201–217). New York and Washington, DC: Routledge and the National Association for the Education of Young Children.

Lerner, C. (2016, March 7). Tips for using screen media with young children. Zero to Three. Retrieved 08/05/18 from: https://www.zerotothree.org/resources/386-tips-for-using-screen-media-with-young-children

Matteson, A. (2016, July 5). When an Ebook is the best book. School Library Journal. Retrieved from: http://www.slj.com/?detailStory=when-an-ebook-is-the-best-book

McLennan, D.P. (2017). Creating coding stories and games. *Teaching Young Children, 10*(3), 18–21.

NAEYC & Fred Rogers Center for Early Learning and Children's Media. (2012). *A Framework for Quality in Digital Media for Young Children: Considerations for Parents, Educators, and Media Creators.* Retrieved from: http://cmhd.northwestern.edu/wp-content/uploads/2015/10/Framework_Statement_2-April_2012-Full_Doc-Exec_Summary-1.pdf

Nemeth, K.N., & Donohue, C. (2015). Technology to support dual language learners. In C. Donohue (Ed.), *Technology and Digital Media in the Early Years: Tools for Teaching and Learning* (pp. 115–128). New York and Washington, DC: Routledge and the National Association for the Education of Young Children.

Neumann, M.M. (2016). Young children's use of touch screen tablets for writing and reading at home: Relationships with emergent literacy. *CAE Computers & Education, 97*, 61–68.

Olmstead, K. (2017, May 25). A third of Americans live in a household with three or more smartphones. Pew Research Center. Retrieved 08/05/18 from: http://www.pewresearch.org/fact-tank/2017/05/25/a-third-of-americans-live-in-a-household-with-three-or-more-smartphones/

Paciga, K.A. (2015). Their teacher can't be an app: Preschoolers' listening comprehension of digital storybooks. *Journal of Early Childhood Literacy, 15*(4), 473–509.

Paciga, K.A., & Donohue, C. (2017). *Technology and Interactive Media for Young Children: A Whole Child Approach Connecting the Vision of Fred Rogers with Research and Practice.* Latrobe, PA: Fred Rogers Center for Early Learning and Children's Media at Saint Vincent College.

Paciga, K.A., Lisy, J.G., & Teale, W.H. (2013). Better start before kindergarten: Computer technology, interactive media and the education of preschoolers. *Asia-Pacific Journal of Research in Early Childhood Education, 7*(2), 85–104.

Pew Research Center. (2017, May 25). A third of Americans live in a household with three or more smartphones. Retrieved 06/0/18 from: http://www.pewresearch.org/fact-tank/2017/05/25/a-third-of-americans-live-in-a-household-with-three-or-more-smartphones/

Piazza, S., Rao, S., & Protacio, M.S. (2015). Converging recommendations for culturally responsive literacy practices: Students with learning disabilities, English language learners, and socioculturally diverse learners. *International Journal of Multicultural Education, 17*(3), 1–20.

Puerling, B., & Fowler, A. (2015). Technology tools for teachers and teaching: Innovative practices and emerging technologies. In C. Donohue (Ed.), *Technology and Digital Media in the Early Years* (pp. 183–198). New York and Washington, DC: Routledge and the National Association for the Education of Young Children.

Ripp, P. (2013). Where in the world are they? Students find out with Mystery Skype. *Learning and Leading With Technology, 40*(5), 30–31.

Robb, M.B., & Lauricella, A.R. (2015). Connecting child development and technology: What we know and what it means. In C. Donohue (Ed.), *Technology and Digital Media in the Early Years: Tools for Teaching and Learning* (pp. 70–85). New York and Washington, DC: Routledge and the National Association for the Education of Young Children.

Roman, S. (2015, July 8). Technology's harmful effects on children. Publicsource. Retrieved from: https://www.publicsource.org/technologys-harmful-effects-on-children/

Screen Sense: Setting the Record Straight. (n.d.). Zero to Three. Retrieved 07/04/18 from: https://www.zerotothree.org/resources/series/screen-sense-setting-the-record-straight

Siegle, D., Amspaugh, C.M., & Mitchell, M.S. (n.d.). Learning from and learning with technology. In J. VanTassel-Baska & C.A. Little (Eds.), Content-Based Curriculum for High-Ability Learners (3rd ed., pp. 437–460). Waco, TX: Prufrock Press.

Stevenson, N.C., & Just, C. (2014). In early education, why teach handwriting before keyboarding? *Early Childhood Education Journal, 42*(1), 49–56.

Strauss, V. (2015). Confirmed: Standardized testing has taken over our schools. But who's to blame? Retrieved 08/05/18 from: https://www.washingtonpost.com/news/answer-sheet/wp/2015/10/24/confirmed-standardized-testing-has-taken-over-our-schools-but-whos-to-blame/

Tangible Tech Collection: Early Childhood Tangible Tech and Robotics Info Sheets. (2017, October 5). Erikson Institute Technology in Early Childhood Center. Retrieved 08/10/18 from: http://teccenter.erikson.edu/publications/infosheets/

US Department of Education and Department of Health and Human Services. (2016). *Early Learning and Educational Technology Policy Brief*. Retrieved from: https://tech.ed.gov/files/2016/10/Early-Learning-Tech-Policy-Brief.pdf

U.S. Department of Justice & U.S. Department of Education. (n.d.). *Questions and Answers: ADA.gov*. Retrieved from: https://www.ada.gov/doe_doj_eff_comm/doe_doj_eff_comm_faqs.htm

Wang, F., McGuire, P., Kinzie, M.B., & Pan, E. (2010). Applying technology to inquiry-based learning in early childhood education. *Early Childhood Education Journal, 37*, 381–389.

Wollscheid, S., Sjaastad, J., Tømte, C., & Løver, N. (2016). The effect of pen and paper or tablet computer on early writing – A pilot study. *Computers & Education, 98*, 70–80.

11 Mirrors, Windows, and Springboards

Choosing and Using Quality Literature with the Young Children We Know

Marie Ann Donovan

Figure 11.1 Finding yourself in books when young pays dividends.

Children's Literature in the 21st Century

Early childhood professionals devote considerable time and talent to insuring their work with young children and families is relevant. Knowing children personally enables us to tailor curriculum, instruction, and assessment in ways that insure our efforts hold meaning for all stakeholders. As we aim to individualize our practices, however, it's not unusual to face difficulty in finding the "right" book or other materials for our particular children (Figure 11.1). Despite decades of increasing diversity in our U.S. school and care center populations, we find the books and other instructional tools available don't always demographically match our children. Moreover, even though U.S. publishers generated 27,309 titles for children alone in 2016 (Barr & Harbison, 2017), not all those titles were written well or contained accurate, authentic content for the children we teach, two hallmarks of quality literature. (See the controversy over the use of invented, stereotyping dialogue in *When We Was Fierce*; Barack, 2016.) Why is this frustratingly so?

When editor and educator Nancy Larrick (1965) conducted her landmark study of children's trade books published during 1962–1964, a decade after the Supreme Court's Brown *vs.* Board of Education of Topeka decision (Sims, 1983), she found a mere 6.7% of those 5,206 books featured any African-American children and their families. Over 50 years later, when we examine the statistics for all books published during 1994–2017 (Lee & Low Publishers, 2018), we see that only 13% of all those titles were either written by, and/or written about, people of color and members of the First/Native Nations. Considering 37% of the U.S. population in 2017 classified themselves as people of color, a *publishing diversity gap,* as this phenomenon is now termed (Lee & Low Publishers, 2018), exists. Additionally, although publishers are slowly increasing their output of titles depicting or concerning LGBTQIA$^+$ children and their families, the numbers do not match the known U.S. population who identify in these ways (Dorr & Deskins, 2018). These statistics are significant. Moreover, they're troubling to us early childhood educators who strive to insure what we do is obviously purposeful and relatable to the children we teach (Brophy, 2008).

Reasons posited for this gap range from a perceived lack of market for more diverse children's books to a severe shortage of experienced authors and illustrators who self-identify as minorities (Low, 2013). More recently, the founder of the leading children's publishing company wholly devoted to books about and by people of color and other minorities, Lee & Low Books, took a different approach to studying the gap. Jason Low (2016) found an intriguing (yet sad) disparity in his 2015 survey of trade book and children's book review journal publishers' staff. Of the 42 companies whose employees responded, in terms of race, 79% identified as White; 4% as Black/African-American; 7% Asian/Native Hawaiian/Pacific Islander; 6% as Hispanic/Latino/Mexican; 3% Biracial/Multiracial; 1% Middle Eastern; and less than 1% as Native or Alaskan Native American. The statistics for employee Gender (e.g., 78% Woman/Cis-Woman), Orientation (e.g., 88% Straight/Heterosexual), and Disability (92% Non-disabled) were proportional to the percentages of authors, illustrators, and featured characters in the books published during 1994–2014 (Low, 2016), save in the case of titles whose characters or authors identified somewhere in the LGBTQIA$^+$ spectrum (Dorr & Deskins, 2018). If the people hiring the creators or reviewers of children's books do not represent the demographics of the children and families reading them, how much longer and how much harder will it be for diverse voices to actually be heard and understood (Horning, 2016; Thomas, Reese, & Horning, 2016)?

Whatever the reasons for the dearth of culturally accurate and relevant books, its reality remains a factor we must recognize and work hard to overcome. Scholar, educator, and social justice activist Rudine Sims Bishop (1990) created a now classic metaphor that sums up best why we cannot discount our need to choose and use diverse texts with young children. It also serves to organize our thinking and planning for finding and sharing these books:

> Books are sometimes windows, offering views of worlds that may be real or imagined.... These windows are also sliding glass doors, and readers have only to walk through in imagination to become part of whatever world has been created.... [A] window can also be a mirror. Literature transforms human experience and reflects it back to us [so] we can see our own lives and experiences as part of a larger human experience.
>
> (Sims Bishop, 1990, p. *ix*)

Books as Mirrors

Early childhood educators naturally seek books whose content reflects the specific learning needs, situations, and aspirations of the young children we teach. What characterizes a title as a Mirror Book depends upon how closely and accurately it depicts the everyday, lived lives of the children with whom it's shared. Do the illustrations resemble any of the children or neighborhood landmarks you know? Does the dialogue sound like your classroom conversations? Are the theme and content relatable to any of the children and adults in the community you serve? The term Mirror Book, then, is relative in large part. What might be a Mirror for one child won't necessarily serve the same purpose for another. Ideally, Mirror Books show us who we are, and how we are, in ways we haven't roundly considered previously. That is what makes them worth reading. The more adept the author and illustrator are in presenting a novel, true way of thinking about our lives somehow, the higher the quality of our Mirror Books.

A quick scan of any classroom's shelves by the casual visitor provides some insight into "who" is part of that learning community, as well as what matters to them. Those shelves also demonstrate who does the choosing: the teacher and/or the purchasing committee members for that site. Apropos the publishing industry statistics listed above, odds are most current shelves and ebook readers are filled predominantly with books about and by White people, or titles whose main characters are animals, rather than books that speak to the array of family constellations and children in that room (Horning, Lindgren, Schliesman, & Tyner, 2018). Educators facing the difficulty of finding sufficient Mirror Books often wonder whether quantity matters. They argue that with intentional teaching of non-Mirror Books, they can connect the theme or content to their students' lives. Yet research into how young children's self-concepts are shaped environmentally demonstrate how critical it is to secure and share Mirror Books instead (Brooks, 2006; Lysaker & Miller, 2013).

In their study of toddlers aged 14–24 months, Botto and Rochat (2018) endeavored to determine when young children first appear to be aware of being evaluated by others, and whether their behavior is affected by that attention. Previous research (Kagan, 1981) concluded that while embarrassment appeared to emerge during these toddler months, children this young typically did not change their behavior when they showed signs of embarrassment; nor did they attempt to secure positive evaluation after having received negative feedback from their audiences, which would indicate they might understand social norms in some way. Botto and Rochat (2018) discovered that children as young as 14 months actually can and do modify their actions when they realize their audience is expressing a negative opinion about what they are doing. Moreover, this self-consciousness leads them to change their behavior in order to elicit future positive responses from their audiences. To wit, even children this young can connect their behavior to what those who care for them prefer, and can self-initiate change in response to the simplest evaluation as well as remember it for later use with those caregivers. These findings remind us that every day is a new set of opportunities to model and affirm our embrace of the diverse lives and voices around the world. Sharing Mirror and Window Books, and discussing whose stories they are or how the content relates to our everyday thinking and doing, sends the message that books—and people—of all kinds matter. Enthusiastically endorsing the rereading of these books inspires children to reengage with them, which deepens their understanding and personal connection to the life lessons contained within (Guthrie, Wigfield, & You, 2012; Taylor, Pearson, Peterson, & Rodriguez, 2003).

Citing research into young children's development of self-awareness, Kemple, Lee, and Harris (2016) observe how during ages 3–5 years, children tend to focus primarily upon physical ("I have brown hair; she has yellow hair") and behavioral ("I can jump up the big step; he can run up the big step") characteristics of themselves and others. The younger the child, the more these self-descriptions and comparisons can only be made in the moment while examining the setting, usually with prompting or other stimulation from peers and adults. In view of this developmental phenomenon, Kemple, Lee, and Harris (2016) argue, it's necessary for adults who work with children during this age span to directly call children's attention to variations in the physical and behavioral characteristics of themselves and others. Drawing their attention in this way is no different than directing them to notice how other aspects of their environment, such as the color and shape of flowers, can be the same or different. Guiding young children to notice their own natural characteristics, and how they are similar as well as different from others, develops their awareness that the world holds a wide range of possible combinations. Children come to appreciate that *difference* is a matter of one not being the same as the other. Reading and discussing Mirror Books featuring children and adults exploring familiar-looking places and facing similar challenges organizes young children's thinking about who they are, not only in terms of what they look like but more importantly, what they can do. Connecting with a character, tracing that character's changing thoughts and feelings across the narrative arc, creates what Lysaker and Miller (2013) term social imagination, the thinking and subsequent planning about how to act in the world. Further: since book language often differs from the child's, sharing Mirror Books introduces children to academic language, the language of school. Choosing books with plots or expositions that scaffold young children's burgeoning comprehension skills in ways that enable independence in rereading fosters their reading habit.

Kemple, Lee, and Harris (2016) also note how children's self-esteem development intensifies during ages 3–5 years. In this stage, they more frequently express degrees of comfort with their physical and behavioral characteristics. Their concepts of "good" and "bad" or "pretty" and "ugly" are formed by the diet of images, objects, and commentaries they're exposed to by peers and adults in their lives. By carefully selecting Mirror Books that reflect our children in positive, myriad ways (i.e., physical, behavioral, situational), we feed their psyches the affirming images they need to counter the toxic manipulations of self-concept that inevitably seep into so many 21st-century lives.

Books as Windows

The specific titles that would serve as Window Books for your children also will vary, depending upon who is in your room and your school or center community. As professionals, we endeavor for every moment of our instructional day to be purposeful and meaningful to our students. We plan each facet whereby it scaffolds challenges for all children to move from realizing what they already know to using it to learn what they need to know next. We recognize that motivation to learn resides in the student, not the materials or the activities (Brophy, 2008). Children increase their motivation when they can see the purpose of what they're learning (Brophy, 2008; Egbert & Roe, 2014), and are shown how it connects to their everyday existence. Mirror Books, with their familiar background settings, characters, and content, build upon children's prior knowledge in ways that deepen their appreciation for their learning capacity. They enjoy reading and discussing them because they are experts about at least some of their content. When used appropriately, Mirror Books foster confidence and refine competence. Window Books do something similar—but require more of a stretch. In a broad Piagetian sense, Mirror Books, when chosen to closely match children's schemata and social-emotional development, require assimilation to comprehend and appreciate. Window Books require accommodation. The aim in planning how you'll incorporate Mirror and Window Books across the instructional week is to find that Vygotskian "sweet spot" where students can use what they learn through their Mirror Books and connected literature responses to engage in learning through their Window Books—with your expert teaching, too, of course. Figuring out which books will serve as Window Books requires knowing your learning community, as well as your book collection, beyond their surface levels. The following sections outline how to begin this essential work.

Analyzing Your Current Collection for
Mirror and Window Books

Rudine Sims Bishop's (1990) coining of the terms Mirror and Window Books was sparked by investigating the deleterious effects on African-American children's social-emotional development resulting from a lack of books about themselves and their families. Today, we apply Sims Bishop's viewing conditions distinctions to literature that also includes other racial, ethnic, linguistic, and gender-defining groups or cultures. The settings, characters, and content of the literature, and how the authors and illustrators depict them, need to explicate, entertain, and educate children in negotiating the complexities of 21st-century life. All children need quality Mirror as well as Window Books in their diets.

American classrooms' diversity demographics are growing at speeds many veteran teachers, especially, never imagined. With all that we're responsible for accomplishing each day, it's not unusual to focus by default on the individual child's school learning needs, rather than considering the range of our students' culturally influenced differences and how they interact to affect curriculum, instruction, and assessment practices. But we must shift our focus. One of the central tenets of culturally responsive teaching (Gay, 2000; Hammond, 2015; Ladson-Billings, 1994) is conducting our planning by basing it on our awareness of the learning perspectives and knowledge resources our students bring to school. If we do not understand how our students make sense of what we teach (and where we fail to connect our content and approaches to theirs), we won't succeed. We need explicit knowledge about our students' cultural diversity (Gay, 2000). We also need to critically examine our own beliefs and values that influence the choices we make in the methods and materials we use, in addition to what we teach. Looking critically and closely at your current collection of books by conducting a diversity audit, using the guidelines described below, will also help you refine other aspects of your anti-bias, anti-racist pedagogy (Derman-Sparks & Ramsey, 2006; Husband, 2012).

Before you begin examining the books in your classroom library and the ones you set aside for read-alouds, accept that a diversity audit has phases and isn't completed in one sitting. (Refrain from analyzing the titles you're required to use for guided reading or any you access electronically. You'll learn a lot just by working with the library and set-aside books.) This is because once you get started, you'll soon find yourself returning to titles you previously considered, realizing you might have missed something in that earlier review. Also, as you work through your books, you'll recall moments when students first encountered them, and how they reacted. You might even find yourself wishing you'd noticed more in those moments, now that you know what you didn't know then about engaging children in Mirror and Window Books. It's these reflections that will partially inform how you find the diversity gaps in your collection. Vow to devote the time you need—and be kind to yourself. This isn't easy, and some of the discoveries you're bound to make can feel uncomfortable. Invariably, you'll discover that your collection skews toward certain types of characters and situations, or topics, or authors and illustrators. You also might see that the majority of your realistic fiction collection has male protagonists with females in supporting roles, or the characters are predominantly White and middle class, or most of the books for younger children have animal, not human, characters (usually illustrated with stereotypical gender distinctions; Horning, Lindgren, et al., 2018). It's okay. It's what publishers have been issuing for decades for young children, as the statistics cited earlier described. These publishing profiles can and will change—with your book diversity advocacy and that of other teachers, as well as numerous organizations (e.g., We Need Diverse Books, https://diversebooks.org/).

The simplest way to initially audit your book collection's diversity and utility is by considering it in two ways:

- whether and to what degree its themes, characters, and other content reflect the children and families your program serves; *plus*
- whether and to what degree your titles enable you to teach children about other people, other experiences, other ways of being in the world.

In other words, *study your books*: which are Mirrors of your children and their lives? Which books provide you a vehicle for opening Windows and Sims Bishop's (1990) Sliding Glass Doors onto other peoples? While this may seem like an overly straightforward approach at first, you'll notice as you make your piles or lists of each type that your holdings do not fully match the cultures and lives of your students. You also may discover books that can serve both purposes, either because of their universal lessons or the wide diversity of your children's lives.

The initial audit is necessary for establishing a baseline working knowledge of your collection. Since most teachers purchase or otherwise amass books over time, it's easy to lose sight of what's in your library as well as who is represented. Make and keep lists of both your Mirror and Window Books—they'll come in handy later, for planning new lessons or units as well as for seeking new titles to compensate for what and who are missing.

The next analysis uses your Mirror Book list. Compare it to results of surveys or questions you pose over time with your families that enable you to learn more about how they interact at home and what they expect their child's learning day to look, sound, and feel like. (Consider asking many of these questions informally, e.g., during drop-off/pick-up, or when sharing report cards/progress reports.) In addition to learning about your families' racial and linguistic backgrounds, probe respectfully about pertinent home situations (e.g., adults' work schedules and how they affect child care; after-school support; homelessness; routines such as weekend worship; transportation to and from school). Also learn about who's expecting a sibling, or where your students are in birth order within the household. Once you have your survey data/questions in hand, skim each family's responses while you consider your Mirror Book list. Do you see titles that match your children and their living situations in various ways? Again, ask: who and what are missing from your shelves?

If you find you have more Window than Mirror Books, do not despair—but look at them in a different way now. It may be that you collected books with the required topics, issues, themes, and genres of your curriculum in mind, which (unwittingly) limited your selections. Also ask yourself critically whether these titles are written from the perspectives of who your children are culturally. (For example, do your books about inventors include mostly White men, perhaps with a few White women featured in what seems like lip service?) Remember: Window Books need to model for students what they might aspire to, as well as how what's in them relates to their lives. If your current Window Books do not match your students' cultural assets, find ways to convert or amend them instructionally whereby children can connect more readily to their content. The next section on finding books details sources where you can find lesson plans to supplement and make more culturally relevant at least some of the titles on your current Window Books list.

If and when you're ready to dig more deeply into your collection, in preparation for doing a more complete diversity overhaul, review the evaluation criteria created by Derman-Sparks (2013), Ehrlich (2014), or Teaching Tolerance (2017). While some of their frameworks may be too granular for your needs or time, scanning their categories and classification prompts may prove helpful in furthering your understanding of the complexities involved in creating a book collection that resonates with each and every child in your care. The Teaching Tolerance (2017) tool is an interactive pdf that enables you to store your findings, which you can share with your school librarian or book purchasing committee to bolster your arguments for new expenditures.

Finding Mirror and Window Books

Fleming, Catapano, Thompson, and Carrillo (2016) advise us that there is an essential difference between multicultural and culturally relevant literature to keep in mind as we rethink our collections. The Cooperative Children's Books Center (Horning et al., 2018) notes that multicultural literature is broadly and loosely defined to mean any literature either written by or about people of color and First/Native Nations. Others (Dorr & Deskins, 2018; Lee & Low Publishers, 2018) expand this definition to also include LGBTQIA+ authors, illustrators, characters, and storylines, plus books by or about people with disabilities. Fleming et al. (2016) explain that while all culturally relevant literature will be multicultural, the opposite does not hold. What distinguishes the two is that culturally relevant literature connects with readers through its setting (e.g., neighborhoods, faith community), plot (e.g., immigration story), concepts, and content in ways that are familiar to one degree or another with these readers' life experiences. This is why in order to insure your classroom library and other texts are culturally relevant to your children, you first must learn more about your students and their families, as well as analyze the books you already have for their fit with your students as individuals. Folktales and songs from "around the world" are not in themselves culturally relevant—but they do have multicultural roots.

Before heading to your laptop to find new Mirror and Window books, realize it's impossible for any one book to be a full-length mirror, as it were. No book can totally capture any one child's life, any one culture's breadth and depth. Nor should you aim to revamp your holdings within a school year. Publishers are still grappling with how to diversify their titles, authors, and illustrators (Lee & Low Publishers, 2018). There's much work underway but, as of yet, no stream of more culturally relevant titles available. As pointed out above, your collection audit will show you the gaps in both types of titles. Using your gap analysis plus your knowledge of your children and the curriculum you must enact, investigate the following sources of potential titles as a start:

- Both the Teaching Tolerance (2018) and the Anti-Defamation League (ADL, 2018) organizations routinely review and feature culturally relevant books, vetted by expert teachers. You'll find their lists are extensive and easy to search for age/developmental stage. They also include lesson plans for thematic units connected to the titles featured. Teaching Tolerance organizes its titles according to the Social Justice Standards' domains of Identity, Diversity, Justice, and Action. The ADL's titles are organized by key aspects of their social activist efforts to foster Communication and Respect while exploring Differences and Identity. They also feature a number of teaching resources for countering Bias and Bullying.
- Fleming et al. (2016) host an interactive site for finding, evaluating, and ordering culturally relevant books, Kids Like Us (2018). They cull and review multicultural literature for children living in urban settings. Their text sets are solid guides for thematic units.
- Lee and Low Publishers' (2018) site and blog offer researched information and perspectives on how to educate the wide range of children and families who populate our centers and schools. All their books have downloadable, free lesson plans. They recently published the first-of-its-kind: A multicultural books' program, the Diverse Reading Leveled Bookrooms, for use with children in kindergarten through eighth grade. The program uses the Fountas and Pinnell levels (A-Z) to indicate text complexities. It features books in Spanish and English, as well as detailed lesson plans for conducting guided reading and interactive read-alouds. The Spanish-language texts are not translations. This enhances their cultural relevance in terms of providing natural language patterns and expressions. There is an even mix of genres and text structures (i.e., expository and narrative) across content disciplines.
- Awards for children's books and other media featuring non-White cultural groups are growing in number and criteria rigor being applied. As part of your book search, visit the Web site of the Association for Library Service to Children (ALSC), a division of the American Library Association

(http://www.ala.org/alsc/awardsgrants). ALSC serves as a clearinghouse for groups and agencies that recognize outstanding quality in children's titles about and for cultural majority as well as non-majority readers.

Public library staff and local booksellers are experts in finding children's books that relate to your local community's demographics and preferences. Invite them to your next professional development day to showcase titles that meet your particular needs. Ask representatives from your book distributors or publishers to do the same. The book industry has finally realized that to turn a profit, they must dramatically change their lists as well as personalize them for different schools and centers.

Using Books as Springboards

We focus much of our daily work on "getting the words" into our children's minds and hearts. Recent cognitive science research on vocabulary acquisition and development is confirming the power and utility of our language-focused practices. Scientists at the University of Edinburgh (Ota, Davies-Jenkins, & Skarabela, 2018) found that infants intentionally exposed from the age of nine months to increased levels of "baby-talk" words such as *tummy* (instead of stomach), and words that were either onomatopoeic (*woof-woof*) or rhymed, had significantly larger total receptive vocabulary sizes for high-frequency words such as *you*, *get*, and *where* by age 21 months, compared to those who were not exposed. The researchers posited that the specific nature of the sounds and their repetitive frequencies influenced development, possibly by establishing sound and meaning pathways in the mind that created an attentional foundation for processing more complex words. Anyone who's shared a nursery rhyme or books such as *Goodnight Moon* (Brown & Hurd, 1947) and *Peek-a-Who?* (Laden, 2000) with infants and toddlers appreciates having her practices reinforced and elucidated by this discovery. Performing read-alouds of rhyming, expressive texts with infants and toddlers on a daily basis, intentionally highlighting phoneme patterns, is a worthwhile practice.

In addition to the sound qualities and frequencies of word inputs influencing language acquisition and development, researchers are fine-tuning what we've known about the value and effectiveness of certain types of verbal exchanges compared to others. Demir, Rowe, Heller, Goldin-Meadow, and Levine (2015) determined that the complexity and range of unique words children hear used during conversations with parents and older family members predicts later vocabulary size and complexity. In particular, preschoolers who participated regularly in conversations about abstract ideas (e.g., pretending to drink juice) and past events (e.g., an episode at school yesterday) were found to have more complex syntactical and narrative knowledge at the kindergarten stage than children who were not part of as many of these conversation types on a regular basis. These decontextualized situation talks served a critical purpose (Demir et al., 2015) in shaping young children's understanding of story as well as their language to use when talking about a story (i.e., academic language). The amounts of words, as well as the types of interactions children were prompted to engage in while using this vocabulary, appeared mutually influential in fostering children's overall language and cognitive development. Reading and talking about books, and referring to them later on in a unit or a school year—all typical teacher practices—are being shown once again to be purposeful, necessary activity for building memory and higher-order thinking skills (Demir et al., 2015).

Just as we do not want to exclude any one race or culture from our shelves, we need to avoid implying that books are the most valued or solely esteemed literary format for children. Teaching children how to orally retell the stories they read, or how to format other "thinking work" into oral pieces to share, reinforces the oral-written language connections so central to maturing thought. Making time in the instructional day for meaningful, authentic oral sharing sparks integration and connection among ideas and people. It also establishes a familiar space for expression preferred by children whose family and community interactions are active-participatory in nature (Gay, 2002).

Dialogic reading, an interactive read-aloud approach for use with older toddlers and preschoolers, structures picture book engagement in such a way that children wind up "telling" the story as much as listening to it. During the initial reading, the teacher uses a set of prompts and follow-up probes that focus children's attention on content and aesthetics, encouraging children to talk about what they see and think as they view each two-page spread. On the subsequent four days with that book, she uses the prompts and probes to further direct children's attention to the book's language and its representation in the illustrations. She also returns to the story arc and how the characters change, again prompting children to pull the book's descriptive words and phrases into their oral responses to her probes. Daily, children revisit their previous understanding and appreciation for the book, through spontaneous retellings and recollection of specific text portions. Research into dialogic reading's effectiveness on older toddlers' and preschoolers' language development is extensive (see reviews in Towson, Fettig, Fleury, & Abarca, 2017; Wasik, Hindman, & Snell, 2016). Dialogic reading is recognized by the U.S. Department of Education's What Works Clearinghouse as an evidence-based (i.e., recommended) practice for fostering children's oral language, print knowledge, and comprehension skills (Towson et al., 2017). By keeping the listeners actively participating in the reading event, dialogic reading teachers model the active nature of reading, of making sense of what's in a book. Also, the probes and prompts connect the book language with the child's natural language, thereby expanding as well as deepening their vocabulary stores.

Closing Thoughts

We—adults and children—all need both Mirror and Window books in our lives. When used in concert with developmentally appropriate instruction, culturally relevant literature of both types supports children in creating their own life roadmaps. By aiming to diversify your literature collection, you avoid the Danger of the Single Story that novelist Chimamanda Ngozi Adichie (2009), in her TED Talk, so passionately exhorted her audience to recognize and rail against. Adichie, like Rudine Sims Bishop and so many others (e.g., Delpit, 1995; Hammond, 2015; Ladson-Billings, 1994), spent years overcoming the stifling effects of an imposed majority-culture literature diet when young. She now sees how "The single story creates stereotypes, and the problem with stereotypes is not that they are untrue, but that they are incomplete." (Adichie, 2009, para. 24). While it's still not easy to find culturally relevant Mirror and Window Books for all our students, commit to doing your utmost to move beyond presenting a single story in your classroom book collection. Make sure your holdings tell the complete story your children need to hear and read.

References

Adichie, C.N. (2009). The danger of a single story. TED Talk. [Video speech]. Retrieved from: https://youtu.be/D9Ihs241zeg

Anti-defamation League. Author. 2018. Books matter: Children's literature. [Blog post]. Retrieved from: https://www.adl.org/education-and-resources/resources-for-educators-parents-families/childrens-literature

Barack, L. (2016). *"When We Was fierce"* pulled as demand grows for more #OwnVoices stories. [Blog post]. Retrieved from: https://www.slj.com/?detailStory=when-we-was-fierce-pulled-as-demand-grows-for-more-ownvoices-stories

Barr, C., & Harbison, C. (2017). *Library and Book Trade Almanac* (p. 313). Medford, NJ: Information Today.

Botto, S.V., & Rochat, P. (2018). Sensitivity to the evaluation of others emerges by 24 months. *Developmental Psychology, 54*(9), 1723–1734.

Brooks, W. (2006). Reading representations of themselves: Urban youth use culture and African-American textual features to develop literary understandings. *Reading Research Quarterly, 41*(3), 372–392.

Brophy, J. (2008). Developing students' appreciation for what is taught in school. *Educational Psychologist, 43*(3), 132–141.

Brown, M.W., & Hurd, C. (1947). *Goodnight Moon*. New York: Harper & Row.

Delpit, L. (1995). *Other People's Children: Cultural Conflict in the Classroom*. New York: Norton.

Demir, O.E., Rowe, M.L., Heller, G., Goldin-Meadow, S., & Levine, S.C. (2015). Vocabulary, syntax, and narrative development in typically developing children and children with early unilateral brain injuries: Early parental talk about the 'there-and-then' matters. *Developmental Psychology, 51*(2), 161–175.

Derman-Sparks, L. (2013). Guide for selecting anti-bias children's books. [Blogpost]. Retrieved from: https://socialjusticebooks.org/guide-for-selecting-anti-bias-childrens-books/

Derman-Sparks, L., & Ramsey, P.G. (2006). *What If All the Kids are White: Anti-Bias Multicultural Education with Young Children*. New York: Teachers College Press.

Dorr, C., & Deskins, L. (2018). *LGBTQAI+ Books for Children and Teens*. Chicago, IL: American Library Association.

Egbert, J., & Roe, M.F. (2014). The power of why. *Childhood Education, 90*(4), 251–258.

Ehrlich, H. (2014). Checklist: 8 steps to creating a diverse book collection. [Blog post]. Retrieved from: http://blog.leeandlow.com/2014/05/22/checklist-8-steps-to-creating-a-diverse-book-collection/

Fleming, J., Catapano, S., Thompson, C.A., & Carrillo, S.R. (2016). *More Mirrors in the Classroom: Using Urban Children's Literature to Increase Literacy* (Kids Like Us). Lanham, MD: Rowman & Littlefield.

Gay, G. (2000). *Culturally Responsive Teaching: Theory, Practice, and Research.* New York: Teachers College.

Gay, G. (2002). Preparing for culturally responsive teaching. *Journal of Teacher Education, 53* (2), 106–116. Gayl

Guthrie, J.T., Wigfield, A., & You, W. (2012). Instructional contexts for engagement and achievement in reading. In: S.L. Christenson, A.L. Reschly & C. Wylie (Eds.), *Handbook of Research on Student Engagement* (pp. 601–634). New York: Springer.

Hammond, Z. (2015). *Culturally Responsive Teaching and the Brain: Promoting Authentic Engagement and Rigor Among Culturally and Linguistically Diverse Students.* Thousand Oaks, CA: Corwin.

Horning, J.T. (2016). When whiteness dominates reviews. [Blog post]. Retrieved from: http://readingwhilewhite.blogspot.com/2016/07/when-whiteness-dominates-reviews.html

Horning, J.T., Lindgren, M., Schliesman, M., & Tyner, M. (2018). Publishing statistics on children's books about people of color and first/native nations and by people of color and first/native nations. [Blog post]. Retrieved from: http://ccbc.education.wisc.edu/books/pcstats.asp

Husband, T. (2012). "I don't see color": Challenging assumptions about discussing race with young children. *Early Childhood Education, 39*(3), 365–371.

Kagan, J. (1981). *The Second Year: The Emergence of Self-Awareness.* Cambridge, MA: Harvard.

Kemple, K.M., Lee, I.R., & Harris, M. (2016). Young children's curiosity about physical differences associated with race: Shared reading to encourage conversation. *Early Childhood Education, 44*(9), 97–105.

Kids Like Us. (2018). Book browser. Retrieved from: http://www.kidslikeus.org/books/

Laden, N. (2000). *Peek-a-Who?* New York: Chronicle.

Ladson-Billings, G. (1994). *The Dreamkeepers.* San Francisco, CA: Jossey-Bass.

Larrick, N. (1965). The all-white world of children's books. *Saturday Review,* September, 63–65, 84–85.

Lee and Low Publishers. Author. (2018). The diversity gap in children's book publishing. [Blog post]. Retrieved from: http://blog.leeandlow.com/2018/05/10/the-diversity-gap-in-childrens-book-publishing-2018/#more-15863

Low, J.T. (2013). Why hasn't the number of multicultural books increased in eighteen years? [Blog post]. Retrieved from: http://blog.leeandlow.com/2013/06/17/why-hasnt-the-number-of-multicultural-books-increased-in-eighteen-years/

Low, J.T. (2016). Where is the diversity in publishing? The 2015 diversity baseline survey result. [Blog post]. Retrieved from: http://blog.leeandlow.com/2016/01/26/where-is-the-diversity-in-publishing-the-2015-diversity-baseline-survey-results/

Lysaker, J.T., & Miller, A. (2013). Engaging social imagination: The developmental work of wordless book reading. *Journal of Early Childhood Literacy, 13*(2), 147–174.

Ota, M., Davies-Jenkins, N., & Skarabela, B. (2018). Why choo-choo is better than train: The role of register-specific words in early vocabulary growth. *Cognitive Science, 42,* 1974–1999.

Sims, R. (1983). What has happened to the 'all-white' world of children's books? *Phi Delta Kappan, 64*(9), 650–653.

Sims Bishop, R. (1990). Mirrors, windows, and sliding glass doors. *Perspectives, 1*(3), ix–xi.

Taylor, B.M., Pearson, P.D., Peterson, D.S., & Rodriguez, M.C. (2003). Reading growth in high-poverty classrooms: The influence of teacher practices that encourage cognitive engagement in literacy learning. *Elementary School Journal, 104*(1), 3–28.

Teaching Tolerance. Author. (2017). *Reading Diversity: A Tool for Selecting Diverse Texts.* Retrieved from: https://www.tolerance.org/magazine/publications/reading-diversity

Teaching Tolerance. Author. (2018). Classroom resources: Lesson plans. [Blog post]. Retrieved from: https://www.tolerance.org/classroom-resources/learning-plans

Thomas, E.E., Reese, D., & Horning, K.T. (2016). Much ado about a fine dessert. *Journal of Children's Literature, 42*(2), 6–17.

Towson, J.A., Fettig, A., Fleury, V.P., & Abarca, D.L. (2017). Dialogic reading in early childhood settings: A summary of the evidence base. *Topics in Early Childhood Special Education, 37*(3), 132–146.

Wasik, B.A., Hindman, A.H., & Snell, E.K. (2016). Book reading and vocabulary development: A systematic review. *Early Childhood Research Quarterly, 37*, 39–57.

12 Mathematics to Promote Critical Thinking

Kathleen M. Sheridan and David Banzer

The Importance of the Teacher's Role in Early Math Success

During childhood, most of us spent time playing with blocks, Legos™, stones from outdoors, or other small groups of objects. Do you remember the joy of sorting, fitting together, stacking, or organizing them by size, shape or color? At the time, you probably did not realize you were using sophisticated mathematical thinking in your play with the objects, but you were! Young children, as early as infancy, can see the difference in quantities of objects. Thus, babies possess what is referred to as an innate primitive number sense. This is an important fact, because it means young children come to the early childhood classroom possessing some mathematical knowledge and skills. It is your job as an early childhood educator to establish a mathematical environment that encourages and facilitates the development of mathematical concepts.

In doing so, your own beliefs and knowledge about math are important. Have you ever heard anyone who claims, "I am just not good at math?" When my college students and teachers tell me this, I always reply by asking "How many times have you had someone tell you, 'I am just not very good at reading'?" Most stop and think, and then respond "never" or "rarely." Because while it seems to be socially acceptable to be "bad at math" it is not socially acceptable to say we are bad at reading. Why do we see this dichotomy in our society? If you believe that you are bad at math, does that mean you believe that you cannot get better at it? I challenge you to think about what makes you believe that you do not like math or are not good at it. And for those of you claiming to be a "math person," what makes you love it? Because mathematical literacy is extremely important for young children, and as their teacher, your own beliefs and attitudes about math influence their thinking, including math in your curriculum is vitally important for their future academic success (Geist, 2015).

A quick review of the research will inform you that early math literacy matters. Duncan et al. (2007) found that attainment of early math concepts such as ordinality and number knowledge are powerful predictors of successful learning as children progress in school. In fact, that what children knew about math at the start of elementary school was the strongest predictor of high school graduation and college attendance. Additionally, a study completed at Vanderbilt in 2014 revealed that both girls and boys who were successful in math early in their schooling reported high levels of life satisfaction and psychological well-being as adults, had leadership roles in their jobs, and reported more creative contributions professionally than their peers who were not successful in early math (Lubinski, Benbow, & Kell, 2014). Thus, as an early childhood educator you have a profound responsibility to foster mathematical literacy and success. You can engage children in a developmentally appropriate play-based curriculum promoting mathematical learning and fostering early math success while developing other important early learning skills such as attention, social, and language skills. In order to do so, you must understand what early math is!

What Is Early Math?

Let's consider the difference between "early math" and mathematics. When reflecting on early math, you may consider your own experiences learning mathematics. While early math is definitely a part of mathematics, your own self-reflections on your experiences around early math might focus on specific lessons or the teaching style you experienced around math in elementary school rather than the mathematical thinking involved in early math.

You might think about sheets of paper filled with addition, subtraction, or multiplication problems and timed tests on how many problems you could answer in a minute or two. You might think about multiplication tables and mnemonic devices to remember mathematical rules. While these activities center around mathematics in general, specifically around number operations, you might not truly remember your early math experiences in great detail. You probably don't remember being an infant and crawling in the direction of a ball that rolled away. You might not remember creating a pile of toy dinosaurs and a separate pile of toy farm animals or stacking blocks on top of other blocks to make a house. But as a young child, you were exploring early mathematical concepts through these activities.

Early math includes much more than number and counting. These early play experiences provide children with rich opportunities to explore math concepts. Think about what you used to enjoy playing as a young child. When you were an infant crawling toward a ball that rolled away, you were exploring spatial relationships, and aware of which direction to find a ball that rolled out of view. When you created piles of separated dinosaurs and farm animals, you were grouping toys by attributes and observing and analyzing which attributes belong to dinosaurs and not farm animals. When you were stacking wooden blocks on top of each other, you were adding more, exploring dimensional concepts of height, and testing out the balance and symmetry of a block house. These experiences provide the basis for internalizing mathematical concepts and understanding abstract mathematical relationships later in children's mathematical thinking.

Early math includes an array of foundational concepts leading to later math learning. These concepts include number sense and operations, spatial awareness, geometry, measurement, patterns, and data collection and analysis, which we will discuss in the following sections. At the core of these mathematical concepts is relationships and symbol systems. Relationships exist between physical objects that can be seen, such as creating a group of red plates and ignoring all other plates in the dramatic play area of a classroom. A child focusing on red plates is mentally creating a group with criteria including specific plates into a group, while excluding other plates. These relationships between physical objects become the first basis for a child to create mental, abstract relationships with math concepts. These relationships can be seen in the following mathematical concepts (Figure 12.1).

Figure 12.1 Child engaging in mathematical thinking through block play.

Number Sense

Most early childhood educators agree that number sense is a key mathematical concept taught and supported in early childhood classrooms. Through activities such as counting the number of children present that day, setting the number of plates needed for lunch, or counting quantities of physical objects, counting can be a practical skill needed daily. However, deep understanding of number sense at a conceptual level is key to developing young children's number sense and deep understanding of number sense involves principles of counting. The number sense principles provide insight into the necessary concepts needed to accurately count and demonstrate number sense.

The principles include one-to-one correspondence, the stable-order principle, cardinality, and the order-irrelevance principle. Children demonstrate one-to-one correspondence when they count an object once and assign a counting tag to the object. For example, a child may point to an object as she says a number aloud, thus tagging the object with a number. One-to-one correspondence involves understanding an object can be counted only once. A child demonstrates stable order in counting when they use the same counting sequence in a consistent manner. For example, a child knows that there is an order to counting by always counting 1, 2, 3, 4, 5, and so on. They know that counting cannot progress in a different order. Cardinality involves an understanding of part-whole relationships that exist in counting, and a larger set is created as counting progresses (Figure 12.2). A child who understands cardinality knows counting to five while pointing to an array of blocks, the number counted aloud represents the block counted combined with all previous blocks

Figure 12.2 Child exploring the concept of cardinality through counting objects.

counted. For example, a child may tag the fifth block counted as five but understands that the overall quantity of blocks includes blocks tagged as 1, 2, 3, 4, and 5 together. After objects have been counted, when asked how many objects there are altogether, a young child who has not developed cardinality will typically re-count the objects as the child cannot coordinate the overall part-whole relationship of the final number counted in a set. The child may think that the block tagged "5" refers only to the name of that block in the set, and does not represent all other blocks counted. Thus, the child does not understand cardinality (Kami, 1982).

Finally, the order-irrelevance principle involves understanding objects can be counted in any order and the final quantity will be the same. For example, objects can be counted left to right and the quantity will be the same if counting went right to left, top to bottom, or counter clockwise. The order in which objects are counted is irrelevant to the overall quantity.

These principles are necessary to developing number sense. Within these principles a child must develop the idea that number involves sets and relationships of physical objects within these sets. Young children typically begin exploring counting concepts by using physical objects as they are unable to consider number in a purely abstract manner, such as counting mentally while connecting these numbers to an overall mathematical quantity. By encouraging children to count objects in their typical environment, connections to the abstract nature of number begins to develop.

Number Operations

When considering number operations, many of us envision worksheets or timed math tests involving addition or subtraction equations. While these worksheets do show operations equations, they lack the necessary connection to what number operations actually are on a deeper level. Mathematics is symbolic in nature and young children need to manipulate objects and create sets to truly understand the meaning behind operations. When children add more playdough to a rolled ball or add unit blocks lengthwise to create a road in the block area, they are manipulating overall quantities of a mass of playdough, or the overall length of a block road. Young children begin exploring these concepts of more and less when playing with typical early childhood materials such as water or sensory materials, clay or playdough, constructive materials such as blocks or magnetic tiles, or during mealtimes when serving themselves food.

At the center of number operations are comparisons between sets of objects. When you ask a child how many red counting bears there are and how many blue counting bears there are, you are asking them to sort and compare two sets of objects. If a child is developmentally ready, you can scaffold his understanding of operational thinking to have him combine the two sets into one set of bears. Children can visually see two set of bears being combined, or added together, into a larger set. This type of mathematical practice can happen

Figure 12.3 Child exploring the concept of how many.

throughout the day. For example, by comparing how many crackers each child has during snack time, children can examine equalities and inequalities of sets of crackers (Figure 12.3). Equality principles includes the language of more and less to describe quantities of objects, such as crackers in this case. These experiences create a foundation for understanding later symbol systems used in written mathematical equations.

Spatial Awareness

Exploring and describing relationships amongst objects in physical space provides a child with foundational experiences for developing geometric concepts in addition to the ability to use descriptive language to describe relationships amongst objects. This language provides opportunities for children to connect abstract language describing relationships with everyday knowledge they have during their daily experiences. This connection between a child's everyday world and the development of abstract knowledge to describe their experiences is key to the development of abstract mathematical thinking.

Think about a child constructing a building with wooden blocks. What does a child need to understand to build? What does a child need to know in order to explain how they built their building? Developing an awareness of spatial relationships is necessary to explain how objects exist in the world. Is there a triangular block on top of a square block? Where is the building's door? It is below the window? Are two small windows next to a large window? Do people walk inside of the building? Do dogs stay outside of the building? Do birds fly above the roof? This descriptive language demonstrates an understanding of relationships between objects and considers how physical objects relate to each other, providing children with opportunities to apply these spatial relations to common experiences and analyze critically how the physical world appears.

Geometry

What do you think of when you hear the word "geometry"? You might remember proofs and theorems, rules about angles, and maybe different types of triangles from your academic experiences. Those experiences are rooted in abstract mathematical processes, but preschoolers use the same process of proofs and theorems when analyzing shapes. Think about common shapes you might discuss with young children. Certainly circles, squares, rectangles, and triangles come to mind. Now, what are the properties of a triangle that make it a triangle? A triangle has three sides, sides are connected at all corners, and there are three angles inside those corners. When a child in preschool classroom identifies a triangle, can the child explain these properties? Certainly, a typical preschooler can identify that a triangle is a triangle, but an early childhood educator needs to delve deeper into why a triangle is a triangle.

This process can occur with every shape. What is the distinction between a square and a rectangle? A square and a rhombus? A cylinder and a sphere? Delving into shapes outside of the typical circle, square, triangle, and rectangle group will yield rich discussions about shapes seen in everyday life. And in that everyday life, we see objects in three dimensions, so it is essential that accurate shape names, those of three-dimensional shapes, be used in language throughout the day (and night!) to describe the world.

Measurement

Measurement might bring up thoughts of measurement tools, such as rulers and yardsticks. Perhaps you needed to measure the size of a room to see whether a piece of furniture might fit somewhere, or you were making something with fabric or wood and needed precise sizes. While measurement in early childhood can include standard measurement tools, non-standard measurement can be used to help young children think about why and how measurement tools actually exist, and what they represent.

As a preschool teacher, I once introduced cloth measuring tapes with only a little background information on standard units of measurement. Preschoolers began measuring objects in the classroom during choice time and would compare what objects were longer than the others, which prompted conversations about what measurement was and what we could use the tools for. This then prompted extended projects using measurement that helped students to think about using measurement for useful purposes. For example, we discussed questions such as, why were children's shadows longer on the east side of the building than the south side, and how much does a child's height change over time? While this use of standard measurement tools was successful in getting children to think about the uses of measurement, it might be more meaningful to have children use objects in the classroom for nonstandard measurement. For example, how many "shoes" long is the carpet? Or, how many "blocks" high is the table top? Consider how measurement fits in with data collection and analysis discussed below.

Patterns

Early math includes concepts of patterns, following the idea of relationships amongst physical objects. Patterning in a classroom might focus on repeating AB patterns, where for example a red circle is followed by a blue circle, repeating with red-blue-red-blue and so on. This ability to repeat the pattern focuses on a child putting red and blue circles into relationships and creating rules for what the pattern may be, then following those patterns to extend these patterns, using paper circles, beads, parquetry blocks, etc.

Simple repeating patterns may be explored using colors or shapes in a classroom but make sure to also consider patterns that exist in daily life. For example, patterns of a daily routine, patterns that exist in the bricks on a building, patterns in fences or sidewalks, and patterns found in natural objects in a child's neighborhood and on clothing all provide opportunities to explore patterns in a concrete sense.

Data Collection and Analysis

Data collection and analysis does not need to be a complex, statistical analysis for young children, but rather a way to present information in a mathematical way and to find out answers to questions. Surveys are a great way to introduce children to data collection and analysis. During group time, a teacher can ask the class if more children are wearing shoes that have laces or Velcro. During this activity, children can create groups of shoes based on whether there are laces or Velcro, and collect data to answer this question. These shoes can then be counted for comparing quantities of shoes to answer the original question. They can collect data on the family toothpaste preference, their favorite food, fruit, or vegetable, or what pets they have at home.

Opportunities to examine and answer questions are abundant in a child's daily experiences. Measurement tools can be used to examine how tall children are, then to display this information by creating a large graph. Asking children their preferences can provide opportunities to use data collection and analysis by creating charts to display whether children prefer apples or oranges, or whether they have a pet in their home. Children can then use other math concepts to analyze the collected data and reach a conclusion about the answers to their questions.

Since the breadth of early math concepts is wide, consider how to prompt children's thinking within typical routines. A teacher's own knowledge of early math concepts is important in understanding how these concepts can be taught. Explore how you might engage children to think mathematically and solve mathematical problems on a daily basis and in different areas of your classroom while reading the next section where we will describe best practice guidelines for optimum facilitation of early math thinking.

Pedagogy

For children's optimum development, early childhood classrooms should have a healthy mixture of both teacher-directed and child-directed learning opportunities. However, both of these concepts are often misunderstood. For example, when you think of teacher-directed learning, do you think about sitting in a lecture room with a teacher talking AT you while you take notes? While this is a form of teacher-directed learning, it is not what we are referring to when we talk about teacher-directed learning in the early childhood classroom. When you think about child-directed learning, do you envision children playing all day with little to no adult interaction? This is not what we are referring to when we talk about child-directed learning in the early childhood classroom. In the early childhood classroom both teacher-directed learning and child-directed learning involve conversations between the adults and children in the classroom, with teachers using "academic language" and asking probing questions to scaffold and make visible a child's intentions and knowledge. Academic language in the preschool classroom involves using appropriate and grammatically correct language when talking to children as well as using the language of the content area you are studying. For math, this means using vocabulary such as "on", "more," "less," and "how many?" As you read the sections below, try to discern the differences between child-directed and teacher-directed activities, and prepare a conversation starter with families explaining why each type of pedagogy is important.

Child-Directed Math Support

When you plan lessons to implement with children, it is important to consider how child-directed math learning can occur. Early childhood classrooms are arranged to allow children's free exploration and play. Within this environment, teachers can support mathematical learning by following the child's lead and participating in their play in a non-intrusive manner. Think about a child in a preschool classroom. What do they like to do? What materials might they choose to play with? What areas of the classroom do they choose to play in? Within these child chosen activities, children take initiative in what they will play with. A teacher interacting with children during this play can support their math development.

Consider a block area in a preschool classroom. Alfredo, a four-year-old boy, chooses to play in this area on a daily basis. He spends time building elaborate castles and adding props such as wooden people and animals throughout his castle. What types of mathematical concepts might he be exploring in this play? What does his play tell us about opportunities for math learning? What does the material, wooden blocks, tell us about possible math concepts he is exploring? Alfredo might be exploring spatial dimensions in creating a three-dimensional structure. He may need to balance and create a structurally sound base to build a tall castle. He could be exploring patterns in the way he is arranging blocks, such as a cylinder on top of a rectangular block in a repeating pattern. While all of these are possibilities, we do not know what Alfredo is exploring until a teacher engages him in a conversation about his play.

When teachers engage children in conversation about their chosen play, children are typically eager to discuss what they have been building, creating, or pretending. In Alfredo's case, the teacher may begin asking him what he has built, and how he has built his castle, leading to the aspects of the construction process that Alfredo has been focusing on. Perhaps he tells the teacher that he has created rooms for each of the wooden people inside the castle and spaces outside of the castle for each animal to sleep in. The teacher, having gained an understanding of Alfredo's thought processes, can naturally draw attention to the numbers of people that can fit inside of the castle, or the number of stalls for animals to sleep in outside of the castle. This could lead to opportunities to connect mathematical concepts to Alfredo's natural interests in his block construction.

Similarly, these types of conversations could occur throughout a preschool classroom during free choice times. These times offer rich opportunities to support children's mathematical development by connecting possible math concepts to children's chosen play activities.

Teacher-Directed Math Instruction

There are times when you might want to focus on engaging all of the children in the classroom in learning a specific mathematical concept. To achieve this goal, you might decide to develop a lesson with a specific objective that every child should attain. For example, you might focus on counting, ways of representing numbers, and one-to-one correspondence so that children increase their mathematical proficiency and fluency. To do this, you create a counting game you discovered on mathathome.org. The game has specific directions and rules that the children must learn and follow. To introduce the lesson, you gather the children together and read a book about counting. For example, you might choose to read the children *Five Apples Up on Top!* by Dr. Seuss. You then tell the children you are going to play a counting game together. You begin by demonstrating the rules and sequence of the game, making sure each child participates. Afterwards, you play the game together and ask probing questions to discover each child's intention and knowledge or to scaffold their learning. For example, you might ask a child or group of children "Who has the most counters?", "Who has the least counters?", "Does anyone have the same number of counters?"

This type of teacher-directed learning is developmentally appropriate and has many benefits for a child's learning. It is fun for children to play games; their knowledge is visible to you and you can focus on a specific learning objective to document. In addition, the social learning involved in game playing is a great benefit for children. There can be some cons if you are not careful to pay attention to where each child is developmentally and to scaffold and support those children who will struggle with the lesson.

Both child-directed and teacher-directed learning have an important place in the early childhood classroom and making sure there is an appropriate balance of each is a part of being an effective and excellent early childhood educator.

Planning Instruction with Professional Standards

Using the National Council of Teachers of Mathematics Standards (NCTM) to design and plan your lessons and units of instruction is a very important step when planning for learning in your classroom. When you use the standards as your starting point in lesson planning, the planning process is called "backwards design" (Wiggins & McTighe 2005).

Instead of creating activities and then trying to match them to a standard, you examine the standards first and determine what it is you want the children to learn. Then, you design lessons and activities that are mapped out with objectives and aligned to the standards.

Go to the NCTM website (http://nctm.org) and take a look at the standards. There you will see standards for the math content areas as well as for the processes that children engage in when learning mathematics (NCTM, 2000). The five content areas for pre-K–grade 2 are: Number & Operations, Algebra, Geometry, Measurement, and Data Analysis & Probability. And the five process standards are: Problem Solving, Reasoning & Proof, Communication, Connections, and Representation. You will need to plan for both the content and the processes standards. It is also helpful to look at what children are expected to know about math when entering the kindergarten classroom. In this way, you will know what you want all of the children to be able to do when they leave your classroom for the world kindergarten.

As you examine the NCTM math standards (shown below as examples), notice that each standard has benchmarks describing what children should master in order to attain the standard. For example, under Number and Operations, children should:

1. understand numbers, ways of representing numbers, relationships among numbers, and number systems;
2. understand meanings of operations and how they relate to one another;
3. compute fluently and make reasonable estimates.

If you look further you will find there are detailed benchmarks to be achieved. For example, under the first expectation:

Understand numbers, ways of representing numbers, relationships among numbers, and number systems, the following benchmarks are to be achieved for children PreK-grade 2:

- count with understanding and recognize "how many" in sets of objects;
- use multiple models to develop initial understandings of place value and the base-ten number system;
- develop understanding of the relative position and magnitude of whole numbers and of ordinal and cardinal numbers and their connections;
- develop a sense of whole numbers and represent and use them in flexible ways, including relating, composing, and decomposing numbers;
- connect number words and numerals to the quantities they represent, using various physical models and representations;
- understand and represent commonly used fractions, such as 1/4, 1/3, and 1/2. (NCTM, 2000)

Obviously, some of the benchmarks are intended for preschool-age children to attain, and others are intended for elementary-age children. You must use your understanding of child development to choose how to create developmentally appropriate lessons around these benchmarks that will help children move from one level of cognitive understanding to another.

When children are ready to move forward from one conceptual understanding to another, they are in "the zone of proximal development" (Vygotsky, 1978). This means that children understand one level of a concept and are developmentally ready to build on that understanding to attain a more complex level of understanding. This happens through a child's experimentation with objects and ideas and interactions with a more knowledgeable other. This process is called scaffolding and is a powerful teaching method. For example, let's imagine that you discover that the children in your class are interested in counting objects. You observe that most of the children have one-to-one correspondence and are able to point at a line of objects, counting one number to one object. Your observations with Sydney reveal that when you ask her how many objects are in her collection of five objects, she carefully counts them one by one, matching each object with a number. After observing these actions, you reply "That's right, Sydney!" Next, you give her a collection of 12 objects and ask her how many she has. You observe that when she has 12 objects she no longer can count each object up to 12 without getting mixed up and counting some objects more than once and skipping others. This observation has informed you that Sydney's sense of one-to-one correspondence is not yet stable, and as the number increases she gets confused. You assist and scaffold her learning by gently helping her point to and touch each object as she counts, making sure that none are skipped or double counted. Your scaffolding helps her to develop a strategy for counting larger numbers of objects. This type of questioning and observation allows you to hear and see how Sydney is actually thinking and gives you a clue as to what types of lessons to plan and what strategic questions to ask in the future to help move her to the next developmental level. Thus, paying attention to the standards, the benchmarks and what the developmental level of the individual child is, is vitally important for creating effective lesson plans and questioning strategies.

In conclusion, make sure to use the professional math standards when planning. Many states have statewide early learning standards as well, and you can also use those standards to guide your planning.

Promoting Math-Thinking in All Areas of the Curriculum

With an understanding of what early math is and how it can be planned, it is necessary to consider how early math can be supported in all aspects of an early childhood curriculum. Within a preschool curriculum, it is important to consider aspects of a daily classroom routine as well as how the classroom environment is intentionally planned to support early math development. The environment includes areas typical to a preschool classroom: a block area, art area, dramatic play area, space for toys, games, and manipulatives, a library, writing center, and a science area. Daily routines to consider include main instructional times such as whole group times, small group lessons, and support in free play. Additionally, mealtimes and transitions should be considered when planning for early math development support.

Block Area

A block area should have blocks! This may seem obvious, but sometimes block areas can get cluttered with other materials. A well-stocked block area should have wooden unit blocks as the main block in the area. Having props such as wooden cars or people can assist with a child's use of the area, but unit blocks should be the main material in the area. These blocks provide natural math explorations as blocks fit together in standard units. Constructing freely allows children to explore spatial dimensions and solve engineering problems. Consider how patterns can be explored with blocks—these occur naturally in a child's building process and they might not even notice until you point it out.

Art Area

An art area should be set up for children to be freely creative in constructing art pieces. While painting and drawing may be typical art area activities, consider keeping three-dimensional materials available, like clay, wooden sticks, or wire for children to create sculptures that utilize spatial dimensions. Measurement tools can be used for creating precise lengths, straight lines or angles, or to mix different proportions of paint. Creating collages, sculptures and other types of art all demand the use of mathematical tools, thinking and skills. Whether mixing colors—1 part red and 2 parts yellow, combining tissue paper geometric shapes—rectangles, circles and triangles—to make a collage, or exploring symmetry through leaf printing, mathematical thinking is at the forefront of making art.

Dramatic Play

A dramatic play area should be a space where children can recreate a variety of locations and situations. While a standard area may be set up to recreate a domestic situation, children should be involved in establishing different ways that a dramatic play area can be set up. Restaurants, stores, post offices, buses, or airplanes could be possible spaces of interest to children, and math development can be supported by identifying mathematical concepts that are connected to daily experiences. For example, how many chairs does a restaurant table need to fit a group of children? Should the bus driver sit in front of passengers, behind, or to the side? Including children in the construction of dramatic play props can also offer rich mathematical conversation.

Toys, Games, and Manipulatives

Toys, games, and manipulatives are typically rich in math concepts. Many manipulatives in fact are marketed as "math" manipulatives. These types of manipulatives lend themselves well to teacher-directed activities around number sense and number operations through grouping and comparing manipulatives.

A variety of constructive materials are available to support children's critical thinking of construction processes, rich in math concepts. Materials can include magnetic tiles, connecting brick blocks, and items with wheels that can be made into vehicles. These open-ended materials allow children to explore and take the lead in an activity and would be best suited with teacher support within child-directed play.

Library

Intentionally stocking a library can help children explore mathematical concepts through independent book browsing or in read-alouds. Make sure to include some math-specific books for your shelves to encourage mathematical exploration. For example, you might choose *Perfect Square* by Michael Hall,

Inch by Inch by Leo Lionni, and *Marta Big and Small* by Jen Arena. You should also consider illustrations as sources of rich mathematical conversations. What patterns are there? How tall are those trees? How many people can fit on that bus? Selecting storybooks around routines and repetition can also focus on patterns of spoken words and rhythm that can reinforce mathematical thinking.

Science Area

Math and science are closely related in early childhood and a science area with life science and physical science materials will naturally be rich in early math concepts. Physical science activities, such as materials to experiment with gravity and motion such as ramps, provide opportunities for children to think about physical experiments using mathematical language. Why did one ball roll farther than another? How fast did the marble go down the ramp?

Natural science materials are also rich in mathematical concepts. Collected items from neighborhood walks can be sources for data analysis. Sorting these objects, such as sorting leaves from smallest to largest, or examining the leaves' different properties, allows children opportunities to describe objects mathematically. These experiences demonstrate children's application of their existing mathematical knowledge.

Whole Group, Small Group, and Individual Instruction

Different times of the day and sizes of a group for an instructional activity will dictate the depth of instruction on math concepts. During a whole group time, such as circle time or a read aloud, mathematical concepts can be introduced generally with the goal of engaging all the children in using mathematical knowledge. Counting children present in the class that day, singing songs with repeating patterns, or asking specific questions about a story that require mathematical thinking could be ways to engage a large group of children.

Small groups and children's free play may be times to support more specific math concepts as the children in a group can engage with each other in addition to the teacher. Teacher-directed activities may be best with smaller groups when each child needs to be able to participate at the same time as their peers, such as creating groups of objects and comparing quantities from child to child. Additionally, the teacher's support of math concepts during a child's chosen play is best done in smaller groups of children. Challenging children's specific knowledge level of math can be done individually when specific math concepts are to be explored deeply.

Daily Routines

When math learning opportunities occur on a daily basis, opportunities for math experiences can occur in all aspects of the daily routine. Think about transitions from one activity to another. How can children be engaged mathematically through transitions? A clean-up time can be a math-rich time for children to use spatial language when they figure where materials should be returned. Prompting how many blocks or toys or manipulatives still need to be put away can prompt children's number sense and operations thinking. Mealtime can be a great time to incorporate math concepts as well. How many scoops of peas did you take? How full is your plate? Should you fill your cup full of milk or only half-full? These types of questions can prompt mathematical conversations during shared mealtimes. What other times of the day can be opportunities for mathematical learning? With careful reflection and planning, math learning can occur in every aspect of a daily schedule.

Project-Based Learning

Long-term projects can serve as a means to connect math learning across days and weeks by allowing children to revisit and expand upon their learning experiences. By exploring buildings over several weeks and using a variety of materials to construct their own buildings, children will gain confidence in their own use of mathematical language to describe buildings in detail, and to solve problems in creating buildings using mathematical thinking. These types of projects follow children's interests and allow children to engage in math concepts across different aspects of a project and apply mathematical knowledge as a project progresses.

Conclusion

Incorporating rich early math experiences in an early childhood classroom is a journey beginning with a teacher's own math identity, tied closely to that teacher's own experiences learning math and their confidence in teaching early math concepts to young children. Because early math is a facilitator of children's later academic achievement, it is important that young children have rich and deep mathematical experiences and are supported in their early mathematics development. In order for these experiences to occur, early childhood educators must first understand what early math is and the appropriateness of mathematics in an early childhood classroom.

The first step in developing a strong math identity is understanding that early math concepts include not only number sense, but also number operations, spatial awareness, geometry, measurement, patterns, and data collection and analysis. The next step involves examining how all of these early math concepts can be taught appropriately. By examining child-directed and teacher-directed opportunities to teach these early math concepts, you can implement math-rich activities and support children's math development through play. By understanding current math standards, classroom environment setup, and daily classroom routines, you can confidently support young children's math development. This exposure to rich math experiences and math language will aid in children's strong math identity and knowledge and prepare them for positive math experiences in later academic settings.

Sample Math Activity

Read through the following teacher-directed lesson plan (Figure 12.4). Can you describe why this lesson is considered teacher-directed? What does the teacher say, plan and do that clues you in?

Beaded Necklaces

Children will create patterns using beads to string a necklace.

Materials Needed:
- Beads and lacing strings
- Bead Pattern Cards (make your own or use pre-made bead pattern cards)
- Book: What Next Nina by Sue Kassirer

Introduce Activity:
1. Say: "We are going to read a book about a girl named Nina. Something happens and Nina needs to restring her sister's necklace exactly like it was. Nina needs to make the SAME pattern with the beads as it was before it broke." "Who knows what a pattern is?" Encourage the children to verbalize what they think a pattern is.
2. Read: What Next Nina by Sue Kassirer
3. Ask children to predict which beads to add to the necklace in order to follow the pattern.
4. Show children that you are going to make a necklace using a pattern. Start stringing the necklace in front of the children verbalizing what you are doing: "I put 2 red beads on, now I want 2 blue beads again and now 2 blue beads. I like my pattern, who can tell me what color to put on next so my pattern stays the same?"
5. Create your own necklace using large beads in front of the group. Have children help you figure out what to add to the necklace in order to complete the pattern.
6. Show children examples of other beaded necklaces and have them tell you which one is NOT a pattern.

Engage the Children:
1. Tell children that they are going to make their own necklaces following a pattern.
2. Direct children to sit in small groups.
3. Give each child a bucket of beads and the lacing strings and bead pattern cards.
4. Tell children to first choose a pattern card and then choose beads that match the pattern card and lay the beads on the card.
5. Ask children to lace the beads in the correct order of the pattern.
6. Encourage them to describe what their pattern is. Some children may be able to create the pattern by placing the beads on the cards appropriately, but may not be able to transfer that to the necklace string. Assist them by verbalizing the pattern out loud.
7. Encourage them to make longer extended patterns.
8. Allow children to wear necklaces for the day and take them off before they go home.

Figure 12.4 Sample lesson plan. www.mathathome.org.

Sample Children's Books

Aboff, M. (2009). *If you were a Triangle*. Minneapolis, MN: Picture Window Books.

Arena, J. (2016). *Marta Big and Small*. New York: Roaring Brook Press.

Baker, K. (2004). *Quack and Count*. Orlando, FL: Harcourt.

Barnett, M. (2017). *Triangle*. Cambridge, MA: Candlewick Press.

Carle, E. (1969). *The Very Hungry Caterpillar*. New York, NY: Philomel Books.

Ehlert, L. (1990). *Fish Eyes: A book you can count on*. Orlando, FL: Harcourt.

Ga'g, W. (1928). *Millions of Cats*. New York, NY: Penguin Putnam Books.

Hall, M. (2011). *Perfect Square*. New York: Green Willow Books.

Jocelyn, M. (2017). *Sam Sorts*. Toronto, Canada: Tundra Books.

Kanninen, B. (2018) *Circle Rolls*. Phaidon.

Leoni, L., (2012). *Inch by Inch*. New York: Alfred A. Knopf.

LeSieg, T., Seuss, D., & McKie, R. (1998). *Ten Apples Up On Top!* New York: Random House.

Murphy, S. (2000). *Beep Beep, Vroom Vroom!* New York, NY: Harper Collins.

Stein D., & Rothman, J. (2018) *Brick: Who Found Herself in Architecture*. Phaidon.

References

Duncan, G.J., Dowsett, C.J., Claessens, A., Magnuson, K., & Huston, A.C., et al. (2007). School readiness and later achievement. *Developmental Psychology, 43*, 1428–1446.

Kamii, C., & National Association for the Education of Young Children. (1982). *Number in Preschool and Kindergarten: Educational Implications of Piaget's Theory*. Washington, DC: National Association for the Education of Young Children.

Lubinski, D., Benbow, C.P., & Kell, H.J. (2014). Life paths and accomplishments of mathematically precocious males and females four decades later. *Psychological Science, 25*(12), 2217–2232.

National Council of Teachers of Mathematics. (2000). *Principles and Standards for School Mathematics*. Reston, VA: National Council of Teachers of Mathematics. Retrieved 9/11/2018 from: https://www.nctm.org/Standards-and-Positions/Principles-and-Standards/Number-and-Operations/

Vygotsky, L. S. (1978) *Mind in society: The development of higher psychological processes*. Cambridge, MA: Harvard University Press.

Wiggins, G.P., & McTighe, J. (2005). *Understanding by Design*. Alexandria, VA: Association for Supervision and Curriculum Development.

13 "But Why?"

Considerations for Encouraging Scientific Thinking in the Preschool Classroom

Anne Pradzinski

"But why?" asks the four-year-old in your classroom. The question can sometimes make us cringe. Maybe it is because we know that the one "but why" has the potential to be followed up by several more why-type questions. Maybe it is because we are afraid we may not know the answer. Or maybe it is because we just don't know how to explain the answer in terms that young children will understand. Young children are curious and ask many questions. This simple fact makes evident how important it is to continue to develop their scientific thinking and learning at a young age in order to provide strong foundations for later school learning in both science and critical thinking. This chapter will begin with a discussion of young children's capabilities around science, followed by the role that teachers can play in supporting children's scientific exploration and thinking, and will conclude with a look at how teachers can support science learning through inquiry in their classrooms.

Young Children's Abilities to Think and Do Science

They may be curious about new objects and are excited to know more. They may be frightened by the unfamiliar sounds and sensations that the world presents to them. They may be sad when something unexpected leads to imperfect consequences. Young children have a unique way of looking at the world around them as they attempt to understand how things work and why things happen. Understanding and relating to how young children think about and explore the world is key to extending their thinking beyond what they already know.

Scientific exploration begins in infancy as babies use all of their senses to explore their environment. They touch and reach for objects, not just with their hands but with their feet, faces and other body parts as well. They recognize familiar voices and sounds, and they attach these sounds to specific people and objects. They react to both familiar and unfamiliar scents. No one teaches infants to explore this way, they do it naturally. Through all of these sensory experiences, children investigate the various attributes of objects and begin to experiment with finding ways to change them. We have all seen the excitement in children the first time they realize they can knock over a tower of blocks or that puddles are made for stomping!

When Kara is sitting in the high chair and drops cereal to the floor she is actually experimenting with her understanding of gravity. Objects fall. If something is in the way when objects fall, whether it is the high chair tray or the floor, it will stop the object. Kara continues to drop her cereal, not to be naughty but to see if the same phenomenon occurs each time. While Kara does not specifically understand gravity and how it works, her experimentation with the way items fall is building the foundations for later understandings of the concept.

Researchers have learned much in recent years about young children's capabilities for abstract thought. While infants and toddlers may require concrete objects in order to form initial schema (cognitive structures) about the qualities of those objects, their ability to reason abstractly about those objects and the possibilities for those objects is much greater than once thought. Returning to Kara in the high chair, when she drops her cereal and the dog comes running into the room to get it, Kara laughs. When the dog leaves, Kara drops another piece to see if the dog can make her laugh again. It is in this way that Kara is not just thinking about what has already happened, but about the more abstract possibilities for what might happen.

Research into children's scientific reasoning has uncovered many related skills that young children are in the process of developing (Brenneman, Stevenson-Boyd, & Frede, 2009; Duschl, Schweingruber, & Shouse, 2007). Like scientists, children can utilize data and analyze patterns in data to make and test their own predictions and theories (Gopnik, 2012). We see young toddlers who are given toys with varying switches, dials, and buttons consider data as they begin to connect which mechanism causes the toy to light up or move.

As they are developing these understandings of cause-and-effect relationships, children can determine the specific cause of particular events when shown non-conflicting evidence (Gopnik, 2012), as well as correctly determine the cause of an event when presented with multiple possible causes. In a study conducted by Koerber, Sodian, Thoermer, & Nett (2005) most four-year-olds were able to correctly determine the color of a chewing gum that made teeth fall out when shown pictures involving different colors of gum. When new evidence is introduced into a situation in which children have already formed conclusions, they may evaluate the new evidence and change their existing theories (Legare, Schult, Impola, & Souza, 2016). This growing ability to evaluate evidence is a prerequisite skill for conducting investigations and evaluating results.

Beyond the evaluation of evidence and causal relationships, children are developing science-specific language abilities to explain scientific phenomena. A significant barrier to such explanation is their limited science vocabulary, yet children are able to describe events, including their predictions and conclusions, based on what they believe may happen or has already happened, using familiar language and language patterns. With support from the adults in their lives, young children are capable of participating in shared discussions about science involving prediction, observation, and explanation. Thus, teachers can enhance their scientific thinking by modeling scientific vocabulary during children's daily experiences in the classroom and with the world.

Children are mini-scientists, constantly forming and testing their own theories about the world around them through their play. Teachers extend this development through the creation of a scientifically interesting, playful environment for exploration. Because science is reflected in children's play as they explore how items in their environment function, make connections to real-world concepts through their imaginative play, and find solutions to problems that may be inhibiting their abilities, the early childhood classroom is the perfect setting for extending children's learning and thinking about science.

What Is Science in an Early Childhood Classroom?

Thinking back to your own early classroom experiences, you may not remember much direct science learning. Whether it be in preschool or high school, effective science instruction actually looks very similar. Considering the multiple aspects of science instruction may be helpful for visualizing how you might provide numerous opportunities for children to experience all the science available both in and outside of the classroom.

Like many content areas, the discipline of science can be broken down into the processes and the content. Put simply, *science content* is what you know about science and *science process* is what you do when you explore science. Science content encompasses the facts, theories, laws, and ideas of science. Science processes involve everything from asking questions and making simple observations to complex laboratory testing procedures. What is important to know about the relationship between content and process in science is that it is virtually impossible to have one without the other. Clearly, when you are involved in the doing of science you are learning new facts and exploring ideas. What may be less obvious is the opposite; developing deep understandings of science content is reliant upon actually doing science.

Understanding science and being able to generate a list of scientific facts are two very different skills that require very different levels of thinking. Current recommendations for effective science instruction have moved beyond a focus on rote facts to a more hands-on, inquiry-based approach as evidenced by the establishment of the Next Generation Science Standards, which make clear that science content is best learned through doing science (NGSS, 2013). This is not a new idea for teachers. Early childhood teachers have understood the benefits of hands-on learning for a long time. The challenge for early childhood teachers, now, is how to extend children's learning of science content through these hands-on experiences.

Children do naturally form scientific ideas through their own explorations of the world around them. However, these ideas are limited by their experiences, prior conceptions, and growing cognitive abilities. These ideas and naive understandings of the world can and do lead to misunderstandings or overly simplistic views of science concepts. For example, many children believe that the sun actually moves across the sky during the day. This misunderstanding is formed because this is what children believe they are actually seeing. Simply telling children that the Earth is moving means little since their prior understanding about movement usually involves being able to feel something move. As such, there are many smaller, prerequisite concepts that children would need to experience and understand before they can even begin to comprehend the movement of objects in our solar system.

Of course, this doesn't mean adults shouldn't talk with children about their misconceptions. It does demonstrate that science instruction isn't as simple as telling children the facts and expecting them to incorporate these facts into their current views of the world and how it works. It also points out the necessity of the foundational ideas required for understanding larger science concepts. Early childhood is the perfect time to begin building these understandings. While young children might not be able to understand the complex relationship between the movement of the Earth and the sun, shining a flashlight onto children in a darkened room as they turn their bodies may help them to understand the differences between day, when we can see the light, and night, when we can't.

The teacher's role is then to move children beyond their everyday ideas toward these more conceptual scientific understandings. If children are allowed to experience science only through their own explorations, without adult interaction and support, it is unlikely that they will develop any higher level scientific understandings.

There are many opportunities throughout the day for teachers to encourage children in their exploration of both scientific processes and content through formal, informal, and incidental sciencing (Neuman, 1972). By utilizing the term "sciencing" as a verb, the doing of science is emphasized which distinguishes it from "science" which is often understood to be only the concepts to be learned or the name of a school subject. *Formal sciencing* occurs when teachers intentionally plan science learning experiences, present the activity and the materials to the children and encourage the children's exploration and discovery. *Informal sciencing* happens in spaces that have been set up by the teacher for children's exploration but are largely self-directed by children's choices. *Incidental sciencing* is not planned by the teacher but occurs when children explore and discover a new interest of their own, which is then followed by support from the teacher. Examples of ways you can support all of these types of science learning opportunities will be discussed in the following sections.

But I Already Have a Science Center...

Think about your science center, or science centers you have seen in other early childhood classrooms. You can probably easily make a list of the items you might find. There will probably be pinecones, shells, plastic dinosaurs and animals, magnifying glasses, plants, and maybe even a fish tank or classroom pet. Ask yourself what children are doing while they are playing in the science center. How often do you see them take out the pinecones or the seashells? What do they do with them if they do? Would you call what they are doing with them science? Researchers find the science "area" of the classroom is one of the areas least frequently utilized by children and is the least likely area for teacher-child interactions to occur (Tu & Hsaio, 2008). Why might this be? If you were to think like a child, or even like an adult, how exciting is a pinecone after the first time you have observed it? What can you really do with a pinecone? Most likely you have seen the children playing with the pinecones as a substitute for other items such as food. The answer to the question "What can you do with a pinecone?" is actually "A lot!" However, it takes more than simply making an item available for children to observe and incorporate in their play to turn it into a science learning experience. Science centers need to be active areas for exploration, supported by adults, in order for them to be effective in providing any type of science-learning opportunities. Many science areas are structured for children's observations, rather than their explorations.

So how can you make a pinecone into a science-learning experience? You could start with an exploration of what a pinecone's purpose is for the tree. The pinecone holds the seeds for the next generation of trees to grow. The pinecone is actually designed to protect the seeds from animals that might eat them and allows the seed to develop to a point where it can grow new trees. Have children dissect the pinecone and ask them to explain what they think the purpose is for the various parts. Comparing the structures of a pinecone to a fruit would provide the basis for several activities useful for understanding seeds, plant growth, and plant adaptations. Did you know that pinecones use temperature to determine when to drop their seeds? Placing damp, closed pinecones in a warm (not hot) oven will cause them to open and expose their seeds. By doing this, children can see how the actual process of seed production and dispersal works. Explore the patterns in the "petals" (which are actually called scales) of the pinecone. There are actually very complicated patterns to the scales of a pinecone so challenge children to find even simple patterns in these structures. While pinecones are readily available in most geographic areas, if you don't have access to pinecones, other seed pods can be investigated in a similar manner.

As can be seen, even the simplest materials currently in the science center can be extended into deep learning experiences beyond simply observing the object. Think about the rest of your materials. What else could you do? Thinking more about the science that these objects hold within them can make the science area into a true learning experience for young children.

Other suggestions for making your science center into a more effective center for learning include making sure to rotate objects in and out often. Teachers often overlook their science center when making these regular changes to their classroom. Take a look at the aesthetics of your science center. Does it scream out to children "I have interesting activities here"? If not, think about how you can make it more inviting. Are all of the objects too small to see from across the room? Is it colorful? Does it include anything that children may never have seen before?

Science tools are integral to children's ability to do science and should be included in the science area of the classroom. There are many tools used by scientists that are appropriate for young children. Try to think about what you would want to explore as a child. Would you want to use those small plastic magnifying glasses that get scratched and are difficult to see through, or would you be more likely to utilize a tool that looks like the ones actual scientists use? Giving students access to the real tools of science encourages them to explore like scientists. If your goal is for children to use actual science items, consider how some of these items may have been made "child friendly" by the manufacturers. Plastic, colorful magnets that are made to look inviting may lose the connection to the science of how magnets work and may lead to misconceptions about magnets being attracted to plastic items. When safety is a concern, breakable tools can be used with adult supervision. Examples of such tools might include real magnifying glasses, child-friendly tweezers that can be used to take objects apart, balance scales, measuring tapes and rulers, flashlights, stopwatches, sorting trays, pipettes, and plastic test tubes.

Materials that encourage exploration might include natural objects such as those pinecones and seashells, as well as tree and flower parts, bones, rocks, birds' nests, and bee honeycomb. Science, Technology, Engineering, and Math (STEM) items that encourage building and engineering include blocks, batteries and child-friendly circuitry, and different types of magnets. Display items that encourage exploration of mixtures and solutions, including water. You can't imagine all of the ideas that children can come up with to test the properties of water!

Finally, a word on children's books about science. There are many great non-fiction picture books for science instruction. Books should be chosen both to get children excited about science and to support the activities that children are already exploring both in and outside of the classroom. Books can never replace science exploration; they serve to foster curiosity and to support hands-on learning. Scientific facts without higher-level connections do not contribute greatly to any type of enduring scientific understandings. For real science learning to occur, children need to connect the facts and pictures in these books with real-life objects and situations. Ask yourself "Are these facts important for children to know as adults?" "Do they provide any type of scaffolding to higher-level science concepts?" "Do they get children excited about science?" If the answer to all of these questions is no, then they may not be as beneficial to children's science learning as you thought.

Inquiry Science in the Early Childhood Classroom

The word inquiry is often thrown around in relation to science instruction and learning but what does it actually mean? We understand what it means to inquire, but inquiry science is much more than just questioning. Inquiry science involves asking questions, testing and experimenting to find answers, evaluating evidence, communicating about the findings from all of the previous steps and asking more questions.

For example, an exploration of plant growth does not simply involve planting seeds in paper cups and observing as the plant emerges from the soil. Children can be prompted to explore the types of materials that seeds might germinate or not germinate in, and they can explore the needs of plants through growing them in light or dark conditions or by feeding them liquids other than water. Allowing children to explore based on their own wonderings allows them to generate their own questions which can be tested and built upon. Children can collect data as they measure the height of the different plants grown in different conditions, they can draw what they observe in science notebooks like real scientists, and they can communicate what they are findings about their plants to their peers and their families.

What becomes important in inquiry science is not arriving at a single, correct answer (e.g. the plant grew because it had water and sunlight) and ending your exploration, but the ongoing processes, the new questions that may be generated, and the ability to explain how answers to these questions are found (e.g. this plant grew better because… but I wonder what would happen if…).

Figure 13.1 is an example of the inquiry process for young children. Notice it begins with the child's own wonderings or explorations, not the teacher's.

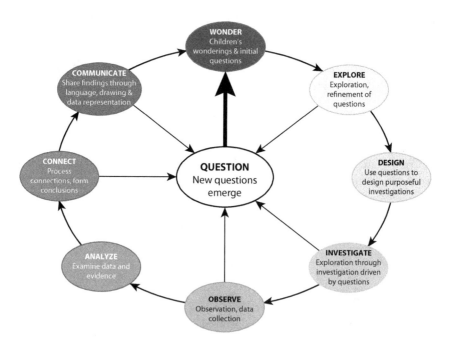

Figure 13.1 Representation of the inquiry model.

By allowing children to first express what they observe, and then to form their own questions for further exploration, children are performing their own inquiry and refining their abilities to think scientifically. The teacher's main role in supporting children's inquiry is to encourage them to think more deeply, to ask questions about the exploration that will lead them to further learning and, when appropriate, to provide and model the scientific language that accompanies the investigation.

Inquiry is a cyclical process in which new questions are constantly being generated, explored, answered (or not), communicated and then repeated. As such, scientific concepts cannot be taught in a single day, themes are fluid, not set in stone, and the children's ideas, not the teacher's, drive the process. Think about some of the most common science "lessons" taught in preschool classrooms. Do you think they are inquiry based?

Sinking and floating is one commonly taught activity. Many teachers present children with a bucket of water and a sampling of pre-selected objects of which about half sink and half float. Children are then told to "test" to see which sinks and which floats. Is this an inquiry experience? Is there any real science that the children have learned through this activity? The answers to these questions are no and very little respectively. Giving students the materials for an experiment, telling them the vocabulary to use and guiding them through a set of directions for that experiment all at the same pace is not inquiry science.

Yet a lesson like sinking and floating can be an inquiry experience for children. The first step is to take away the idea that developing an understanding of sinking and floating can be accomplished in just one day. True inquiry takes time as new ideas and questions are formed and explored. Next, adults need to relinquish some of the control over what happens and allow it to unfold based on the children's interests, questions, explorations, and findings. By responding to the children rather than the activity, the exploration is supported by the adult based on the children's own prior knowledge and encouragement to them to think for themselves rather than simply following a set of directions. By providing children a container of water and allowing the children to choose items from the classroom they want to test for the ability to sink or float, children are driving the investigation and may, in fact, begin to investigate in ways that teachers may not have planned or considered. Depending on the age of the children, data could be recorded by simple methods like sorting and comparing objects and picture charts to more complex written recordings of the findings.

Questioning is one of the most effective ways to support children's scientific inquiry. Open-ended questions of the "why" and "how" variety, rather than questions that require children to simply recall a fact, have been shown to be the most likely to contribute to their learning. Unfortunately, research has shown that only five to six percent of the questions asked in preschool settings are of the open-ended nature (Siraj-Blatchford & Manni, 2008). Open-ended questions require children to engage in conversation, think about possible future actions, and reveal to the listener much more about their ideas and thinking. Some questions that are beneficial to inquiry science might include:

Why do you think that happened?
How could you (*make something work*)?
What do you think will happen if?
How could you change (*an object or result*)?
How are they similar/different?
Why did you do it that way?
What if you tried it another way?
What else could you do?

Asking questions like these during the sinking and floating activity transforms the activity from a simple teacher-directed experiment, which results in little learning other than a working definition of sink and float, into a true inquiry activity where children learn more about the types and characteristics of items that sink or float, how items may sink or float, and may even begin to make lasting connections to real-life sink-and-float objects like boats.

One reason teachers may avoid teaching concepts like sink/float is because they lack their own understanding of the science behind it. Density of objects and buoyancy are hard concepts to understand for many adults and are much too difficult for young children. The object of the inquiry is to encourage children's thinking and build initial understandings of simple science concepts, not to understand fully every scientific concept behind it. Rather than worrying about having all of the answers about difficult science concepts, teachers can focus on the inquiry process for children and model the vocabulary and simple, conceptual understandings. The goal is not to have all of the answers but instead to build the foundation for understanding the world through the concepts and processes of science and to encourage the development of scientific thinking.

The National Science Teachers Association has several recommendations for how teachers of young children can support young children's inquiry (NSTA, 2014). Among them are

- tap into, guide, and focus children's natural interests and abilities through carefully planned, open-ended, inquiry-based explorations;
- provide numerous opportunities every day for young children to engage in science inquiry and learning by intentionally designing a rich, positive, and safe environment for exploration and discovery;
- emphasize the learning of science and engineering practices, including asking questions and defining problems; developing and using models; planning and carrying out investigations; analyzing and interpreting data; using mathematics and computational thinking; constructing explanations and designing solutions; engaging in argument from evidence; and obtaining, evaluating, and communicating information

While it is easy to see how inquiry fits in the design of formal science experiences when teachers begin with a certain concept in mind and present it in a formal manner to either a whole class or small group of children, encouraging inquiry in less formal settings might be more challenging for teachers unfamiliar with such science instruction. In practice, incorporating inquiry into informal and incidental science might be easier than you think if you simply look for those opportunities.

Inquiry in Incidental Science

Incidental science happens in the early childhood classroom quite frequently but can easily go unnoticed by the adults in the room. Children are constantly exploring science concepts as they play, pretend, imagine, build, and move. These explorations and discoveries provide numerous opportunities every day for teachers to help children understand, explore further, and think more deeply about their discoveries.

A commonly seen example might involve light and shadows. When out on the first walk of the springtime, Matthew sees a figure on the ground which seems to move along with him. Matthew is confused because he knows that this figure is not usually attached to him. One of the first things Matthew might do is to try to step on his shadow. Maybe he even tries to jump on it. It causes no pain so it must not be attached, but it keeps moving. Maybe he notices that the child next to him has one too, and tries to jump on that one, causing a bit of commotion in the line. When the class turns the corner, the shadow seems to disappear. Matthew wonders where it went and forgets about it until next time.

This interaction with light and shadows could easily have gone unnoticed by the adults supporting Matthew's learning. They may have even scolded him for disrupting the line. However, Matthew's interaction with his own shadow provides a perfect starting point for his teachers to deepen his understanding of shadows and more specifically the concept of light. In the moment, the teacher could have Matthew talk about what he is observing. By encouraging Matthew to travel in different directions while asking him questions about what he thinks is happening, he can see where his shadow goes and can begin to express his ideas about what might be causing the shadow. Encouraging him to try taking different positions with his arms and legs would help him to see that in some way he can control the shape of the shadow. However, understanding shadows outdoors can be a difficult concept since children have a hard time understanding that light comes from the sun in the same way as it comes from the lights in our homes and schools.

When the children get back to the classroom, encouraging Matthew to use flashlights to create shadows can help him make the connection between the shadows created in front of the flashlight and the shadow he saw outside. He might even begin to understand that shadows require light. Children love to make shadow figures with their hands and could use puppets or other items to perform a shadow puppet play on the wall. Through these additional explorations based on a single, outdoor discovery, Matthew and his classmates begin to develop an understanding of light and shadows.

Incidental science occurs as children build with construction materials, dig in the sandbox, explore the outdoors, and even in unexpected places such as at the lunch table. While eating lunch, John begins to mix together everything on his plate. It begins with just ketchup and mustard and ends with mashed potatoes and peas. You ask yourself, "why can't he just eat like a normal person?" Well, John is actually eating like a normal young child. John is actually doing science while he eats. He wants to know what happens when items are mixed together. Why can he still see the peas when he mixes them in the mashed potatoes but the ketchup turns the mashed potatoes red? John is exploring solutions and mixtures, an important foundational concept for chemistry. By asking John questions about his mixtures and encouraging this messy exploration, you could help John develop a better understanding of solutions and mixtures. While you may not approve of children playing with their food, it is unlikely that allowing a four-year-old to explore at the lunch table will lead to an adult thinking it is appropriate to do the same.

It is important to note here that by not understanding the inquisitive perspective of a young child, adults often inhibit young children's scientific curiosity and growth. Social norms and fear of injury can lead adults to require young children to follow certain rules that can prevent their deeper inquiries. It is important to think about and balance what children may be learning versus how we want them to behave or how we can keep them safe. For instance, Jacquie wants to build a tower as high as she can before it falls down. She has been practicing building with the large motor blocks and now can build a tower to her shoulders (the classroom rule) with ease. She has already learned the fundamentals of structures but only for structures two feet high. Without an exception to the classroom rule of "not above your shoulders," Jacquie will likely lose interest in building these structures at a critical time for her to be learning more about this important interest of hers. Are the classroom rules preventing her from learning? Think about ways to adapt the rules so that Jacquie could both build safely and taller. Perhaps an adult could assist her while she tries to build a safe and taller structure. Additionally, a teacher could encourage Jacquie to build in other ways to extend her learning of structures while observing the classroom rules.

Inquiry in Informal Science

There are so many areas of the classroom where the possibility to learn and explore science are present. Some of the most common areas you might think of would be the sensory/water table, the block/construction area, fine motor building materials, and of course the science center. You have purposely placed objects in these areas for children to explore during their choice/free play time hoping that they will get some sort of science learning out of them. Maybe they will and maybe they won't. You can ensure and extend the learning possibilities within these areas through encouragement, modeling, and collaboration with the children.

Let's consider the water table. What science learning is possible at the water table? Obvious possibilities include measurement, properties of water, conservation and water flow. Returning to the discussion of everyday science concepts, what will children learn about these concepts through their own exploration at the water table? Most likely they will make new observations about materials and practice existing skills. What is missing from this scenario is the adult interaction required to extend their learning beyond their everyday concepts. While it is certainly possible for young children to conduct an inquiry at the water table on their own by asking questions, testing predictions, evaluating results and asking follow-up questions, the addition of an adult to facilitate the learning by asking deeper questions, modeling the scientific language and answering children's questions, provides the necessary scaffolds for extending the child's science learning beyond their everyday conceptual understandings.

The water table can be a source of inquiry into deeper concepts such as bubbles, mixtures and solutions, dissolving, evaporation, the water cycle and more. By placing new objects in the water table other than those that are the same old reliables, children can begin to think of new ways to use and test these materials both new and old. Asking questions and encouraging exploration moves the water table from a place of observation to a place of inquiry, new conceptual learning, and scientific thinking.

Likewise, the sensory table can provide children with numerous science-learning experiences, given the right materials and adult guidance. Think about all of the science ideas that are held within the materials you choose to place in the sensory table. Natural materials showing characteristics of living (and formerly living) objects, and physical objects of differing sizes, can be used to explore volume, space and movement, and the sensory table is the perfect place to set up materials that can be combined, taken apart, and engineered into usable objects given the right challenges.

Materials placed in the dramatic play area can provide opportunities for children to role play important science concepts and provide important conversational opportunities and explorations around these concepts. For instance, when pretending to cook, references to the changes that food items undergo as they are cooked provide a foundation for concepts of heat transfer, changes of state, and mixtures—all important chemistry concepts. When role playing a doctor or a parent, opportunities exist for examinations of the human body and body systems as well as health, germs and even genetics. Putting out imaginary fires while playing firefighter creates opportunities for discussing burning, water pressure, and fire safety.

One of the strongest possibilities for early physics learning occurs in the block area. Much of the science that can be learned here is clear: how to build tall structures, how to make items balance, bridges, ramps, simple machines, and the list goes on. Teachers are often quite comfortable in this area, encouraging children to build taller and longer, to add windows and other structural components, and to use their imagination and creativity. One activity you may not have thought of is to encourage further exploration of ramp and car play. Children may have learned they can make the cars go faster by raising the ramps, but can they make them go slower? There are many options for experimenting with ramps and cars, including comparing the speeds of cars of different sizes, adding weight to the cars, and changing the surface of the ramps with carpet, sandpaper or other coverings the children want to try. Why not teach the children to use a stopwatch? They probably won't be able to use it accurately but they will develop a better understanding of how to conduct an experiment using a real science tool. These explorations will build foundational understandings for later physics concepts including friction, forces, and Newton's laws.

Informal science is abundant in the classroom. If the children can play with and explore it, there is some sort of science within it. The goal for teaching science through these informal experiences is simply to explore concepts more deeply, develop creative, scientific ways of thinking, and most importantly learn that science is fun!

Conclusion

Exposing young children to science is developmentally appropriate and builds a strong foundation for learning the concepts and processes encountered in elementary school and beyond. As shown here, children explore science every day in the early childhood classroom whether you as the teacher plan it or not. A rethinking of what it means to teach science shows that science instruction occurs through both formal and informal activities. Much of your instruction in science may come from your interactions with the children during their unplanned time. Even though these are informal, unplanned instructional times, teachers still need to plan for science instruction by considering the materials and environment that make science learning accessible to children during these choice explorations. Additional planned, formal science activities can support young children's learning of important science concepts and processes when presented through inquiry-based experiences in which children are given time and freedom to explore, theorize, wonder, test, experiment, evaluate, and communicate. Science in the early childhood classroom is messy and requires time, but when done well, extending children's explorations through questioning, modeling, and encouraging further investigations, it can provide children with strong scientific thinking skills, foundational concept learning and, most importantly, it can be fun. Remember that science in the early childhood classroom doesn't end with observation: observation is where science begins!

References

Brenneman, K., Stevenson-Boyd, J., & Frede, E.C. (2009). Math and science in preschool: Policies and practice. *Preschool Policy Brief, 19*, 1–12.

Duschl, R.A., Schweingruber, H.A., & Shouse, A.W. (2007). *Taking Science to School: Learning and Teaching Science in Grades K-8*. Washington, DC: National Academies Press.

Gopnik, A. (2012). Scientific thinking in young children: Theoretical advances, empirical research, and policy implications. *Science, 337*(6102), 1623–1627.

Koerber, S., Sodian, B., Thoermer, C., & Nett, U. (2005). Scientific reasoning in young children: Preschoolers' ability to evaluate covariation evidence. *Swiss Journal of Psychology / Schweizerische Zeitschrift Für Psychologie/Revue Suisse De Psychologie, 64*(3), 141–152.

Legare, C.H., Schult, C.A., Impola, M., & Souza, A.L. (2016). Young children revise explanations in response to new evidence. *Cognitive Development, 39*, 45–56.

National Science Teachers Association (NSTA). (2014). *NSTA Position Statement: Early Childhood Science Education.*

Neuman, D. (1972). Sciencing for young children. In K.R. Baker (Ed.), *Ideas that Work with Young Children*. Washington, DC: National Association for the Education of Young Children.

NGSS Lead States. (2013). *Next Generation Science Standards: For States, by States*. Washington, DC: The National Academies Press.

Siraj-Blatchford, I., & Manni, L. (2008). "Would You Like to Tidy up Now?" An Analysis of Adult Questioning in the English Foundation Stage. *Early Years: An International Journal of Research and Development, 28*(1), 5–22.

Tu, T.-H., & Hsiao, W.-Y. (2008). Preschool teacher-child verbal interactions in science teaching. *Electronic Journal of Science Education, 12*(2), 199–223.

14 Studying Social Studies and Visual Literacy to Foster Identity and Community

Mark Newman

Figure 14.1 Child's drawing of family.

Whether in or out of school, drawing their family is a common activity for young children. While the task seems simple, more is involved than just sitting down with paper and colored pencils, crayons, or markers. As is true of every picture, the drawing above tells a story (Figure 14.1). Let's look at that story.

A starting point is identifying the artist. It appears a young girl drew the picture. She presents herself as a happy only child living with her mother and father. Note that her figures are the same shape. All have heads with hair. Rectangles form the clothing out of which arms and hands extend, and they wear shoes. Legs comprise most of their bodies. They stand next to their home, a multi-story house it seems.

The whole tone of the picture is happiness. The family members are smiling. A bright sun shines in the sky and we see a flower. The artist's story is of a happy family.

When we probe deeper into what the young girl needed to know and be able to do to create this picture, the story gains multiple dimensions. She did not just sit down and begin drawing; the process was more complex. It drew upon many experiences over time. While our discussion goes into detail describing the process, she probably intuitively but thoughtfully drew the picture in a short period of time.

First, she had to compose a mental picture of what the drawing would look like. Prior knowledge played a role. She had looked at her parents and herself over time to identify certain traits. She recognized that the father was the tallest family member, followed by the mother and then herself. She drew upon many experiences to decide what feelings she wanted to portray, leading to smiling faces.

Next, she moved to composing the scene. Where should everyone be? She made a conscious decision to place herself between her mother and father. By having everybody stand outside amid flowers on a sunny day, the artist reinforced the idea of the happy family.

After seeing the picture in her mind, she had to transfer it to paper. Here, she also built upon prior experience related to drawing pictures over a long period of time. Her skill had progressed to the point that our artist could draw recognizable figures and background. Everyone could read the story of her family.

The drawing represents a culmination of knowledge, experiences, and skills that climbed Bloom's taxonomy to its highest level, create. To climb those levels, the artist exercised a range of visual literacy skills that had her read, make sense of, and communicate with visuals. The drawing also focused on an important social studies topic in preschool and primary grades, the family, and it touched upon identity and community, two basic social studies themes.

This chapter explores how social studies and visual literacy can help preschool and primary grades children foster a sense of identity and community. As the analysis of the drawing indicates, an important step is overtly recognizing that much of what young children know and do connects directly to social studies and visual literacy. Too often, such connections are neglected.

The discussion begins by establishing context, examining social studies and visual literacy. Social studies is defined and its role in early childhood education is explored, stressing the connection to identity and community. Next, visual literacy is discussed as a basic skill in preschool and primary grades. The skill of visual literacy is defined and we examine how and why it works in early childhood education. The third section offers a few classroom strategies and activities related to fostering identity and community with an explicit social studies and visual literacy learning context.

Social Studies in Perspective

It's unlikely that the first thing a teacher thinks about when students enter the classroom is, "Let's do social studies." But applying social studies concepts may be the first thing that students do when they come through the door. Not by studying academic content; rather, their behavior relates to social studies. Do your students follow a routine when they come into your classroom? How do they know what to do? We can look at a simple example to see how social studies works in the classroom. We can also see how what students do connects to identity and community.

Examine the photo in Figure 14.2. Is this similar to what you have students do in your classroom? When you ask a question, do they respond by raising their hands, so they can be called upon to answer? Why do teachers have students raise hands to speak? It is a matter of order rather than of potential chaos with everyone talking at the same time. But there is much more to it.

Students assume the identity of a respectful, polite member of the classroom community. As community members, they follow established rules knowing that by following those rules, they gain certain rights. In this instance, they have the right to speak. Over time this raising hand rule can evolve into a classroom norm, a pattern of expected behavior in a community.

A foundation of our society is that people have an identity as a member of a community and that membership involves certain responsibilities and rights. Hand raising and other behavior is learned in the initial years of schooling and continues throughout one's education and life. We learn what a community is, that our identity includes being a member of various communities. In essence,

Figure 14.2 Group of elementary age schoolchildren answering question.

the classroom acts as a microcosm of our larger society, a training ground for students to be productive citizens in the future. And this is what social studies is about.

Social studies is a multi-dimensional subject. Its value extends beyond building skills and learning content to important classroom management functions. Figure 14.3 offers insight into the academic side of what it teaches us about ourselves, our communities, our nation, and our world.

Looking at Figure 14.3, what do you notice about the connection between what social studies teaches and the related disciplines? Examine the questions, how important is it for students to gain answers to these queries? Equally important, how might these questions and answers change as students possess more knowledge and experience? What other questions does Figure 14.3 raise?

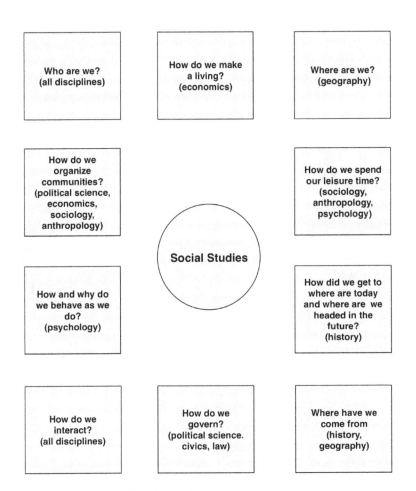

Figure 14.3 What social studies teaches.

Figure 14.3 provides a visual representation of the National Council for the Social Studies (NCSS) definition of social studies: "the integrated study of the social sciences and humanities to promote civic competence." Its primary purpose is to "help young people develop the ability to make informed and reasoned decisions for the public good as citizens of a culturally diverse, democratic society in an interdependent world." (NCSS, 2018)

The first sentence of the NCSS statement makes a direct connection between academic learning and behavior. Students learn social studies content so they can act as competent citizens in society. The classroom is one of the first communities young children join. To learn grade-appropriate content, students must also learn how to behave appropriately.

In terms of academic subjects, the NCSS statement shows that social studies is a blend of several disciplines. Together, these disciplines supply a framework to study people. Social studies is the only school subject whose purpose is to study people. An important aspect of studying people is examining their identity and their communities.

The first realization of many teachers is that the content of social studies is overwhelming. While in later grades the subject areas narrow their focus to such disciplines as history or geography, that is not true of the earlier grades. For example, the Illinois Social Science Standards identify themes for elementary grades, K-5 as follows:

- Kindergarten: My Social World
- First Grade: Living, Learning, Working Together
- Second Grade: Families, Neighborhoods, and Communities
- Third Grade: Communities Near and Far
- Fourth Grade: Our State, Our Nation
- Fifth Grade: Our Nation, Our World

These themes align with all the social studies disciplines. They represent a revision of the traditional expanding environment curriculum structure that began with the student and radiated out progressively to the world. The expanding environment structure might stress home, family, and school in kindergarten and first grade, expanding to neighborhoods in second grade. The progression would continue to communities in third grade and the state in fourth. The United States and the world would be studied in some organized fashion in grades five through eight. (Maxim, 1999, pp. 20–21; Chapin & Messick, 1999, p. 23)

Recent developments have further defined the structure and organization of social studies teaching. In 2013, the NCSS published the C3 (College, Career, Civic Life) Framework. One of its goals was to provide states with guidance in developing social studies standards. (https://www.socialstudies.org/c3 p. 6)

The C3 Framework addressed the issues of content and pedagogical approach. It whittled down the core disciplines to four— civics, economics, geography, and history— relegating psychology, sociology, and anthropology to secondary status. It also established an inquiry arc based on the following four "dimensions:"

1. Developing questions and planning inquiries.
2. Applying disciplinary concepts and tools.
3. Evaluating sources and using evidence.
4. Communicating conclusions and taking informed action.

The Framework divides each core discipline into subtopics and supplies college, career, and civic readiness (CCR) anchor standards for each core subject subtopic. Connections to Common Core standards are also made. But there are so many anchor standards that it borders on overkill. For grades K-2, there are 64 standards. The overwhelming majority, 49, relate to dimension 2 on applying disciplinary concepts and tools. The suggestion is to use the C3 Framework as a guide and focus on the 15 subtopics in dimension two. Refer to individual anchor standards as needed or consult state standards if available.

Following the publication of the C3 Framework, many states revised their standards. In Illinois, the Illinois State Board of Education developed three sets of guidelines and standards for different age groups and school levels:

- *For Children Birth to Age Three: Illinois Early Learning Guidelines*;
- *For Preschool 3 years old to Kindergarten Enrollment: Illinois Early Learning and Development Standards* (2013): and
- *Illinois Social Science Standards* (2016).

Social studies is included in the preschool standards and the K-12 social science standards.

The K-12 social science standards are divided into two categories: inquiry skills and disciplinary concepts. They include anthropology, psychology, and sociology along with the four C3 Framework core disciplines.

The Illinois standards are manageable. For primary grades, they are divided by grade level. As Table 14.1 below shows, Kindergarten has six inquiry skills and seven content standards.

It is important to remember that not every standard needs to be met in each unit. Rather, standards are met as students study content multiple times over the school year.

What does My Social World mean? Understanding this phrase is key to planning effective teaching and learning. "My" indicates that that the student is at the center of teaching and learning. Everything has to connect to the student in some way. "Social" indicates teaching and learning will focus on how and why the student fits and interacts with others in various contexts. "World" is more difficult to define. It can include the student's total experience; the people, places, and events that the student has been exposed to personally. Or, it can extend beyond the student's experience to other peoples, places, and even times.

Table 14.1 IL Social science standards (2016), Illinois state board of education 10-12, 16, 19, 22, 25

Inquiry Skills	**SS.IS.1.K-2.** Create questions to help guide inquiry about a topic with guidance from adults and/or peers.	**SS.IS.2.K-2.** Explore facts from various sources that can be used to answer the developed questions.	**SS.IS.3.K-2.** Gather information from one or two sources with guidance and support from adults and/or peers.	**SS.IS.4.K-2.** Evaluate a source by distinguishing between fact and opinion.	**SS.IS.5.K-2.** Ask and answer questions about arguments and explanations.	**SS.IS.6.K-2.** Use listening, consensus-building, and voting procedures to decide on and take action in their classrooms.
Civics	**SS.CV.1.K.** Describe roles and responsibilities of people in authority.	**SS.CV. 2.K.** Explain the need for and purposes of rules in various settings, inside and outside of the school.				
Economics	**SS.EC.1.K.** Explain choices are made because of scarcity (i.e., because we cannot have everything that we want).					

Geography	**SS.G.1.K.** Explain how weather, climate, and other environmental characteristics affect people's lives.	**SS.G.2.K.** Identify and explain how people and goods move from place to place.
History	**SS.H.1.K.** Compare life in the past to life today.	**SS.H.2.K.** Examine the significance of our national holidays and the heroism and achievements of the people associated with them.

Knowing what My Social World means is the first step to effective planning. The next concerns are content and method. If needed, standards can provide assistance.

Kindergarten can introduce many of the content topics and themes that students will study in other grades. By examining the subjects of other grade levels, first and second in particular, teachers can identify those topics and themes. As they study their social world, students could explore how and why people live, learn, play, and work together in families, neighborhoods, and various communities. They could study their own family, neighborhood, and community along with others past and present in the United States and other parts of the world.

Identity and community are two important themes that can be introduced in kindergarten.

Studying their social world can help students better understand who they are as an individual. This is who I am, where I live, learn, and play. They also learn about the groups and communities that they belong to, how they interact with people and places. They gain insight into what events help build the community and how these events may have influenced their identity. They learn about rules, rights, responsibilities, traditions, etc. that define who they are and where they fit in the community.

The next question is: what is a viable method for teaching and learning social studies? The standards and common practice mandate inquiry-based learning. Inquiry stresses posing questions and seeking answers to study a topic and coming to a conclusion that explains or synthesizes what was learned.

With guidance from the teacher, students open the study of a topic by posing questions. The questions should incorporate what they want to learn and other queries that probe into such areas as cause and effect as well as significance. For our purposes, significance may stress why it is important to learn about this topic, looking into its relevance to the students. Students could also pose questions on how to pursue the study of the topic, including activities and the products developed to show learning.

Having set up the course of study, students proceed through the inquiry cycle. They consult sources to help answer the questions. They gather pertinent information. They evaluate the information by distinguishing fact from opinion. Throughout the process, students discuss ideas and seek explanations by asking and answering questions. They use such consensus-building techniques as voting to reach agreements. (Cole & McGuire, 2011, p. 27) The last step involves taking action by completing the final product and reporting findings. In many cases, projects are developed across the unit and then shared at the end, possibly with parents or others.

Inquiry also strengthens knowledge of identity and community. Students are active participants, making decisions. Some students may assume leadership roles that become part of their identity. As leaders or as members, they learn how to interact with the teacher and other students to discuss matters related to the topic of study, following rules and norms. If voting is used, they practice an essential function of a community, learning that as individuals their actions can have an impact.

When group work is involved, students learn how communities can be organized to complete a specific task. While working on the task, the rules and norms of the classroom community apply. After the task is completed, students can feel a sense of pride as individuals and as cooperative members of the group.

Throughout the inquiry experience, effective social studies instruction makes special reference to who the individual student is and how that student fits in that subject area. Relevance to the student is an important aspect of social studies instruction. The basic question that teachers must answer for the student is: why do I care? If students do not understand how and why what they are studying fits into their lives, they are less likely to be motivated to learn.

So, why should you teach social studies? From a practical perspective, as the hand raising example shows, it supplies basic foundations of effective class-room management. Obviously, other reasons exist related to content and skills related to the goal of developing competent citizens.

In addition, the expansive nature of social studies makes it a likely core topic for a thematic unit that encompasses all subject areas. Gilbert, Huddleston, and Winters (2018) described a second-grade project on building a model house that integrated social studies with math and science. Cole and McGuire (2011) wrote about a kindergarten project on creating a mural for an imagined play-ground that integrated knowledge "from all of the disciplines in the humani-ties, sciences, and arts." (p. 25) Do you have units or projects in your classes that bring various disciplines together, including social studies?

Another hallmark of effective education is active student engagement. A corollary of active involvement is ensuring that students enjoy what they are doing. In many grades, but certainly from pre-K-2, engaging in activities that students enjoy can be a recipe for chaos. Channeling the boundless energy, enthusiasm, and short attention span of young learners into productive pursuits can be a challenge. The application of social studies concepts related to rules and community can help.

Remember Figure 14.3, about what social studies teaches and the questions it raises? Hopefully, the discussion above helped you develop some answers. We move now to another often-overlooked foundation of education that plays a pivotal role in early childhood and social studies education: visual literacy.

Visual Literacy

So far, this chapter has featured a drawing by hand, a photo, a concept map, and a table. Four different types of visuals but all are similar in that each pro-vides a picture of something.

Over the last 50 or so years, visuals of all types have become more perva-sive in our lives, transforming how we communicate. Today's students live in a world of emojis, icons, and streaming video, among other things related to technological advances. They also meet traditional visuals, including photos, cartoons, maps, stickers, and stamps, etc. No wonder some scholars say that we are experiencing a visual turn, meaning that visuals are becoming more important as a means of communication. (Mitchell, 1994).

Based on your experience, have you seen an increasing intrusion of visuals in your lives? In the lives of your students? Three-year-olds may not be able to read letters and words but they can manipulate an iPad or make pictures using stickers and stamps. In education, we have seen an increase in the use of visuals as documents to access information and as graphic organizers to make sense of the data. In preschool and primary grades, visuals play a pivotal role in all areas of education.

The proliferation of visuals led to the recognition that we need to be able to use them effectively. In 1968, John Debes coined the term visual literacy. Over time, a body of literature, strategies, and practices has developed so that visual literacy is becoming recognized as an important component of education at all levels. As a result, teachers have to improve their understanding of visual literacy. They need to know what it is, how it works, why it is important, and where it fits in preschool and primary grades education.

What is visual literacy? No consensus definition exists. Though the wording may vary, most agree that

Visual literacy is the ability to read, make sense of, and communicate with visuals.

In many classrooms, working with various visuals (pictures, maps, photos, charts, emojis, etc.) is part of the regular routine. Teachers design activities where students read, analyze, interpret, and evaluate a visual. Students also create two and three-dimensional visual products to show what they learned. In the process, visual literacy skills are developed.

In essence, many teachers have their students practice visual literacy without explicitly identifying it as such. This chapter opened with a discussion of the drawing of family that was. examined from a visual literacy perspective in two ways. First, we inquired into the picture to get its story by reading it for content and interpreting its message. Second, we explored the creation of the drawing examining the prior content and skills practice needed to create the drawing. Raising hands followed a similar approach of reading and analysis, but it was connected to appropriate behavior.

Think of activities in your classroom, could you examine any from a visual literacy perspective? Could you identify how students drew on prior knowledge, how they read pictures or actions to gain knowledge? Did they discuss what they read to understand it, and then did they create a visual product to show their learning? Have you done explicit literacy activities related to reading letters, word, and stories? How are they similar to what was done with the family drawing? What was different?

Literacy has certain common concepts and strategies. It can be defined as the ability to read, think, and communicate. Overwhelmingly, the context is with printed text. The suggestion is to apply some of the same ideas and importance to visuals, adapting strategies and practices to becoming visually literate.

Figure 14.4: A Visual Literacy Curriculum details the stages involved in studying a visual. Since effective learning requires practice, the curriculum works best when connected to a progressive learning sequence. Three levels follow a continuum of scaffolding to independent work. Student competency determines what level is used. Begin with heavy instructor facilitation, possibly in whole class instruction. Moderate facilitation, perhaps working in groups follows. The highest level involves independent completion.

How does the visual literacy curriculum work? We will go through the first three stages of the curriculum, leaving the final stage of communicating learning to you.

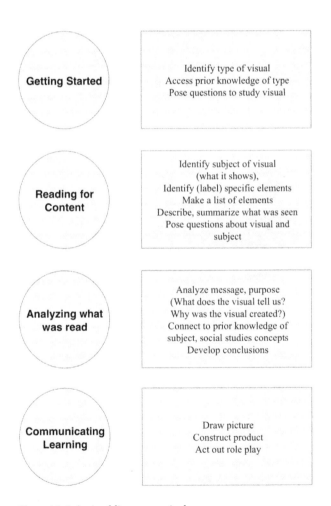

Figure 14.4 A visual literacy curriculum.

It is first grade, near the beginning of the school year. The unit is community helpers and the topic is firefighters. Identity and community are themes for social studies across the course.

The previous class discussed community helpers generally and identified those who would be studied. The unit inquiry question is: how and why do community helpers help our community? The lesson is the first of five on firefighters and they are the first community helper to be studied.

Assume students have some experience with the visual literacy curriculum. But they are not that familiar with it or the use of a graphic organizer to identify and label elements of the visual. As a result, teacher facilitation is needed. All labels are provided here. Depending upon skill proficiency, teachers may supply some labels to help orient students to the graphic organizer and to the task. It also aids English Language Learners and students with special needs to learn important vocabulary terms (Figure 14.5).

The title of the lesson is Firefighters. The objectives are to:

1. Identify who firefighters are.
2. Label correctly various parts of the firefighter uniform.
3. Describe the functions of the various parts of the firefighter uniform.

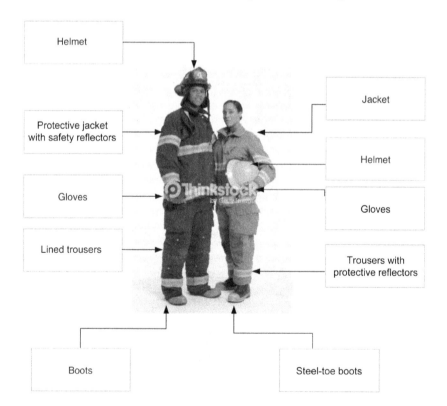

Figure 14.5 Firefighters.

The visual acts as a prompt to facilitate discussion and to evaluate student ability to read a visual for content. Throughout the exercise, the teacher can record answers and questions that can act as guides as students pursue their study.

Stage One: Getting Started opens by projecting a picture of the firefighters, asking the class what type of visual it is. If needed, the teacher provides clues, so a photograph is identified. Questions are asked about what photographs are and what experiences students have had with them. Identifying the type of visual is an important aspect of visual literacy. Students typically work with various types. Knowing that there are different types and what each kind is provides important contextual information.

Next, the teacher has the students identify the people in the photo. Students discuss what they know about firefighters. The information provides a foundation for future study, offering teachers insight into what students need to learn. If desired, create a list of what they know. The list may include important vocabulary words perhaps connected to a visual that depicts the term. For example, fight fires could be the caption for a picture of a firefighter using a hose to extinguish a flame.

The third task is having students pose questions about what they want to learn about firefighters. The teacher should guide the students, so their questions focus on who can be a firefighter, what they wear and why they wear the clothes they do, where they live while they work, what they do at a fire, etc. Not all of the questions will be addressed in the lesson, but they will be answered over the course of the following lessons.

Stage Two: Reading for Content moves to the photo of the two firefighters and completing the graphic organizer. Grade level and student ability determine how the graphic organizer is completed. It might be done as a whole class with the teacher filling in the answers on a large version of the photo/graphic organizer. Or, employing the organizer as a handout, the teacher could facilitate students completing the organizer individually or in pairs.

Using the pertinent questions posed by the students earlier and perhaps others related to the task, discuss who the firefighters in the photo are. Have students identify the articles of the uniform. Next, have students summarize their findings in one or two sentences. The last task in Stage Two is posing questions for further study. Depending on the original questions, the queries should focus on who can be a firefighter and what the purposes of their clothing are. Stage Three: Analyzing What Was Read involves higher levels of thinking. Asking who can be a firefighter has students draw upon what they learned from the photo; they can see that community helper occupations are open to both genders and members of any ethnic group.

Discussing the clothing has students use prior knowledge to make observations and inferences. The helmet protects the firefighter's head from anything that might fall on it. The gloves, jacket, and pants help protect them from heat and fire. The boots keep their feet dry and protect them from fire and stepping on things that might hurt their feet. Here, too, a list of words and pictures might prove helpful. The conclusion is that the uniforms protect them when they fight fires.

Stage Four: Communicating Learning has students apply what they know by creating a visual. What would you have students do? Draw a picture? Create a role play? Something else?

While we have gone through the entire visual literacy curriculum as written, it can be adopted to meet classroom needs. Students could use a picture as part of an exercise to create a concept map of prior knowledge. The topic is placed in the center in a circle and as students identify what they know, each item is placed in a circle around that center. The picture and graphic organizer might be the assessment at the end of a lesson.

No matter how the curriculum or its components are used, the teacher has created a pattern of learning that used over time will improve student learning. As students become more familiar with the process and the resources, they will need less facilitation. They could study more complex visuals and complete activities independently. They will understand what a visual is, what a graphic organizer is, and how both work. They will be able to read, to make sense of, and to create visuals to show what they have learned. Through practice over a school year, students will become more visually literate.

Studying Identity and Community

Chances are that you already teach much about identity and community in your classes and that visuals are important resources. But are those units and lessons explicitly connected to social studies? Is the use of visuals directly related to visual literacy? Do teaching and learning follow a clear progressive learning curriculum? Readers probably have mixed answers to these questions.

The early childhood literature on identity and community is vast. It extends over a wide range of topics for various grade levels that connect to numerous social studies topics. Many feature prominent use of visuals, but few focus on visual literacy or even mention it. Williams (2007) noted that interest in visual literacy was high in middle and high school but found little evidence of its use in primary grades. He considered the lack of evidence ironic since "visual images may be more accessible to younger children." (p. 637)

Do students read, make sense of, and communicate with visuals? In many cases, yes, but the literacy functions are implicit rather than explicitly taught. In researching this chapter, several years of the NCSS journal *Social Studies and the Young Learner* were reviewed. Between 2011 and 2018, 13 articles related to identity and community were published. All had a visual component, but none mentioned visual literacy. One purpose of this chapter is to make the teaching of visual literacy explicit, to strategically integrate it into the teaching and learning routine.

The following activities fit within the progressive, sequential curriculum discussed above. The first activity involves a single task while the second provides a framework for building visual literacy skills over time. They can be adapted by teachers for other grade levels.

My Favorite Things (Preschool)

While the push for young children in preschool to learn to use iPads and other devices is important, the need remains for hands-on, tactile activities. Among other things, small motor skills are developed. *My Favorite Things* is a beginning activity for use at the start of the school year to assess small motor and visual literacy skills, among other things. Our discussion will stress the visual literacy component to provide an added context.

Begin by questioning students about their favorite things, such as food, toys, colors, perhaps a princess or a superhero. Next, provide the students with sheets of paper and relevant stamps, stickers, and/or markers. Have them create pictures of their favorite things and present what they drew to the class.

While the students are creating the picture, walk around the room, offering help as needed. Observe how each child is going about creating the picture. Are they just using stamps? Stickers? Markers? Are they using more than one and, if so, and for what purposes? Are they filling the entire page or are they focusing on one part of the sheet? Is the paper crowded with stickers, stamps, or drawing; or are there just a few on the page? Do you see a child stop and think about the next step or continually work? Do they move stickers around?

Answers to these questions can provide insight into student ability to work with visuals. You likely will see that student ability ranges along a spectrum of experience of working with visuals and the materials provided. You can assess how well students draw and work with stickers or stamps. While observing the students creating the picture, ask them about what they are doing and why they are using a sticker, etc.

During the presentations, watch how the pictures compare with their oral description. See if they point to certain stickers, etc., as they talk about their favorite things. Observe other aspects of the presentation that relate to the visual they created.

This activity provides insight into student familiarity with materials they can use to create a visual. It also provides a snapshot of visual literacy skills that teachers can use to plan future instruction. Students need to be able to read each sticker and stamp, connecting it to the specific favorite thing or things. What they use and the final product helps the teacher understand how well a student translates a mental picture to paper.

Neighborhoods (Second Grade)

Often, in primary grades, students engage in longer projects that have them create a book or other portfolio-like project, either in physical or electronic format. Our discussion shows how such projects can help students build visual literacy skills progressively over time.

Neighborhoods has students study varied examples, their own, one from the past, and possibly one in a different country. Using the Illinois social science standards as a guide, students will have studied families, so neighborhoods would come later and precede communities. Assume the school year is 36 weeks and each quarter is nine weeks, with families studied in the first quarter and neighborhoods in the second.

The unit project is to create a book on neighborhoods that includes a map, various pictures, and written work. Our focus is on the maps. Over the unit, students will work with three maps in a progressive fashion that has students assume more complex and difficult tasks.

One scenario moves from labeling elements to coloring maps. With some items identified, have students name and label items such as streets, school, parks, any businesses, any municipal buildings on the map of the neighborhood being studied. For the map of the second neighborhood, depending upon student proficiency, they can label all the items without any being identified. The third activity moves to a higher level. Have students color different elements and create a key showing different colors for the various items on the map. Parks can be green, streets gray, the fire station red, and so on.

If students are familiar with maps, they could draw the last map. Prior map activities would build to the drawing. Labeling might be the first activity with the second adding coloring and the key. Various options exist.

In all cases, the instruction stresses building visual literacy skills progressively. To label a map requires the ability to read different elements. Coloring and the key move to the higher level that involves not just labels but organizing elements by function. Drawing rises to the top of the visual literacy taxonomy.

But student proficiency determines next steps. If students cannot identify and label elements, they cannot move to coloring and the key. If they cannot color and create the key, they won't be able to draw the map.

The map activities help students gain a visual perspective of a certain type of community, a neighborhood. They learn about the institutions and services, places, and transportation routes that make up the neighborhood. They also may learn about where they fit by discussing the elements on the map and how these elements relate to them.

Conclusion

A "play" on the old adage that a picture is worth a thousand words offers some final thoughts. A picture depicting student identity, or a community is only worth those 1,000 words if students can read and make sense of the picture. Connecting the picture to social studies content provides added context, enhancing understanding and building appreciate classroom behavior.

Further Reading

Adams, E. (2015) Civics in the grocery store: A field trip of awareness and agency. *Social Studies and the Young Learner* 27(4), 16–18

Brownlee, J., Johansson, E., Walker, S. & Scholes, L. (2017) *Teaching for Active Citizenship: Moral Values and Personal Epistemology in Early Years Classrooms*. London and New York: Routledge.

Dykstra Van Meeteren, B. (2013) Looking for social studies…and finding a democratic community in the classroom. *Social Studies and the Young Learner* 25(3), 27–31.

Fantozzi, V., Cottino, E. & Gennarelli, C. (2013) Mapping their place: Preschoolers explore space, place, and literacy. *Social Studies and the Young Learner* 26(1), 5–10.

Gleeson, A. & D'Souza, L. (2016) Expanding local to global through ESRI story maps. *Social Studies and the Young Learner* 29(2), 14–16.

Lopatovska, I. (2016) Engaging young children in visual literacy instruction. ASIST 2016, Copenhagen, Denmark, pp. 1–5.

Milica, J. (2014) Developing a sense of identity in preschoolers. *Mediterranean Journal of Social Sciences* 5(22), 225–234.

Mulrey, B., Ackerman, A. & Howson, P. (2012) "Boss of the United States" Kindergarteners' concept of voting: Five scaffolded lessons that build understanding. *Social Studies and the Young Learner* 25(1), 27–32.

National Council for the Social Studies (NCSS). (2013) *The College, Career, and Civic Life (C3) Framework for Social Studies State Standards: Guidance for Enhancing the Rigor of K-12 Civics, Economics, Geography, and History.* Silver Spring, MD: NCSS.

Payne, K. (2015) Who can fix this? The concept of "audience" and first graders' civic agency. *Social Studies and the Young Learner* 27(4), 19–22.

References

Chapin, J. & Messick, R. (1999). *Elementary Social Studies: A Practical Guide*, 4th edition. New York: Longman.

Cole, B. & McGuire, M. (2011). The challenge of a community park: Engaging young children In powerful lessons in democracy. *Social Studies and the Young Learner* 24(1), 24–28.

Debes, J. (1968). Some foundations of visual literacy. *Audio Visual Instruction*, 13, 961–964.

Gilbert, S., Huddleston, T. & Winters, J. (2018). Design, build, and test a model house: Using the C3 framework to explore the economics of constructing a dwelling. *Social Studies and the Young Learner* 30(4), 24–27.

Illinois Early Learning and Development Standards. (2013). https://illinoisearlylearning. org/ields/ e

Illinois Social Science Standards. (2016). Illinois State Board of Education. https://www. isbe.net/Documents/K-12-SS-Standards.pdf

Maxim, G. (1999). *Social Studies and the Elementary Child*, 6th edition. Upper Saddle River, NJ: Merrill.

Mitchell, W. J. T. (1994). *Picture Theory*. Chicago, IL: University of Chicago Press.

National Council for the Social Studies (NCSS). (2018). https://www.socialstudies.org/ about

Williams, T. (2007). Reading the painting: Exploring visual literacy in the primary grades. *The Reading Teacher* 60(7), 636–642.

15 The Strength in Strategy

Planning for High-Quality Professional Learning Communities

Megan Schumaker-Murphy and Ravi Hansra

As a classroom teacher and a direct service early intervention provider, one of our favorite things about the start of the new school year was the renewed energy and passion we felt as we participated in professional learning communities (PLCs). In fact, now that we've transitioned into leadership roles outside of the classroom, PLC participation focused on our own learning is one of the things we miss the most. Imagine our surprise when speaking with a teacher, Mr. Collier, as he lamented how much he dreaded his district's back-to-school kick-off professional development. Mr. Collier described feeling these two days of professional development (PD) sessions a complete waste of time, because the PD lacked focus and alignment to the actual needs of the teachers in the district. Unfortunately, Mr. Collier's experiences aren't uncommon. In fact, fewer than 30% of teachers are happy with the professional development offerings available at their school, and most teachers feel that available professional development doesn't help to prepare them for the changing needs of their students (Bill & Melinda Gates Foundation, 2014).

What made our experiences so different than Mr. Collier's? After deep dialogue over this common quandary, unpacking the commonalities and differences in our professional learning experiences, we both had one positive experience in common: engagement in professional learning communities (PLCs). According to Stoll et al., a true PLC is "a group of [educators] sharing and critically interrogating their practice in an ongoing, reflective, collaborative, inclusive, learning-oriented and growth promoting way" (Stoll et al., 2006, p. 229). By definition, this kind of professional learning is more meaningful than "drive-through" PD sessions often presented as lectures by an expert on a topic, which may or may not relate to our classroom context or the areas we are most interested in improving in our daily teaching practices. This chapter discusses the opportunity for teacher PD as one valuing and accounting for a teacher's professional journey. This PD is a systems approach starting with understanding the professional development needs and desires of teachers. We offer concrete steps to establishing professional learning communities as teacher-driven and, ideally, system-supported.

However, one can create informal PLCs should the PD offered in your setting not match your needs.

Establishing Common Lexicon

To understand the difference between PD and PLCs, we need to understand education terms and associated abbreviations. Teachers hear a ton of acronyms thrown around: IEP, LRE, UDL, RTI, PLC, PD. Sorting terms and acronyms is further complicated when there is disagreement regarding the meaning of terms or how we abbreviate them. Let's begin by establishing a common language for this chapter. The alphabet soup of relevant acronyms for this chapter are PD, PLC, UbD, and RP.

Professional Development (PD)

Professional Development refers to any of the learning opportunities pedagogically focused and aimed at elevating the knowledge and skill of the educators.

Professional Learning Communities (PLC)

Effective Professional Learning Communities are content- and context-specific, teacher-driven, and focus on using a collaborative method aimed at elevating the quality of teaching and learning. The term "Professional Learning Community" first emerged in education in 1995 (Myers & Myers) and is now used so freely and often that it tends to lose its true meaning. Thus, we will subscribe to Stoll et al.'s definition, which is "a group of [educators] sharing and critically interrogating their practice in an ongoing, reflective, collaborative, inclusive, learning-oriented and growthpromoting way" (Stoll et al., 2006, p. 229).

Understanding by Design (UbD)

Understanding by Design (UbD) is a framework created by Jay McTighe and Grant Wiggins (2005). It offers practitioners a method for planning, beginning with the end result in mind. Starting with desired results helps to focus lesson and PLC planning to meet emergent needs and interests of teachers while staying on course toward our the North Star of desired end result.

Reflective Practice (RP)

Reflective practice is an intentional process of thinking about your teaching, connecting it to theory and using a cycle of thoughtful planning, implementation, and assessment for personal and professional growth (Bassot, 2016). RP is a part of what distinguishes PLCs from other forms of more traditional drive-through professional development.

Pros of PLCs

Traditional forms of professional development—generally short seminars, workshops or conferences—are not particularly effective at helping teachers incorporate new practices into their daily teaching routines (Easton, 2008; Bayer, 2014). Researchers found these short sessions frequently focus on topics dictated by experts, and often provide information that is too general to be helpful to individual teachers' real-life classroom contexts. Additionally, these short sessions don't allow enough time for teachers to plan to transfer any new knowledge into their practice (Bayer, 2004). Conversely, a true PLC's content is determined by its members based on their group and individual needs as a community of educators. The content can be differentiated to meet the individual needs and skill levels of the participants. The PLC participants set goals specific to their individual levels of experience, pedagogical strengths, and areas for growth, then dive deeply into content over a longer period of time: usually a school year or longer. PLCs often incorporate nontraditional forms of PD found more effective than purely "drive-through PD"; such practices include coaching, peer observations, and reflective practice (Bayer, 2014). Although PLCs take more time and commitment than drive-through PD, that is precisely what makes them more effective vehicles for teacher learning. In fact, a sustained duration is a key factor in ensuring the effectiveness of teacher professional development (Darling-Hammond, Hyler, & Gardner, 2017). Building strategies including reflective practice, coaching, and peer observations or peer modeling creates an opportunity for intentional transfer of new knowledge and skills into daily teaching practices.

Components of Effective PLCs

Recently, a group of researchers reviewed 35 studies related to teacher professional development. They determined that effective PD has seven key elements that can and should be incorporated into a true PLC model (Darling-Hammond, Hyler, & Gardner, 2017). The key elements include the following:

1. Content focus. Successful professional development dedicates time to understanding relevant content rather than sharing new procedures and policies.
2. Active learning strategies. Effective PLCs don't use tired methods like PowerPoint lectures: they invite more hands-on learning, group close reads, reflective journaling, modeling, and small-group planning.
3. Collaboration between peers. A main component in professional learning communities in the community! Almost all meaningful learning takes place within relationships (Bronfenbrenner & Morris, 1998).
4. Provision of strong models. Models are a great way to bridge theory into practice and to demystify new strategies. Models can be created during PLCs through role play or video of teacher practice, or by job-embedded coaching or by observing a peer or mentor.

5. Coaching. Coaching models often use an experiential learning cycle (Kolb, 1984; 2014) to engage teachers in a process of practice, reflecting on the practice, determining what went well, and what to tweak for next time. It can be done formally with an instructional or content area coach, or with a peer mentor who is skilled in the focus area.

6. Reflection and feedback loops. Reflective practice is a key component for bringing about positive change in your daily teaching practices. This can be done through reflective journaling, reviewing video of your teaching practices, or verbally after a coach, peer, or administrator observation of your teaching.

7. Sustained duration. Change doesn't happen overnight and experts aren't made in a day. The best professional development allows teachers enough time to dig deeply into the content and engage in experiential learning cycles supported by reflective supervision.

Depending on available resources and teacher needs, these elements can be utilized in a variety of combinations.

Getting Started

Ideally, PLCs would be a part of the school district or agency culture and supported by paid, protected time for professional learning. While this is the best-case scenario, individual administrators, teachers, or early intervention providers can start PLCs by grouping two or more educators with a common goal. There can even be multiple PLCs running in a school at the same time based on teacher needs and interest. For example, one group of teachers may be focused on classroom management using restorative justice practices, while another group may be interested in integrating literacy blocks into their teaching, and yet another may be interested in implementing Universal Design for Learning. Once you've established a group of educators with a common goal, you can start your PLC by planning your end goals and setting up protected, consistent times to meet and collaborate (Figure 15.1).

Unfortunately, not all educators have the formal structures in place to create PLCs. For example, Dr. Hansra experienced a formal PLC, which utilized a district and school-wide systems approach to professional learning, while Dr. Schumaker-Murphy accidentally created an informal PLC while working as an independent contractor in early intervention. She began by reaching out to early intervention colleagues who then started meeting once a month over potluck dinners to dive into best practices, including routines-based therapy strategies. Each shared our particular area of expertise with one another while supporting each other with real experiences from the field. Those two years of potluck dinners impacted my practice much more than any session of traditional professional development ever did. It was only later as I grew in my career that I realized we created our own professional learning community.

Values underlying cultural competence	What do I need to do to apply culturally relevant practices in my classroom?
1. Equitable classroom processes build cultural competence for all children 2. As their teacher, I understand their home cultures as well as their strengths and needs 3. As teachers, we become aware of our biases, so we do not apply them in the classroom,	1. Apply culturally relevant teaching strategies 2. Evaluation books already in the classroom and add additional children's literature to reflect our classroom community 3. Become aware of personal biases and avoid applying them in the classroom
How do I know I have succeeded?	**What external validation of my progress can I gather?**
1. Review Documentation Panel of Children's Work 2. Examine children's learning portfolios, including art and dramatic play observations 3. Keep a reflective journal of my learning and practice.	1. Review CLAS S[1] and ECERS[2] Acceptance of Diversity Scores 2. Provide a video of my interactions with children for my coach to discuss with me. 3. Invite my colleague to observe a lesson.

Figure 15.1 A sample showing the planning process using the principles of UbD.

Planning for Successful Professional Learning Communities

Creating a Professional Learning System of Support

Once you've found other folks with the same professional learning goals, it's time to come together and start planning. We recommend using a planning strategy based on Understanding by Design (UbD) (Wiggins & McTighe, 2005). A model of UbD planning is available in this chapter's spotlight.

The UbD process starts with determining an essential question to guide your learning. Essential questions are based on big ideas that can be argued, are immediately related to your daily teaching practices, and are understood with more clarity over time (Wiggins & McTighe, 2005). In the PLC of early intervention providers, the essential question was "How does the use of routines-based intervention and bagless therapy sessions improve early intervention outcomes for families?" Each of the early interventionists came into the PLC with their own intentions for professional growth, but were able to work together toward gaining a better understanding of how to implement strategies related to routines-based interventions. While we no longer teach in classrooms, we remember the goal-setting aspect of effective PLCs, and use UbD to facilitate our work with practitioners.

Now as leaders, we're immersed in work focused on the essential question "How can anti-bias education and culturally relevant pedagogy improve learning and development for educators, children, and their families?" It's a big question. Each educator who engages in the PD process with one of us brings personal experiences, pedagogical strengths, teaching philosophies and personal teaching goals related to the topic. Because we enter into our PLCs with a strong North Star for all teachers, guided by this question, we can facilitate active learning strategies meeting each teacher's personal starting point while remaining confident we're all on a path toward the same North Star.

Once you identify your North Star by drafting an essential question, you can begin a master plan for the duration of your PLC. How often will you meet? Who will lead your sessions? What readings and other resources will you consult? How will you establish accountability to yourselves and each other? Which of the seven key components to effective PD can you access to support the learning in PLCs? How will you use data to inform your planning? What data will you use? How will you get it? These are all questions that are easier to answer once your focus is clearly established in an essential question.

When planning ongoing PLCs, using multiple data points to inform direction and content will make intentional, relevant, and systemic learning opportunities. For example, student data, teacher expertise, teacher knowledge and skill gap, district priorities, and school-based priorities should be considered when identifying the content-focus of the professional learning for the year. By assessing where teachers are in their learning journey, leadership can plan for the starting point. For example, by digging into student data (e.g., social, behavioral, academic), you may identify a pedagogical gap in teachers' knowledge and skill regarding cultural competence. Thus, prior to engaging in a PLC, teachers may need to experience some high-quality, informationally based PD to close a basic knowledge and skill gap. Then PLCs can be implemented to start the experiential learning cycle.

Once you've reviewed data and an essential question is crafted, the PLC participants will establish emerging theory regarding how they believe change will take place over time within a professional learning system. This emerging theory is called a Theory of Change and should be grounded in evidence-based literature related to the PLC's essential question. A theory of change sounds fancy, but it can be simplified into a sort of mad lib: if we have [resources], then we can [implement pedagogical focus of PLCs] and then [desired outcome]. For example, the theory of change for the essential question "How can anti-bias education and culturally relevant pedagogy improve learning and development for educators, children, and their families?" would be "If we have the opportunity to participate in PLCs focused on deepening our understanding of culturally relevant pedagogy that incorporates the experiential learning cycle and reflective practice, then our students will have deeper connections to learning materials and improve academic achievement." Often, a theory of change emerges clearly when following the UbD process outlined in the chapter spotlight.

Experiential Learning Cycle and Power of Reflection

It's likely that you engage in experiential learning cycles with your students all the time (Figure 15.2). For example, when teaching a student how to divide crackers for snack time into equal portions, you'll watch your students attempt their own strategy of putting two crackers onto each plate and being left with a giant pile of extra crackers. Through thoughtful questioning, you ask the child what they did (e.g., gave everyone two crackers), what happened when they did that (e.g., lots of extra crackers), why that happened (e.g., there's enough for everyone to have more than two crackers), and what they'll do differently next time (e.g., maybe give everyone one cracker at a time over and over until all the crackers are gone). Adults benefit from this process, too. A formal structure for supporting the experiential learning cycle in your PLCs is the use of reflective practice.

Once your PLCs are up and running, you'll start to incorporate new knowledge and skills into your daily teaching practices. Some of them will instantly work just like the source material said they would, but most of them won't. This is where reflective practice comes in. Taking time to honestly reflect on what you did, what the immediate outcome was, and why that outcome occurred are important catalysts for you to be able to plan what you're going to do next. You can do these reflections verbally with a coach or peer mentor, in writing with yourself, or with a coach or peer, reading and providing feedback or through watching yourself on video and processing what happened with your PLC group. Reflection is perhaps the most important part of the experiential learning cycle and the PLC process. It's largely the lack of time to reflect and plan that prevents drive-through PDs from being effective.

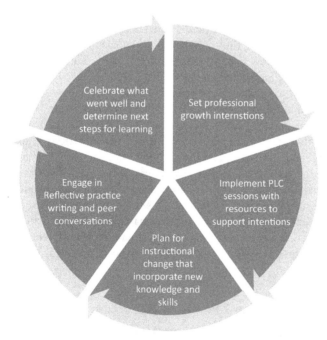

Figure 15.2 In PLCS, learning occurs in an ongoing cycle of planning, implementation, reflection, and celebration.

Onward Together

Ideally, all our professional learning opportunities would be supported by the schools and districts; however, as long you can find a few growth-oriented colleagues, set your intentions, and make a plan, you can create and facilitate a successful professional learning community that meets your unique professional development needs.

References

Bassot, B. (2016). *The Reflective Practice Guide: An Interdisciplinary Approach to Critical Reflection*. New York: Routledge.

Bayer, A. (2014). The components of effective professional development activities in terms of teachers' perspectives. *International Journal of Educational Sciences, 6*(2), 319–327.

Bill & Melinda Gates Foundation. (2014). Teachers know best: Teachers' views on professional development. Retrieved from: http://www.teachersknowbest.org/reports

Bronfenbrenner, U. & Morris, P.A. (1998). The ecology of development process. In W. Damon (Series ed.) & R.M. Lerner (Vol. ed.), *Handbook of Child Psychology: Vol. 1. Theoretical Models of Human Development* (5th ed., pp. 939–991). New York: John Wiley.

Darling-Hammond, L., Hyler, M.E., & Gardner, M. (2017). *Effective Teacher Professional Development*. Palo Alto, CA: Learning Policy Institute.

Easton, L.B. (2008). From professional development to professional learning. *Phi Delta Kappan, 89*(10), 755–761.

Kolb, D. (1984). *Experiential Learning: Experience as the Source of Learning and Development*. Upper Saddle River, NJ: Prentice Hall.

Kolb, D. (2014). *Experiential Learning: Experience as the Source of Learning and Development* (2nd ed.). Upper Saddle River, NJ: Pearson.

Stoll, L., Bolam, R., McMahon, A., Wallace, M., & Thomas, S. (2006). Professional learning communities: A review of the literature. *Journal of Educational Change, 7*(4), 221–258.

Wiggins, G., & McTighe, J. (2005). *Understanding by Design* (2nd ed.). Alexandria, VA: ASCD.

Conclusion

Teachers Succeeding in the Face of Challenges

Gayle Mindes

This book is chock full of ideas to contemplate and strategies to implement in your program. Chapter experts shared the latest research and recommendations based on their various professional roles. The authors are united in their support for responsive developmentally appropriate practice—an approach to education fostering young children's identities in a community of learners, considering all aspects of development and various learning styles and capacities. Developmentally appropriate beliefs about learning start with the relationship between teacher and child, as well as child-to-child interactions, in a social environment and are the driver in emphasizing the importance of social-emotional learning as the foundation for achievement. Ideas presented show how to practice skillful observation to interpret behavior, as well as language, to ensure capacity building in the social world of the school. This developmentally responsive approach calls for respectful interactions with young children and their families from diverse cultures, languages, ethnicities, abilities and socio-economic situations. You learned how collaboration with families, which connects childcare and education settings, makes children feel safe and secure. For families, your efforts to learn about them and their goals for their children secures a foundation for lifelong appreciation of family involvement in various educational settings.

Implementing responsive developmentally appropriate practice in a prepared learning environment by using early learning standards, employing multiple assessments and practicing culturally sensitive differentiated instruction facilitates the education of each child within your program. Thus, your interactions with children, as you show empathy and an interest in each child's cultural heritage, set the stage for school success. Strategies for instruction presented ways to support curious learners, inquiry, and an integration of all curricular areas. Examples of holistic planning across curricular areas, beginning with Understanding by Design (UbD), provided the groundwork for accountability in your settings. Illustrations of teachers' utilization of digital play, digital media, and tools for children in their work were provided. Finally, you learned how teachers in the bioecological system can support each other and grow through professional learning communities.

After reading, reflecting upon and implementing the ideas and strategies presented in this book, you are positioned to realize best practice in early childhood education and to tackle the challenges of our contemporary society. Programs built upon respectful relationships with children and families, and appreciation of our contemporary society's rich diversity, set the standard for overcoming the everyday challenges you face. We know you do this work with children in the face of many social problems, some beyond your capacity to change, and we hope the ideas presented here will allow you to continue to face obstacles presented. The experts here provide the wisdom for you to recognize your strengths, which we hope will enable you to persevere in a spirit of optimism and hope for future generations, beginning today with the children you serve.

Index

Page numbers in **bold** denote tables, in *italic* denote figures.

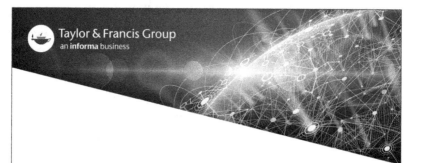

CPSIA information can be obtained
at www.ICGtesting.com
Printed in the USA
LVHW082104210521
688023LV00026B/499

9 781138 312265